JOHN O'DONOHUE

Eternal Echoes

*Celtic Reflections on Our Yearning
to Belong*

Perennial
An Imprint of HarperCollinsPublishers

A hardcover edition of this book was published in 1999 by Cliff Street Books, an imprint of HarperCollins Publishers.

HarperCollins books may be purchased for educational, business, or sales promotional use. For information, please e-mail the Special Markets Department at SPsales@harpercollins.com.

First Cliff Street Books/HarperPerennial edition published 2000.

Reprinted in Perennial 2002.

Designed by Ruth Lee

ISBN 0-06-095558-9

23 24 25 26 27 LBC 36 35 34 33 32

Eternal Echoes

OTHER BOOKS BY JOHN O'DONOHUE

Anam Ċara

For Josie, my mother,
In appreciation of all her warmth and love
Which helped us to discover our longings within
a kind shelter of belonging.

And for all those who inhabit lives
Where the belonging is torn
And the longing is numbed.

"Stabant orantes primi transmittere cursum
Tendebantque manus ripae ulterioris amore"
(So they all stood, each praying to be ferried
across first
Their hands stretched out in longing for the
further shore)

VIRGIL, Aeneid (V1, 313)

"Behold, I am the Ground of thy Beseeching."
JULIAN of Norwich

"A single beat from the heart of a lover is
capable of driving out a hundred sorrows."
NAGUIB MAHFOUZ

Matins

I.

Somewhere, out at the edges, the night
Is turning and the waves of darkness
Begin to brighten the shore of dawn.

The heavy dark falls back to earth
And the freed air goes wild with light,
The heart fills with fresh, bright breath
And thoughts stir to give birth to colour.

II.

I arise today

In the name of Silence
Womb of the Word,
In the name of Stillness
Home of Belonging,
In the name of the Solitude
Of the Soul and the Earth.

I arise today

Blessed by all things,
Wings of breath,
Delight of eyes,
Wonder of whisper,
Intimacy of touch,
Eternity of soul,
Urgency of thought,
Miracle of health,
Embrace of God.

May I live this day

Compassionate of heart,
Gentle in word,
Gracious in awareness,
Courageous in thought,
Generous in love.

Contents

3. PRISONS WE CHOOSE TO LIVE IN

Acknowledgments

I WISH TO THANK: DIANE REVERAND, my editor at HarperCollins; Kim Witherspoon and her agency, for her confidence in the work and for its effective mediation; John Devitt, who read the manuscript and offered a creative and literary critique; Dr. Lelia Doolan, who gave a wonderfully encouraging and rigorous critical response to the text; David Whyte, for his brotherly care and our conversations about the world of the imagination; Barbara Conner, for all her work and support; and especially Marian O'Beirn, who suggested this book on longing and "our hunger to belong" and who read and reread successive drafts, keeping a critical eye on structure and content and whose friendship and inspiration are generosity itself; the memory of my former teachers Professor Gerard Watson and Professor Tom Marsh and Miceal O'Regan, O.P., for his wisdom of spirit; to my family, for the shelter, support, and understanding; to Conamara and Clare, for their mystical spirit which awakens such longing and offers such a tenderness of belonging. Agus do mo cáirde a thug foscadh, solas agus solás.

Prologue

I REMEMBER AS A CHILD discovering the echo of sound. It was the first time that my father took me up the mountain to herd the cattle. As we passed a limestone cliff, he called out to the cattle in the distance. His call had barely ended when it was copied exactly and sent forth again by the stone. It was a fascinating discovery. I tried out my own voice and the echo returned faithfully every time. It was as if the solid limestone mountains had secret hearing and voice. Their natural stillness and silence suddenly broke forth in an exact mimic of the human voice, indicating that there is a resonant heart in the depths of silence; the stone responds in a symmetry of sound. Hearing one's echo out among the lonely mountains seems to suggest that one is not alone. Landscape and nature know us and the returning echo seems to confirm that we belong here. We live in a world that responds to our longing; it is a place where the echoes always return, even if sometimes slowly. It is as if the dynamic symmetry of the echo comprised the radius of an invisible but powerful circle of belonging.

The hunger to belong is at the heart of our nature. Cut off from others, we atrophy and turn in on ourselves. The sense of belonging is the natural balance of our lives. Mostly, we do not need to make an issue of belonging. When we belong, we take it for granted. There is some innocent child-like side to the human heart that is always deeply hurt when we are excluded. Belonging suggests warmth, understanding, and embrace. No one was created for isolation. When we become isolated, we are prone to being damaged; our minds lose their flexibility and natural kindness; we become vulnerable to fear and negativity. The sense of belonging keeps you in balance amidst the inner and outer immensities. The ancient and eternal values of human life—truth, unity, goodness, justice, beauty, and love are all statements of true belonging; they are the also the secret intention and dream of human longing.

Wherever there is distance, there is longing. Yet there is some strange wisdom in the fact of distance. It is interesting to remember that the light that sustains life here on earth comes from elsewhere. Light is the mother of life. Yet the sun and the moon are not on the earth; they bless us with light across the vast distances. We are protected and blessed in our distance. Were we nearer to the sun, the earth would be consumed in its fire; it is the distance that makes the fire kind. Nothing in creation is ever totally at home in itself. No thing is ultimately at one with itself. Everything that is alive holds distance within itself. This is especially true of the human self. It is the deepest intimacy which is nevertheless infused with infinite distance. There is some strange sense in which distance and closeness are sisters, the two sides of the one experience. Distance awakens longing; closeness is belonging. Yet they are always in a dynamic interflow with each other. When we fix or locate them definitively, we injure our growth. It is an interesting imaginative exercise to interchange them: to consider what is near as distant and to consider the distant as intimate.

Our hunger to belong is the longing to find a bridge across the distance from isolation to intimacy. Every one longs for intimacy and dreams of a nest of belonging in which one is embraced, seen, and loved. Something within each of us cries out for belonging. We can have all the world has to offer in terms of status, achievement, and possessions. Yet without a sense of belonging it all seems empty and pointless. Like the tree that puts roots deep into the clay, each of us needs the anchor of belonging in order to bend with the storms and reach towards the light. Like the ocean that returns each time to the same shore, a sense of belonging liberates us to trust fully the rhythm of loss and longing; it also shelters us from the loneliness of life. Though we may not reflect too frequently on the vast infinity that surrounds us, something within us is always aware of it. Such infinity can be anonymous and threatening; it makes us feel inconsequential and tiny. Unknown to us this intensifies our hunger to belong. The universe is too big for us; we long for a sure nest to shelter. The sense of belonging also shelters us from the inner infinity which each of us secretly carries. There is a huge abyss within every mind. When we belong, we have an outside mooring to prevent us from falling into ourselves.

Each one of us journeys alone to this world and it is our nature to seek out belonging. Each of us carries a unique world within our hearts. Each soul is a different shape. No one feels your life as you do; no one experiences things the way you do. Your life is a totally unique story and only you really know it from within. No one knows what your experience is like. The experience of each of us is opaque and inaccessible to outsiders. Yet no individual is sealed off or hermetically self-enclosed. Though each soul is individual and unique, by its very nature the soul cannot cut itself off from the world. The deepest nature of the soul is relationship. Consequently, it is your soul that longs to belong; it is also your soul that makes all belonging possible. No soul is private or merely mortal. As well as being the vital principle of your individual life, your soul is also ancient and eternal and weaves you into the great tapestry of spirit that connects everything everywhere. There is a lovely balance at the heart of our nature: each of us is utterly unique and yet we live in the most intimate kinship with everyone and everything else. Belonging is not merely shelter from being separate and different. Its more profound intention is the awakening of the Great Belonging which embraces everything. Our hunger to belong is the desire to awaken this hidden affinity. Then we know that we are not outsiders cut off from everything, but rather participants at the heart of creation. Each of us brings something alive in the world that no one else can. There is a profound necessity at the heart of individuality. When your life awakens and you begin to sense the destiny that brought you here, you endeavour to live a life that is generous and worthy of the blessing and invitation that is always calling you.

In post-modern culture there is a deep hunger to belong. An increasing majority of people feel isolated and marginalised. Experience is haunted by fragmentation. Many of the traditional shelters are in ruins. Society is losing the art of fostering community. Consumerism is now propelling life towards the lonely isolation of individualism. Technology pretends to unite us, yet more often than not all it delivers are simulated images. The "global village" has no roads or neighbours; it is a faceless limbo from which all individuality has been abstracted. Politics seems devoid of the imagination that calls forth vision and ideals; it is becoming ever more synonymous with the functionalism of economic pragmatism. Many of the keepers of the great religious traditions now seem to be frightened functionaries; in a more uniform culture, their management skills would be efficient and successful. In a pluralistic and deeply fragmented culture, they seem unable to converse with the complexities and hungers of our longing. From this perspective, it seems that we are in the midst of a huge crisis of belonging. When the outer cultural shelters are in ruins, we need to explore and reawaken the depths of belonging in the human mind and soul; perhaps, the recognition of the depth of our hunger to belong may gradually assist us in awakening new and unexpected possibilities of community and friendship.

In a universe of absolute stillness, there would be no question about belonging. Everything would be at one in the same eternal still life. The sway of nature and the swerve of thought means that space and distance are alive with longing. No thing can be itself completely without the other. No one can be herself without the other sisters and brothers. The one who dreamed the universe loved circles and created everything with such beautiful incompletion that we need the others to complete the circles of identity, belonging, and creativity. Life is full of magnetic interims that call what is separate and different to become one, to enter into the art and presence of belonging.

Our world is suffused with beauty. There are landscapes, oceans, paintings, and music whose beauty awakens in our hearts a sense of the eternal. Yet nowhere do we feel so deeply encountered as we do in the presence of another human being. There is something in another human presence that is equal to our longing and soul. The human heart is a theater of longing. One of our deepest longings is to find love and friendship. In the Celtic tradition there was the beautiful notion of the Anam-Ċara. Anam is the Irish word for "soul" and Ċara is the word for "friend." In the Anam-Ċara friendship, you were joined in an ancient way with the friend of your soul. This was a bond that neither space nor time could damage. The friendship awakened an eternal echo in the hearts of the friends; they entered into a circle of intimate belonging with each other. The Anam-Ċara friendship afforded a spiritual space to all the other longings of the human heart.

There is a divine restlessness in the human heart. Though our bodies maintain an outer stability and consistency, the heart is an eternal nomad. No circle of belonging can ever contain all the longings of the human heart. As Shakespeare said, we have "immortal longings." All human creativity issues from the urgency of longing. Literally and physically, each of us is a child of longing—conceived in the passionate desire of our parents for each other. All growth is the desire of the soul to refine and enlarge its presence. The human body is a temple of sensuous spirit. In every moment our senses reach out in longing to engage the world. Movement, colour, and shape engage the affections of the eye; tone, sound, and silence call continually to our hearing; touch, fragrance, and taste also bring us into intimacy with the world. Our sensuous longing is inevitably immediate and passionate: the caress on the skin, the twilight that enthrals your seeing, Fauré's *Requiem* which suffuses the depths of your hearing, the unexpected fragrance of a perfume, the icon of the face that you love. As long as we live in the temple of the senses, longing will eternally call us.

In the inner world, thoughts are, as Meister Eckhart said "our inner senses." The eros of thought is the longing that voyages inwards to discover the secret landscapes of soul, mind, and memory. Through our thoughts, we discover who we are and which presences inhabit our hearts. Thought puts a face on experience and probes the mystery of things. It looks below the surface and seeks the substance. Everything humans have done on earth is an expression of thought. Without thinking none of it would have happened. From the ancient monuments to modern architecture, from the cave paintings to e-mail, from the Druids to modern ritual, human thought has continually incarnated human longing. The world that we have fashioned with its history and cul-

ture expresses the diversity and complexity of human long-
ing. Work is human desire in action.

Many of the really powerful forces in contemporary cul-
ture work to seduce human longing along the pathways of
false satisfaction. When our longing becomes numbed, our
sense of belonging becomes empty and cold; this intensifies
the sense of isolation and distance that so many people now
feel. Consumerism is the worship of the god of quantity;
advertising is its liturgy. Advertising is schooling in false
longing. More and more the world of image claims our long-
ing. Image is mere surface veneer. It is no wonder that there
is such a crisis of belonging now since there is no homeland
in this external world of image and product. It is a famine
field of the Spirit. Despite all the energy and development
that have taken place many areas in modern life are losing
their nature and grace.

The restlessness in the human heart will never be finally
stilled by any person, project, or place. The longing is eternal.
This is what constantly qualifies and enlarges our circles of
belonging. There is a constant and vital tension between
longing and belonging. Without the shelter of belonging, our
longings would lack direction, focus, and context; they would
be aimless and haunted, constantly tugging the heart in a
myriad of opposing directions. Without belonging, our long-
ing would be demented. As memory gathers and anchors
time, so does belonging shelter longing. Belonging without
longing would be empty and dead, a cold frame around
emptiness. One often notices this in relationships where the
longing has died; they have become arrangements, and there
is no longer any shared or vital presence. When longing dies,
creativity ceases. The arduous task of being a human is to
balance longing and belonging so that they work with and
against each other to ensure that all the potential and gifts
that sleep in the clay of the heart may be awakened and real-

ized in this one life. All our longing is but an eternal echo of the Divine Longing which has created us and sustains us here. Sheltered within the embrace of that Great Belonging we can dare to let our longing lead us towards the mountain of transfiguration.

In Greek mythology, the theme of longing and belonging finds poignant expression in the story of Echo. The nymph called Echo could only use her voice in repetition of another. Echo was one of the many who fell in love with the beautiful Narcissus. One day, she secretly follows Narcissus as he goes out hunting with friends, and although she longs to address him, she is unable to do so because she cannot speak first. Her chance to speak comes when Narcissus loses his friends. Alone and isolated, he calls and Echo seizes the opportunity to speak by repeating his words back to him. But when Narcissus calls to his friends, "Let us come together here," Echo misunderstands him and, rushing to embrace him, reveals herself. Narcissus brutally rejects her and she is doomed to spend the rest of her life pining in demented longing for him.

Narcissus, of course, finally beholds his beauty in his reflection in a pool and falls in love with himself. But this love is torture to him, for, falling in love with himself, he is caught in an unbearable contradiction. In the figure of Narcissus, self and other collapse into one: he is both lover and beloved in one body. Unable to endure the torment of such desperate love that is its own object and can, therefore, never possess itself, he breaks the circle by killing himself. Echo is there at his death to repeat his desolate dying words.

In the subtle wisdom of Greek mythology it is no accident that Narcissus and Echo are paired. It is as if she externalizes the fatal symmetry of Narcissus's self-obsession and his life path, which is littered with those he has rejected. The irony here is that he too will have to reject himself as well, with the same ferocity. Trapped within a sealed circle of self-belonging, his longing for himself leads to self-annihilation. He is unable to build any distance or otherness into his own self-love. It tells us much about the nature of Echo that her fate is twinned with his. She is totally vulnerable because she cannot speak first. Her name and nature are one. She longs for him and when he rejects her, she is doomed to a life of demented longing which reduces her to little more than a lonely, desperate voice.

A book is barely an object; it is a tender presence fashioned from words, the secret echoes of the mind. This book attempts a poetic and speculative exploration of the creative tension between longing and belonging. The text has a dual structure: a first layer of image, story, and reflection, and underlying this a more philosophical subtext which might invite a more personal journey of reflection. The modest hope is that in a broken world full of such eerie silence, this little reflection might clear a space in the heart so that the eternal echoes of your embrace in the shelter of the invisible circle of belonging may become audible. A true sense of belonging should allow us to become free and creative, and inhabit the silent depth within us. Such belonging would be flexible, open, and challenging. Unlike the loneliness of Echo, it should liberate us from the traps of falsity and obsession, and enable us to enter the circle of friendship at the heart of creation. There is a resonant heart in the depth of silence. When your true heart speaks, the echo will return to assure you that every moment of your presence happens in the shelter of the invisible circle. These eternal echoes will transfigure your hunger to belong.

Awakening in the World:
The Threshold of Belonging

The Belonging of the Earth

In the beginning was the dream. In the eternal night where no dawn broke, the dream deepened. Before anything ever was, it had to be dreamed. Everything had its beginning in possibility. Every single thing is somehow the expression and incarnation of a thought. If a thing had never been thought, it could never be. If we take Nature as the great artist of longing then all presences in the world have emerged from her mind and imagination. We are children of the earth's dreaming. When you compare the silent, under-night of Nature with the detached and intimate intensity of the person, it is almost as if Nature is in dream and we are her children who have broken through the dawn into time and place. Fashioned in the dreaming of the clay, we are always somehow haunted by that; we are unable ever finally to decide what is dream and what is reality. Each day we live in what we call reality. Yet the more we think about it, the more life seems to resemble a dream. We rush through our days in such stress and intensity, as if we were here to stay and the serious project of the world depended on us. We worry and grow anxious; we magnify trivia until they become important enough to control our lives. Yet all the time, we have forgotten that we are but temporary sojourners on the surface of a strange planet spinning slowly in the infinite night of the cosmos. There is no protective zone around any of us. Anything can happen to anyone at any time. There is no definitive dividing line between reality and dream. What we consider real is often precariously dreamlike. One of the linguistic philosophers said that there is no evidence that could be employed to disprove this claim: The world only came into existence ten minutes ago complete with all our memories. Any evidence you could proffer could still be accounted for by the claim. Because our grip on reality is tenuous, every heart is infused with the dream of belonging.

Belonging: The Wisdom of Rhythm

To be human is to belong. Belonging is a circle that embraces everything; if we reject it, we damage our nature. The word "belonging" holds together the two fundamental aspects of life: Being and Longing, the longing of our Being and the being of our Longing. Belonging is deep; only in a superficial sense does it refer to our external attachment to people, places, and things. It is the living and passionate presence of the soul. Belonging is the heart and warmth of intimacy. When we deny it, we grow cold and empty. Our life's journey is the task of refining our belonging so that it may become more true, loving, good, and free. We do not have to force belonging. The longing within us always draws us towards belonging and again towards new forms of belonging when we have outgrown the old ones. Postmodern culture tends to define identity in terms of ownership: possessions, status, and qualities. Yet the crucial essence of *who* you are is not owned by you. The most intimate belonging is Self-

Belonging. Yet your *self* is not something you could ever own; it is rather the total gift that every moment of your life endeavours to receive with honor. True belonging is gracious receptivity. This is the appropriate art of belonging in friendship: friends do not belong *to* each other, but rather *with* each other. This *with* reaches to the very depths of their twinned souls.

True belonging is not ownership; it never grasps or holds on from fear or greed. Belonging knows its own shape and direction. True belonging comes from within. It strives for a harmony between the outer forms of belonging and the inner music of the soul. We seem to have forgotten the true depth and spiritual nature of intimate belonging. Our minds are oversaturated and demented. We need to rediscover ascetical tranquillity and come home to the temple of our senses. This would anchor our longing and help us to feel the world from within. When we allow dislocation to control us, we become outsiders, exiled from the intimacy of true unity with ourselves, each other, and creation. Our bodies know that they belong; it is our minds that make our lives so homeless. Guided by longing, belonging is the wisdom of rhythm. When we are in rhythm with our own nature, things flow and balance naturally. Every fragment does not have to be relocated, reordered; things cohere and fit according to their deeper impulse and instinct. Our modern hunger to belong is particularly intense. An increasing majority of people feel no belonging. We have fallen out of rhythm with life. The art of belonging is the recovery of the wisdom of rhythm.

Like fields, mountains, and animals we know we belong here *on* earth. However, unlike them, the quality and passion of our longing make us restlessly aware that we cannot belong *to* the earth. The longing in the human soul makes it impossible for us ever to fully belong to any place, system, or project. We are involved passionately in the world, yet there is nothing here that can claim us completely. When we forget how partial and temporary our belonging must remain, we put ourselves in the way of danger and disappointment. We compromise something eternal within us. The sacred duty of being an individual is to gradually learn how to live so as to awaken the eternal within oneself. Our ways of belonging in the world should never be restricted to or fixated on one kind of belonging that remains stagnant. If you listen to the voices of your own longing, they will constantly call you to new styles of belonging which are energetic and mirror the complexity of your life as you deepen and intensify your presence on earth.

Why Do We Need to Belong?

Why do we need to belong? Why is this desire so deeply rooted in every heart? The longing to belong seems to be ancient and is at the core of our nature. Though you may often feel isolated, it is the nature of your soul to belong. The soul can never be separate, its eternal dream is intimacy and belonging. When we are rejected or excluded, we become deeply wounded. To be forced out, to be pushed to the margin, hurts us. The most terrifying image in Christian theology is a state of absolute exclusion from belonging. The most beautiful image in all religion is Heaven or Nirvana: the place of total belonging, where there is no separation or exclusion anymore. A Buddhist friend once gave a definition of Nirvana: the place where the winds of destiny no longer blow. This suggests that it is a place of undisturbed belonging. We long to belong because we feel the lonesomeness of being individuals. Deep within us, we long to come in from separation and be at home again in the embrace of a larger belonging. The wonder of being a human is the freedom offered to you through your separation and distance from every other person and thing. You should live your freedom to the full, because it is such a unique and temporary gift. The rest of Nature would love to have the liberation we enjoy. When you suppress your wild longing and opt for the predictable and safe forms of belonging, you sin against the rest of Nature that longs to live deeply through you. When your way of belonging in the world is truthful to your nature and your dreams, your heart finds contentment and your soul finds stillness. You are able to participate fully in the joy and adventure of exploration, and your life opens up for living joyfully, powerfully, and tenderly. Conversely, when you are excluded or rejected, your life inevitably tends to narrow into a concern and sometimes an obsession with that exclusion and the attempt to change it.

The shelter of belonging empowers you; it confirms in you a stillness and sureness of heart. You are able to endure external pressure and confusion; you are sure of the ground on which you stand. Perhaps your hunger to belong is always active and intense because you belonged so totally before you came here. This hunger to belong is the echo and reverberation of your invisible and eternal heritage. You are from somewhere else, where you were known, embraced, and sheltered. This is also the secret root from which all longing grows. Something in you knows, perhaps remembers, that eternal belonging liberates longing into its surest and most potent creativity. This is why your longing is often wiser than your conventional sense of appropriateness, safety, and truth. It is the best antidote to the fear of freedom, which is second nature to many people. Your longing desires to take you towards the absolute realization of all the possibilities that sleep in the clay of your heart; it knows your eternal potential, and it will not rest until it is awakened. Your longing is the divine longing in human form.

Restless and Lonesome

Where do we get our idea of belonging from? What is true belonging? It seems that the whole origin of belonging is rooted in the faithfulness of place. Each one of us awakens on the earth in a particular place. This place was and remains full of presence and meaning for us. As a child, one of the first things you learn is your name and where you live. If you were to get lost, you would know where you belong. When you know where you belong, you know where you are. Where you belong is where you inevitably continue to return. In some strange way, you long for the stability and sureness of belonging that Nature enjoys. As you grow, you develop the ideal of where your true belonging could be— the place, the home, the partner, and the work. You seldom achieve all the elements of the ideal, but it travels with you as the criterion and standard of what true belonging could be. You travel certainly, in every sense of the word. But you take with you everything that you have been, just as the landscape stores up its own past. Because you were once at home somewhere, you are never an alien anywhere. No one can survive by remaining totally restless. You need to settle and belong in order to achieve any peace of heart and creativity of imagination.

We live in times of constant activity and excitement. The media present endless images of togetherness, talk shows, and parties. Yet behind all the glossy imagery and activity, there is a haunted lonesomeness at the vacant heart of contemporary life. There is a desperate hunger for belonging. People feel isolated and cut off. Perhaps this is why a whole nation can assemble around the images of celebrities. They have no acquaintance with these celebrities personally. They look at them from a distance and project all their longings onto them. When something happens to a celebrity, they feel as if it is happening to themselves. There is an acute need for the reawakening of the sense of community. It is true that neighbours are not necessarily close to you. They do not need to be friends, but humans who live in clusters with each other are meant to look out for and look after each other, rather than live in such isolation. This is a primal sense of duty. You often notice that when something happens to someone on the street or in the village, neighbours who had never been in the house before come to help and support. In Ireland, this is especially apparent at a time of bereavement. People simply gather around so that you are not left alone with the shock and silence of death. While drawing little attention to itself, this support brings so much healing and shelter. It is something you would never forget, and the beauty is how naturally it happens. During times of suffering, the shelter of belonging calms us. The particular shape of belonging must always strive to meet our longing.

The Voices of Longing

Every human heart is full of longing. You long to be happy, to live a meaningful and honest life, to find love, and to be able to open your heart to someone; you long to discover who you are and to learn how to heal your own suffering and become free and compassionate. To be alive is to be suffused with longing. The voices of longing keep your life alert and urgent. If you cannot discover the shelter of belonging within your life, you could become a victim and target of your longing, pulled hither and thither without any anchorage anywhere. It is consoling that each of us lives and moves within the great embrace of the earth. You can never fall out of the shelter of this belonging. Part of the reason that we are so lonesome in our modern world is that we have lost the sense of belonging on the earth.

If you were a stone, you could remain still, gathered in silent witness in the same landscape. The infinite horizons would never trouble you. Nothing could draw you out. As a human, your daily experience is riven with fracture and fragmentation. You wander like a nomad from event to event, from person to person, unable to settle anywhere for too long. The day is a chase after ghost duties; at evening you are exhausted. A day is over, and so much of it was wasted on things that meant so little to you, duties and meetings from which your heart was absent. Months and years pass, and you fumble on, still incapable of finding a foothold on the path of time you walk. A large proportion of your activity distracts you from remembering that you are a guest of the universe, to whom one life has been given. You mistake the insistent pressure of daily demands for reality, and your more delicate and intuitive nature wilts. When you wake from your obsessions, you feel cheated. Your longing is being numbed, and your belonging becoming merely external. Your way of life has so little to do with what you feel and love in the world but because of the many demands on you and responsibilities you have, you feel helpless to gather your self; you are dragged in so many directions away from true belonging.

I was once at a wedding at which an incident occurred; in fact, it was more an event. The wedding breakfast was over, and the music had begun. An older woman was there. She was a quiet person who kept to herself, a shy country woman who was invited because she was a next-door neighbour of the bride. Everyone knew that her husband was an upright person, but mean and controlling. They suspected that she had a very hard life with him. There always seemed to be a sadness around her. Though he was quite wealthy, she never seemed to have anything new to wear. She had married young in a culture and at a time when if you made a huge mistake in your choice of partner, there was no way out. You continued to lie on your bed of thorns and put a face on things for the neighbours. At the wedding, she began to have a few drinks. She had never drunk alcohol before, and it was not long until the veneer of control and reservation began to fall away. The music was playing but there was no one dancing. She got up and danced on her own. It was a wild dance. It seemed that the music had got inside her and set her soul at large. She was oblivious of everyone. She took the full space of the floor and used it. She danced in movements that mixed ballet and rock. Everyone stood back, watching her, in silence. Her poor dance was lonesome, the fractured movements, the coils of gesture, unravelling in the air. Yet there was something magical happening in it too. Often there is a greater kindness in gesture. Here she was dancing out thirty years of captive longing. The façade of social belonging was down. The things she could never say to anyone came flooding out in her dance. In rhythm with the music, the onlookers began to shout encouragement. She did not even seem to hear them; she was dancing. When the music stopped, she returned to her table blushing, but holding her head high. Her eyes were glad, and there was a smile beginning around the corners of her mouth.

The Feeling That Something Is Missing

The human heart is inhabited by many different longings. In its own voice, each one calls to your life. Some longings are easily recognized, and the direction in which they call you is clear. Other voices are more difficult to decipher. At different times of your life, they whisper to you in unexpected ways. It can take years before you are able to hear where exactly they want to call you. Beneath all these is a longing that has somehow always been there and will continue to accompany every future moment of your life. It is a longing that you will never be able to clearly decipher, though it will never cease to call you. At times, it will bring you to tears; at other times, it will set your heart wild. No person you meet will ever quell it. You can be at one with the love of your life, give all of your heart, and it will still continue to call you. In quiet moments in your love, even at moments of intimacy that feel like an absolute homecoming, a whisper of this longing will often startle you. It may prod you into unease and make you question your self and your ability to love and to open yourself to love. Even when you achieve something that you have worked for over the years, the voice of this longing will often surface and qualify your achievement. When you listen to its whisper, you will realize that it is more than a sense of anti-climax. Even when everything comes together and you have what you want, this unwelcome voice will not be stifled.

What voice is this? Why does it seep with such unease into our happiness? Deep down in each of us is a huge desire to belong. Without a sense of belonging, we are either paralyzed or utterly restless. Naturally, when you enter lovely times of belonging, you would love to anchor and rest there. At such times your heart settles. You feel you have arrived, you relax and let your self belong with all your heart. Then, the voice whispers and your belonging is disturbed. The voice always makes you feel that something is missing. Even when everything you want is on your table, and everyone you love is there in your life, you still feel something is missing. You are not able to name what is missing. If you could, you might be able to go somewhere to get it, but you cannot even begin. Something that feels vital to you lies out of your reach in the unknown. The longing to fill this absence drives some people out of the truth and shelter of love; they begin a haunted journey on a never-ending path in quest of the something that is missing. Others seek it in the accumulation of possessions. Again this small voice leads other people into the quest for the divine.

The voice comes from your soul. It is the voice of the eternal longing within you, and it confirms you as a relentless pilgrim on the earth. There is something within you that no one or nothing else in the world is able to meet or satisfy. When you recognize that such unease is natural, it will free you from getting on the treadmill of chasing ever more temporary and partial satisfactions. This eternal longing will always insist on some door remaining open somewhere in all the shelters where you belong. When you befriend this longing, it will keep you awake and alert to why you are here on earth. It will intensify your journey but also liberate you from the need to go on many seductive but futile quests. Longing can never be fulfilled here on earth. As the Un-Still Stones sang so memorably some decades ago: "I can't get no satisfaction." The beauty of being human is the capacity and desire for intimacy. Yet we know that even those who are most intimate remain strange to us. Like children, we often "make strange" with each other. This keeps our longing alert.

Our Longing to Be Loved

One of the deepest longings in the human heart is the desire to be loved for yourself alone. This longing awakens you completely. When you are touched by love, it reaches down into your deepest fibre. It is difficult to realize actually how desperately we do need love. You inhabit your life; you seem to be in control. You live within an independent physical body. From the outside, you seem to be managing very well. Because you present this face to the world, no one suspects that you have a different "inner body" called the heart, which can do nothing for itself if it is not loved. If our hearts were our outside bodies, we would see crippled bodies transform into ballet dancers under the gaze and in the embrace of love. It is difficult to love yourself, if you are not first loved. When you are loved, your heart rushes forth in the joy of the dance of life. Like someone who has been lost for years in a forgotten place, you rejoice in being found. When you are discovered, you then discover yourself. This infuses your whole life with new vigour and light. People notice a difference in you; it is nice to be around you. Love somehow transfigures the sad gravity of life. The gloom lifts, and your soul is young and free. Love awakens the youthfulness of the heart. You discover your creative force. It is quite touching to see love bring someone home so swiftly to herself. The Conamara poet Caitlin Maude writes:

> His little beak
> Under his wing
> The thrush of our love.
> *Author's translation*

Even without the outside lover, you can become the beloved. When you awaken in appreciation and love for your self, springtime awakens in your heart. Your soul longs to draw you into love for your self. When you enter your soul's affection, the torment ceases in your life. St. Bonaventure says in *The Journey of the Mind to God*: "Enter into yourself, therefore, and observe that your soul loves itself most fervently."

Soul: The Beauty of the Broken Circle

The one who dreamed the universe loved circles. There is some strange way in which everything that goes forward is somehow still travelling within the embrace of the circle. Longing and belonging are fused within the circle. The day, the year, the ocean's way, the light, the water, and the life insist on moving in the rhythm of the circle. The mind is a circle, too. This is what keeps you gathered in your self. If you were just a point in space, you would be forever isolated and alone. If your life were simply a line through time, you would be always trapped at this point with all past and future points absent. The beauty of the mind is its circular form. Yet the circle of the mind is broken somewhere. This fracture is always open; it is the secret well from which all longing flows. All prayer, love, creativity, and joy come from this source; our fear and hurt often convert them into their more sinister shadows.

This breakage within us is what makes us human and vulnerable. There is nothing more sinister than someone whose mind seems to be an absolute circle; there is a helpless coldness and a deadly certainty about such a presence. When you discover this inner well of longing, it can frighten you and send you into flight from yourself. If you can be tranquil, amazing things can flow from it. Your body is open physically to the world and the well of your mind flows out of ancient ground. This is reminiscent of the mountains here in the Burren, in the west of Ireland, where there are many wells. The face of the well is on the surface; it is such a pure and surprising presence. Yet the biography of the well is hidden under eternities of mountain and clay. Similarly, within you the well is an infinite source. The waters are coming from deep down. Yet as long as you are on this earth, this well will never run dry. The flow of thought, feeling, image, and word will always continue. The well of soul flows from the fracture in the circle of the mind. This is, in a sense, a frightening inner opening—anything can flow through from the distant and unknown mountains. Part of the wonder of living a real life is to make peace with this infinite inner opening. Nothing can ever close it. When you listen to the voices of your longing, you will begin to understand the adventure and the promise of life with which you are privileged.

Our Longing for Nature

Celtic spirituality reminds us that we do not live simply in our thoughts, feelings, or relationships. We belong on the earth. The rhythm of the clay and its seasons sings within our hearts. The sun warms the clay and fosters life. The moon blesses the night. In the uncluttered world of Celtic spirituality, there is a clear view of the sacrament of Nature as it brings forth visible presence. The Celts worshipped in groves in Nature and attended to the silent divinity of wild places. Certain wells, trees, animals, and birds were sacred to them. Where and what a people worship always offers a clue to where they understand the source of life to be. Most of our experience of religion happens within the walled frame of church or temple. Our God is approached through thought, word, and ritual. The Celts had no walls around their worship. Being in Nature was already to be in the Divine Presence. Nature was the theatre of the diverse dramaturgies of the divine imagination. This freedom is beautifully echoed in a later lyric poem:

> Ah, blackbird, it is well for you,
> Wherever in the thicket is your nest,
> Hermit that sounds no bell,
> Sweet, soft, fairylike is your note.
> *Translated by Myles Dillon*

The contemplative presence of Nature is not ostentatious nor cluttered by thought. Its majesty and elegance drift into voice in the single, subtle note of the blackbird.

The Sanctuary of a Favourite Place

To awaken a sense of our ancient longing for Nature can help us to anchor our longing. When we go out alone and enter its solitude, we return home to our souls. When you find a place in Nature where the mind and heart find rest, then you have discovered a sanctuary for your soul. The landscape of the West of Ireland offers welcoming shelter to the soul. You can go to places in the limestone mountains where you are above the modern world; you will see nothing from the twenty centuries. There is only the subtle sculpture that rain and wind have indented on the stone. When the light comes out, the stone turns white, and you remember that this is living stone from the floor of an ancient ocean. Your eye notices how the fossils were locked into its solidification. Some of the stone, particularly at the edges, is serrated and shattered. In other places, the long limestone pavement is as pure and clear as if it had just been minted. Swept clean by the wind, these pavements are smooth and certain. The eye is surprised at the still clusters of white, red, and yellow flowers amidst the applause of rock. Moments of absolute blue startle the eye from the nests of gentian. Purple orchids sway elegantly in the breeze. Over the edge of the mountain, you can hear the chorus of the ocean. Its faithful music has never abandoned this stone world that once lived beneath its waters. Perhaps Nature senses the longing that is in us, the restlessness that never lets us settle. She takes us into the tranquillity of her stillness if we visit her. We slip into her quiet contemplation and inhabit for a while the depth of her ancient belonging. Somehow we seem to become one with the rhythm of the universe. Our longing is purified, and we gain strength to come back to life refreshed and to refine our ways of belonging in the world. Nature calls us to tranquillity and rhythm. When your heart is confused or heavy, a day outside in Nature's quiet eternity restores your lost tranquillity.

The Longing of the Earth

There is an ancient faithfulness in Nature. Mountains, fields, and shorelines are still to be found in the same places after thousands of years. Landscape is alive in such a dignified and reserved way. It can keep its memories and dreams to itself. Landscape lives the contemplative life of silence, solitude, and stillness. It carries and holds its depths of darkness and lonesomeness with such perfect equanimity. It never falls out of its native rhythm. Rains come with intensity and surprise. Winds rise and keen like lost children, and grow still. Seasons build and emerge with such sure completion, and give way. Yet Nature never loses its sense of sequence. Tides clear the shore and seem to push the sea out, then turn and with great excitement adorn the shore with blue again. Dawn and dusk frame our time here in sure circles. Landscape is at once self-sufficient and hospitable; we are not always worthy guests.

Though its belonging is still and sure, there is also a sense in which Nature is trapped in the one place. This must intensify the longing at the heart of Nature. A little bird alights and fidgets for a minute on a massive rock that was left behind in the corner of this field by the ice thousands of years ago. The miracle of flight is utter freedom for the bird; it can follow its longing anywhere. The stillness of the stone is pure, but it also means that it can never move one inch from its thousand-year stand. It enjoys absolute belonging, but if it longs to move, it can only dream of the return of the ice. Perhaps the stone's sense of time has the patience of eternity. There is a pathos of stillness in Nature. Yet all of us, its children, are relentlessly moved by longing; we can never enter the innocence of its belonging. Where can we behold Nature's longing? All we see of Nature is surface. The beauty she sends to the surface could only come from the creativity of great and noble longing. The arrival of spring is a miracle of the richest colour. Yet we always seem to forget that all of these beautiful colours have been born in darkness. The dark earth is the well out of which colour flows. Think of the patience of trees: year after year stretching up to the light, keeping a life-line open between the dark night of the clay and the blue shimmer of the heavens. Think of the beautiful, high contours of mountains lifting up the earth, the music of streams, and the fluent travel of rivers linking the stolid silence of land masses with the choruses of the ocean. Think of animals who carry in their dignity and simplicity of presence such refined longing. Think of your self and feel how you belong so deeply to the earth and how you are a tower of longing in which Nature rises up and comes to voice. We are the children of the clay, who have been released so that the earth may dance in the light.

The great Irish writer Liam O'Flaherty was born in Gort nag Capall in Inis Mor in Aran. He left there as a young man and had never returned. Shortly before he died, he returned to that little village. A lifetime of changes had occurred, most of those he once knew were now dead. On his way into the village, he saw the big rock which had been there for thousands of years. O'Flaherty hit the old stone with his walking stick and said, "A Chloich mhóir athním tusa," i.e., O great stone I recognize you. In silence and stillness, the stone held the memory of the village. Stone is the tabernacle of memory. Until we allow some of Nature's stillness to reclaim us, we will remain victims of the instant and never enter the heritage of our ancient belonging.

Our Longing to Know

When we emerged from the earth, not only were we given a unique inner well, but we were also given a mirror in our minds. This mirror is fractured, but it enables us to think about every thing. Our thoughts can gather and ask themselves questions and probe mysteries until some new light is quarried. Because you are human, you are privileged and burdened with the task of knowing. Our desire to know is the deepest longing of the soul; it is a call to intimacy and belonging. We are always in a state of knowing, even when we do not realize it. Though the most subtle minds in the Western tradition have attempted to understand what it is that happens when we know something, no one has succeeded in explaining how we know. When we know something, we come into relationship with it. All our knowing is an attempt to transfigure the unknown—to complete the journey from anonymity to intimacy. Since each one of us lives behind the intimacy of a countenance, we long to put a personal countenance on our experiences. When we know what has happened to us, we will come closer to ourselves and learn more about who we are. Yet the world is not our mirror image. Knowledge, including the knowledge we have of each other, does not abolish the strangeness. True knowledge makes us aware of the numinous and awakens desire.

Aristotle said in the first sentence of his *Metaphysics*, "All men by nature desire to know." This is the secret magic and danger of having a mind. Even though your body is always bound to one place, your mind is a relentless voyager. The mind has a magnificent, creative restlessness that always brings it on a new journey. Even in the most sensible and controlled lives there is often an undertow of longing that would deliver them to distant shores. There is something within you that is not content to remain fixed within any one frame. You cannot immunize yourself against your longing. You love to reach beyond, to discover something new. Knowing calls you out of yourself. Discovery delights the heart. This is the natural joy of childhood and the earned joy of the artist. The child and the artist are pilgrims of discovery. When you limit your life to the one frame of thinking, you close out the mystery. When you fence in the desires of your heart within fixed walls of belief, morality, and convention, you dishonour the call to discovery. You create grey fields of "quiet desperation." Discovery is the nature of the soul. There is some wildness of divinity in us, calling us to live everything. The Irish poet Patrick Kavanagh said, "To be dead is to stop believing in / The masterpieces we will begin tomorrow."

Discovery Is the Nature of the Soul

The presence of a person who has stillness and contentment of heart engenders trust. They can sift from the chaff of talk and select what has weight and worth. Sometimes the dignity of their composure can bring the company of those present to a finer level of attention and worthiness. Conversely, you become uneasy in the presence of someone whose stillness and contentment are forced. Their composure only endures because it operates within a very limited frame of self-protection and denial. It is difficult to feel that you can be yourself in the company of such efficiently quelled longing. When you open your heart to discovery, you will be called to step outside the comfort barriers within which you have fortified your life. You will be called to risk old views and thoughts and to step off the circle of routine and image. This will often bring turbulence. The pendulum will fix at times on one extreme, and you will be out of balance. But your soul loves the danger of growth. In its own wise trust, your soul will always return you to a place of real and vital equilibrium.

The very nature of the universe invites you to journey and discover it. The earth wants our minds to listen attentively and gaze wisely so that we may learn its secrets and name them. We are the echo-mirrors of contemplative Nature. One of our most sacred duties is to be open and faithful to the subtle voices of the universe which come alive in our longing. Aristotle said that the reason we can know anything is that there is a morphic affinity between us and Nature; this is the intimate and precise affinity of form. Animals, trees, fields, and tides have other duties. For this alone have we been freed and blessed. Either we are in the universe to inhabit the lovely eternity of our souls and grow real, or else we might as well dedicate our days to shopping and kill time watching talk shows.

Life as a Pilgrimage of Discovery

Ideally, a human life should be a constant pilgrimage of discovery. The most exciting discoveries happen at the frontiers. When you come to know something new, you come closer to yourself and to the world. Discovery enlarges and refines your sensibility. When you discover something, you transfigure some of the forsakenness of the world. Nature comes to know itself anew in your discoveries. Creative human thought adds to the brightness of the world. Yet there is a strong seam of thought which has always de-animated nature and reduced the earth to a mere playground for the worst fantasies of human greed. Why is this? Such blind and destructive perception is often secretly driven by guilt. There is profound but subtle cosmological guilt in human beings. We even communicate guilt to our dogs! Yet the animal world often offers images of pure discovery. My neighbour's pony had a beautiful brown foal early in the spring. In the first days, she followed her mother awkwardly on the uneven ground with her long, new, gangly legs. One afternoon as they were both lying down, the new foal got up and moved away on her own a little more confidently, and then more swiftly with every step. Then, suddenly, she found she could move faster, and then she discovered that she could run. It was a marvelous sight. She started to run so swiftly and gracefully, her head held high, circling round and round the stony field. She was utterly ecstatic at the discovery of her new swiftness. She would come back time and again and halt before her mother as if to say: "Hey see what I can do." Each one of us has made a huge discovery that we have never gotten over. This is the discovery of the world. Our first journey was the journey to the earth and we are still travelling.

The First Journey Creates the Traveller

We are always on a journey from darkness into light. The journey from anonymity to intimacy is one we continually travel. Indeed, the human self, both body and mind, arrives in the world through this journey. We come out of anonymity into light. By some strange destiny, seeds engage each other in the darkness of the womb. It is startling that the infinite intimacy of the human person begins in this unknown encounter between two individuals. Our parents set us on this journey when they make love and conceive us. We forget that our very conception emerged out of the passionate act of their longing for each other. It is no surprise that we are filled with desire. Each of us is literally a child of longing. On its journey to humanity, the embryo actually travels through all the shapes of evolution. Each of these embryonic shapes becomes ever more personal until the blur of forms finally clarifies as the baby's body, and the intimacy of a human countenance emerges. It is no wonder that we have such hunger to belong. The very formation of our tiny bodies as babies was itself a journey of the most precarious longing.

Already in you as a little dot of presence, some powerful longing knew how to guide original belonging to undertake the journey from nowhere towards the intimacy of becoming an individual with your own world within. Usually on a journey you leave a point and travel through a place until you arrive at an intended destination. Your journey into this planet was different from any other journey you will ever make. The journey actually created the one who travelled and created the inner landscape of mind and soul of the traveller. The elemental metamorphosed into the human. This is an instance of the astounding symmetry in Nature. The inner sphere of the womb mirrors and completes the outer journey of evolution. There was some ancient pre-conscious sense of belonging alive in you which already felt enough connection with the mother to start on this dangerous path. Nothing remained the same. All the changes happened in the blind darkness, and the transition to each new stage entailed such complete transformation. The depth and poignant consistency of your hunger to belong can be traced to this forgotten journey between the worlds.

In the womb something inside you already knew you were growing towards belonging. The hunger to belong is not merely a desire to be attached to something. It is rather sensing that great transformation and discovery become possible when belonging is sheltered and true. Belonging is a call to integrity and creativity. The structure of this call illuminates the very nature of belonging. The first belonging is to the body of the mother. Only when desire and destiny help realize this belonging does the embryo grow into self-identity and reach the threshold of belonging to itself. This first belonging is a blind and vulnerable struggle. It is a secret growth in the darkness. Without this primal longing to belong, no individual could ever come into being. When we normally think about people, we inevitably forget that each person actually grew out of this original impulse to belong. This pre-conscious longing grew to become the mind, body, and spirit of a person. This belonging was not a static, fixed attachment. It was alive with desire and the wish to become the one you dreamed.

Even as a little micro-essence of tissue you cling internally to the mother until you develop your own body to cross the next threshold into the distance-filled world. Despite all the scientific inventions that can provide information on the unborn child, the truth is, the really important things remain unknown. Something within you already knows the infinities that lie in wait outside the mother and recognizes that the only way of traversing them is to become a body. To be born is an incredible event, a great disturbance. You are cast out; thrown from the cave into the light. It is interesting that your first moment of experience is a moment of disturbance. In its abrupt dislocation, birth already holds the echo of death. The rhythm of this moment prefigures the subsequent rhythm of your life: parting and coming together. There can be no union without separation, no return without parting. No belonging is permanent. To live a creative and truthful life, it is vital to learn the art of being separate and the generosity of uniting.

Imagining the Time Before Coming Here

Despite its endless and vital artistry, Nature maintains great secrecy and reserve. When we see a pregnant woman, we know that some new person is coming here. Everything else remains unknown. Who that person is, and what she will bring to her family, and world, and what kind of life she will have remain unknown to us and even to the mother, the carrier and the labyrinth of this creativity. This is one of the great privileges of women, to be able to give birth. Mothers are the priestesses of the greatest Eucharist. In and through the mother, empty space is changed into person. The anonymous water element becomes face, body, soul, life, and inner world. To give birth can also be a great burden. Sometimes the weary face of a pregnant mother reveals how her essence is being rifled and her body and mind become implicated in the baby's destiny. A bond is being developed from which she will never be released. In a sense, she can never part from the one she has carried under her heart. To be involved in Nature's most powerful mystery can also destroy all illusions and innocence. A friend told me recently that her moment of bleakest disillusionment was in hospital shortly before she went into labour with her first child. She walked out onto the hospital fire escape, looked into the night, and realized her absolute isolation and saw opening before her a never-ending path of responsibility.

There is no other way into the universe except through the body of the woman. But where were you before you were conceived and entered the womb? This is one of the most fascinating in-between times in any life. It is also the one we know least about. Yet it is a journey that each of us has made. In the Western and Oriental traditions, we have a vast architecture of theory regarding life after death; there are bardos, purgatories, Nirvana, and beatific visions. There is a carefully thought-out path of continuity, transfiguration, and final homecoming after death. It is interesting to note the substantial absence, especially in the Christian tradition, of any geography of the time before we were conceived. Maybe it sounds ridiculous to explore this, since we did not exist before we were conceived. This may be true, but it is surely too simple to imagine that one moment there was no sign of you, everything was blank and empty, and then the next moment you began to be there. If you came out of somewhere, then you had to be somewhere before you came. There can be no such apparitions or pure beginnings. As well as having an "afterwards" every person has a "before." The difficulty in imagining this is that the other world is invisible, and all we have are intimations of our invisible past.

Each of us comes from somewhere more ancient than any family. Normally, if someone asks you where you are from, you can name a house, a street, a landscape. You have an address, parents, and family. This is indeed where you are from now, but this information becomes weak when the question deepens to where you are ultimately from. When you think even simply about your parents' life, they had a whole life as strangers before they ever knew each other. You were not even a twinkle in their eyes then. Even when they came together, there was no sign, talk, or notion of you. When you reflect further, you begin to see that your ultimate address is Elsewhere. Though you are now totally here, you are essentially not from here. You are a child of the invisible. You were not in any physical form before you were conceived. You emerged in seconds from the invisible and began to grow within darkness. This is why birth is always a surprise. It is the first sighting of the invisible one. Everyone wants to see the new baby. Suddenly, there is someone here who has never been seen before. In the excitement of the new baby's arrival, we often fail to notice the silent wound in the invisible world which allowed the new arrival to come through. We also forget the whole background which the new baby has had in the invisible world: the dream of its destiny, body, face, life, and temperament. Many silent questions accompany a birth: Why did this baby come here now, to this family? What changes will it bring? Who is this new person? In each new heart a bridge between the invisible and the visible world opens.

The Invisible World Is All Around Us

That which we can see is the visible; that which we cannot see is the invisible. Within us and around us there is an invisible world; this is where each of us comes from. Your relationship to the invisible influences so much of your life. When you cross over from the invisible into this physical world, you bring with you a sense of belonging to the invisible that you can never lose or finally cancel. When you cross this threshold, you come into the gravity that rules the visible world. Space and time now set the frame for most of your experience. Once you come here, you can never stop experiencing things. Every second of your life something new is going on: you notice a tree, remember a phrase someone said last night, daydream of holidays or wonder what is making you so uneasy. Everything that you experience is now framed in a very definite way. All your experience happens someplace and always at a definite time. As you live here you build a new section of your biography each day. You trust what you see and know what you hear. You know your real life is happening here. Yet your longing for the invisible is never stilled. There is always some magnet that draws your eyes to the horizon or invites you to explore behind things and seek out the concealed depths. You know that the real nature of things is hidden deep within them. When you enter the world, you come to live on the threshold between the visible and the invisible. This tension infuses your life with longing. Now you belong fully neither to the visible nor to the invisible. This is precisely what kindles and rekindles all your longing and your hunger to belong. You are both artist and pilgrim of the threshold.

Forms of the Invisible

The invisible is one of the huge regions in your life. Some of the most important things about you and your life are invisible. What you think and the way you think control how you feel, how you meet people, and how you see the world. Yet your thoughts are invisible. One of the most fascinating questions about your thinking is, Why do you have the thoughts that you do, and why do you link them together in these patterns? The secret bridges from thought to thought are invisible. No surgeon operating on a brain has ever found a crevice full of thoughts. What you believe about yourself determines how people treat you. Yet you can never see your beliefs. Belief is invisible. Your feelings make you sad or happy, yet the feelings are invisible, too. The greatest presence from whom all things come and who holds all things together is also invisible. No one can see God. Because the invisible cannot be seen or glimpsed with the human eye, it belongs largely to the unknown. Still there are occasional moments when the invisible seems to become faintly perceptible. Sometimes, over a fire built out in the open, one can glimpse layers of air trembling. Or when a candle seems to make the air quiver. Maybe this is why we love colours. They bring the longing at the heart of the invisible to such passionate expression.

Under the guise of emptiness, the invisible keeps its secrets to itself. Yet the invisible remains the great background which invests your every gesture and action with possibility and pathos. The artistic imagination brings this out. We see this especially in sculpture. The shape of the sculpture evokes the shape of the emptiness around it. Also in dance we see how the body creates fluent sculpture in the air. It draws out the hospitality of the invisible. There is something quite courageous in the endurance of human presence against the vast canopy of the invisible. We endure the invisible by forgetting it—for as long as we can. When you become aware of the invisible as a live background, you notice how your own body is woven around your invisible soul, how the invisible lives behind the faces of those you love, and how it is always there between you. The invisible is one of the most powerful forms of the unknown. It envelopes our every movement. It is the region out of which we emerged and the state we are destined for, yet we never see it. There is no map with which to discern territories of the invisible. It is without texture. This is probably why we long to ignore the invisible. There is a sense in which the invisible is the home of fear. We tend to be afraid of what we cannot see or know.

The Mystery of Resemblance

In Conamara, when someone asks a child who he is, the child is not simply asked for his name. The question is, "Cé leis thú?" i.e., To whom do you belong? There is a recognition in the language that your identity is not merely your own personal marker. You are both an expression and extension of an already acknowledged family line. This tradition is further intensified in Conamara through the use of patronymics. If a person is called Sean O'Malley and his father was Tom and his grandfather was Páraich, Sean O'Malley could be known as Séan Tom Pháraich. His name becomes an articulation of the line of ancestry to which he belongs. The language is an echo of this belonging. Its constant use reinforces the reference and brings the presence of the ancestors to word. A long chain of belonging comes alive in the clink of a name.

The universe is full of differences. No two stones or flowers or faces are ever the same. There is such an intricate tapestry of differentiation in even the simplest places. On the seashore, no two seashells are ever quite the same. When you focus your attention, the texture and range of the differences in Nature becomes more visible. Against this perspective the discovery of resemblance is startling, especially in human beings. Each individual carries a totally separate world in his or her heart. When you reflect on how differently you feel and think about life, it is a wonder that we can talk to each other at all. Even between the closest people, there are long bridges. This makes us attractive and fascinating to each other. To see a resemblance between people in the one family is interesting, a child's resemblance to an ancestor. For a moment in a gesture, a way of walking, looking, responding, or saying something, you glimpse the presence of an uncle or grandparent. Resemblance has a certain pathos. You behold the gesture, the looks of one person in another. However, each person is a different world. Although the resemblance indicates continuity, it also reveals the distance of the two lives from each other. Resemblance remains a startling index of the way in which two people can so obviously belong to the same clan. There can sometimes be a striking resemblance between people who do not belong to the same family. An old man I know who has been quite ill was making his first journey to Ireland recently. As his daughter picked him up at the airport, he pointed to a woman who seemed to be his recently deceased mother. When the woman turned around, the resemblance vanished. For a moment, the resemblance had startled both father and daughter.

Home as the Cradle of Destiny

There are many places of power in the world: the Pentagon, the Kremlin, the Vatican. Yet the most powerful place of all barely draws attention to itself. This is the family home. One evening, I remember going for a walk. As I came home, the light was ebbing slowly. As the black tide of night was filling the valley, lights began to come on in the houses. The little lights seemed so fragile against the onrush of the night. This has always remained with me as an image of the vulnerability of human presence against the darkness of anonymity. Anywhere the tenderness gathers itself, life often seems to assemble in threat about its nest. This is why all the major thresholds in human life have blessing structures around them in the religious traditions: birth, initiation, illness, marriage, and death. There is a fragility and pathos in light when darkness encircles it. When you drive through a village at evening and the lights come on before the curtains are drawn, for a second you are allowed a glimpse into individual homes. The inhabitants become visible as they move about or sit down together to dinner. Within these walls a unique set of lives is framed and formed. Behind the guise of normal interaction, they are having a huge influence on the hearts and minds of each other. While the home may be a powerful cradle influencing mind and personality, the lack of home is also a huge influence. So many children in poverty-stricken areas are homeless. Some are in institutional care. Imagine how difficult it must be for these little vulnerable ones to develop minds and hearts where they can rest and feel the warmth and shelter of self-belonging. Being deprived of intimate shelter at such a crucial time must cast a lonesome shadow over their future struggle to belong within society.

The Family as Nest of Belonging

The family is the most powerful structure of human belonging in the world. Within the limited compass of the home, a wide range of energies is simultaneously awakening. Limited space inevitably forces form. Their belonging together offers an outer unity to the world. In the family, the emergence of individuality is complex and always accompanied by either a latent or explicit struggle between the different family members. Later in life, when one begins to explore one's identity, it is surprising to learn how the roots of one's personality inevitably lead back to the unsuspecting home. The sources of your potential and the secrets of your blindness lie concealed there. The family is the first place where you stretch and test your essence. A family is not a monument to an extended egotism; it must be pervious, open in communication with the larger world. However, it is never a clear space where you can move as you wish. Family is a warm but cluttered space. Each family member must earn his own room in competition with the others. Yet amidst the cut and thrust of life, especially when times are difficult, it is great to know that you have your family.

A home is a place where a set of different destinies begin to articulate and define themselves. It is the cradle of one's future. Home is the place where the stranger arrives, the place where you see things for the first time. Here you first begin to know that you have a body. You come to know smell, touch, and hearing. Home is the place where your infant senses are fostered. You have been on a long journey; now you settle and learn to recognize things. Here you learn how to cry and begin to notice how the cry and the smile get you attention. Home is where you first notice others, where you first sense that you are separate and different. It is the place where you first recognize your own gender. The fascinating thing about home is how it functions, without the superintendence of consciousness, yet different gifts are being quietly received by each member of the family. Gifts that will take a full lifetime to unwrap and recognize.

Home Is Where You Belong

The word "home" has a wonderful resonance. Home is where you belong. It is your shelter and place of rest, the place where you can be yourself. Nature offers wonderful images of home. It is fascinating in springtime to watch the birds build their nests. They gather the twigs and weave them into a nest. The floor and walls of the nest are padded with wool, moss, or fur. In the wall of a shed near my house, a swallow returns from Africa every year and finds her way back into the opening between the same two stones under the side wall. There she builds her nest and hatches out her young. No journey is too long when you are coming home. In Irish we say, "Níl aon tinnteán mar do thinnteán féin," i.e., There is no hearth like the hearth at home.

There is such wisdom in Nature. Often it carries out its most miraculous work quietly under the veil of the ordinary. Sometimes we achieve the most wonderful things when we are not even aware of what we are doing. If we did know it, we might only paralyze ourselves and ruin the flow of natural creativity. If parents were fully aware of their effect, they could never act. If they could see the secret work of mind formation in the home and the harvest it will eventually bring, they could never achieve the neutrality that allows normal home life to happen in a natural way. Parents are generally wonderful people who give all their hearts and energy to the little people they have called into the universe. Parents must act in good faith—without excessive anxiety or self-rebuke. They must induct their children into the larger community.

Childhood as a Magic Forest

To a child, the parents are gods. Children are totally vulnerable. They are still only at the threshold of themselves.

During your life on earth, childhood is the time of most intense happening. Yet ironically, it is also the most silent time in your life. You are having immense experiences of wonder, discovery, and difficulty, but the words and thoughts to name them have not yet arrived. This time of fermentation and change will influence so much of your later life, yet you have so little access to the integrating power of thoughts and words. Consequently, the depths of your experience as a child remain opaque. Childhood is a forest we never recognize while we are in it. Our minds and imagination and dreams constantly return there to explore the roots of our personality and presence. We try to unravel from the forest of first feelings and first events the secret of the patterns which have now become our second nature.

Childhood is an absolute treasure house of imagination. It is the forest of first encounters to which we can never again return. We have become too used to the world; wonder no longer animates us as it did then. There is so much that we can find out about the magic of our souls by revisiting these memories of first acquaintance. Never again do we experienceso directly and powerfully the surprise and the fresh tang of novelty. The forest of childhood is also the territory where our dreams, imagination, and images were first seeded. So much happened to us there under the canopy of innocence. It was only later that we could notice that the shadows were present too. The memory of childhood is so rich that it takes a lifetime to unpack. Again and again, we remember certain scenes, not always the most dramatic, and gradually come to a kind of self-understanding and an understanding of our parents. When we are as old as they were when we first knew them, whose face do we see in the mirror—ours or theirs?

The Belonging of Childhood

Innocence is precious and powerful. It is expected and acknowledged as a natural fact that a child is innocent. Yet innocence is more sophisticated than mere ignorance, lack of knowledge, or lack of experience. It is not accidental that the manner of our arrival in the universe is shrouded in innocence. This first innocence protects us from knowing the sinister negativity of life. It also immunizes us against recognition of how strange it is to be here, thrown into a world which is crowded with infinities of space, time, matter, and difference. It should be frightening to be a child in such a vast and unpredictable universe, but the little child never notices the danger directly. Innocence is a state of unknowing and the readiness to know. The wisdom of the human mind, especially in the child, ensures that knowing the world happens in stages. The innocence of childhood never breaks completely in one vast bright or dark epiphany. It only gives way gradually to new recognitions and experiences. Even when severe trauma occurs, it is somehow integrated; though it does deep damage, it still rarely extinguishes the flame of innocence. There is a poignant sense in which the child must keep its innocence alive in order to continue to grow and not allow the darkness to swamp its little mind. Innocence minds us. It only lets us become aware of what we are able to handle. Innocence permits the child to belong in the world. This is the secret of the child's trust; it assumes that belonging is natural and sheltering. Experiments have shown that young children who have been thoroughly cautioned against the danger of strangers can still be coaxed and will walk off with a stranger in a public place while the parent is momentarily occupied. The innocence of childhood renews that of the parents and quickens their instinct to preserve it.

Innocence Keeps Mystery Playful

Innocence has a lyrical continuity. A child cannot turn it on and off. The fractures in innocence are partial. In different moments, thresholds are crossed into experience. Yet innocence manages to hold off the full recognition of how broken the human journey will be. The innocence of the child is its immediacy and nearness to everything. Rilke says that in all our subsequent life we will never again be as close to anything as we were to our toys in childhood. The toy becomes your friend and closest confidant. Before and below words, you invest the delight and concern of your heart in the toy. If you are clearing out an attic and you come across one of your old toys from childhood, it can release a flood of memories. The child lives in the neighbourhood of wonder where innocence keeps mystery playful. Each new event and encounter is all-absorbing. No overall perspective on life is available. The child lives in the house of discovery. The unconscious innocence of the child assembles new experiences. It is their cumulative gathering which eventually signals the end of childhood. Brick by brick, the house of innocence falls to ruins. Once that threshold into adulthood is crossed, one may never return again to the kingdom of innocence. Innocence always urges the child to explore and continues to pace and shelter this exploration until the child is finally adult and ready to stand alone in its new knowing. In contrast to how a child belongs in the world, adult belonging is never as natural, innocent, or playful. Adult belonging has to be chosen, received, and renewed. It is a lifetime's work.

Childhood experience is deeply infused with longing. The adventure of being here is utterly engaging. There is longing to explore, to play, and to discover. Because the sense and contour of the self are only coming into definition, the child's sense of longing is largely unrefined. This is often evident in the way children play with each other. Their play is never merely chaotic. It is inevitably governed by self-conscious and elaborate rules which they stipulate. Perhaps these delineate safe zones in which new experience becomes possible.

The Longing of Childhood Is Akin to Dream

The imagination of early childhood has no limits. This is why children are fascinated by stories. A story has permission to go anywhere. Its characters can have any powers and do anything they like. The child rarely experiences the story as an observer. The child enters the story, experiencing its drama from within. Often a child will explicitly ask to be included as one of the characters in a story: "Which am I, Daddy?" The wonder and imagination of the child are awakened and engaged. Perhaps the shape of story fascinates the child, because it takes the child's longing to wild and dangerous frontiers where it cannot go in its day-to-day life. The story allows the child to act with a power and strength which are impossible in the limitation of its present little body. Anything and everything is possible in a story. The longing of the child lives in the realm of pure possibility. All doors are open. All barriers are down. Because it is a story with a beginning, middle, and end, it offers a form of belonging in which the full adventure of longing can be explored. Narrative is a dramatic form of continuity created by longing, and it is also a place where human desire can come home. Great stories retain resonance because they embody the "immortal longings" of the heart; our longing to enter them comes from the child-like side of our hearts.

Childhood's Dark Innocence

The innocence of childhood is never simply pure. Childhood also has a dark innocence. In its unknowing, the child senses the presence of negativity and evil. The fascination with monsters and sinister goblins often grips the little mind. Children are not interested in stories which lack the dimension of fear. This accounts for the subtle depth of fairy tales.

The Red Bush of Ancestry

As individuals, we are cut off from the dense and intricate networks of life within us. A simple instance of this is when you cut your finger, the surprise of seeing your own blood flow. We forget the tree of bone and the bush of blood that flows within us. Blood is one of the most ancient and wisest streams in the universe. It is the stream of ancestry. An ancient bloodline flows from the past generations until it reaches and creates us now. Blood holds and carries life. From mythic times, blood has been at the heart of sacrifice; life was offered both as plea and praise to the deities. The Catholic Eucharist still centres on the transfiguration of the wine of the earth into the divine blood of the Redeemer. This consecration is not merely a memorial of the past event. The divine presence in the Eucharist is understood as an actual participation in the ongoing memory of God.

Superficially, a family might look like an accidental gathering of individuals called together by the chance meeting of a man and a woman who fell in love and wanted to express the depth of their love in procreation. At a deeper level, a family is an incredible intertwining of multiple streams of ancestry, memory, shadow, and light. Each home hosts the arrival of history and assists the departure of new destiny. The walls of the home contain immense happenings that occur gradually under the subtle veil of normality. Though each family is a set of new individuals, ancient relics and residues seep through from past generations. Except for our parents and grandparents, our ancestors have vanished. Yet ultimately and proximately, it is the ancestors who call us here. We belong to their lifeline. While they ground our unknown memory, our continuity bestows on them a certain oblique eternity. In our presence we entwine past and future. Virgil underlines the beautiful value of "pietas." It means much more than duty; it is prospective as well as retrospective. Though Aenaeas is utterly committed to his huge and painful destiny, he is concerned for his son as well as his father.

The loneliness and creativity of being a parent is the recognition that family is inevitably temporary. Good parenting is unselfish and, to encourage independence in a child that has received unconditional love, acts to reinforce the sense and essence of belonging. Nothing, not even departure, can sever that intrinsic sense of belonging. Children are created to grow and leave the nest. Family provides the original and essential belonging in the world. It is the cradle where identity unfolds and firms. Such belonging outgrows itself. Home becomes too small and too safe. The young adult is called by new longing to leave home and undertake new discovery. The difficulty for parents is letting them go. In a certain sense, parents and children never leave each other; this is a kinship that no distance can sever. However, in a substantial sense, part of the task of maturity is to become free of one's parents. Clinging to parents causes a destructive imbalance in one's life. One never achieves an integral sense of self-possession if one's parents continue to dominate large regions of one's heart. To grow is to come to know their fragility, vulnerability, and limitation. There is great poignancy and pathos in parents' difficulty in letting go.

Kahlil Gibran says, "Your children are not your children. They are the sons and daughters of Life's longing for itself."

Parents as Memory Holders

Parents have such incredible power to confirm and influence the inner life of the child. Identity is fashioned in the inner life. The child's sensibility is like a sponge. It absorbs everything. Without knowing it, we drink in the voices of our parents at that stage. We have not yet developed any kind of filter to sift the creative from the destructive. There is no such thing as perfect parents. Without wanting to, and often without knowing it, all parents leave some little trail of negativity for their children; this belongs naturally to life's ambivalence. There is never anything absolutely pure in the valley of tears, but we still love our parents in their imperfection. As Robert Frost says, "We love the things we love for what they are."

Children come here without knowing where they are landing. A little child has no power. In these times, terrible stories are emerging. Children have been violently abused both mentally and sexually. Outwardly, the home appeared normal, but it was in fact a quiet torture chamber. Sick and violent parents have turned their innocent little children into targets of their own demented psyches. Such violence marks a person for life. It shakes the inner ground of the psyche. This violation of the innocent is one of the most sinister forms of evil. It is a deeply troubling question. Why would a kind and loving divine power allow the innocent goodness of a child to be delivered into the hands of such twisted violence? It is a massive spiritual task for those who have been abused to love and reclaim themselves. Abuse wants to turn the abused child against itself. To learn to break this inner reflex of violence is a task that can be achieved only with the help of a wise and caring healer and the kindness of grace. The abused child must learn to see himself as lovable by loving himself, and, in time, others. In a home where this love and space exist a child has a wonderful introduction to life. You are encouraged and your gifts are awakened. For years, you will be able to live from the perennial nourishment of this creative, initial belonging. You will be able to embrace and inhabit other styles of belonging demanded by the different stages of your journey.

Styles of Belonging

We have suggested that the sense of belonging ultimately derives from place and persons. Landscape provides location; this makes it possible to know and approach things and persons. If there were no place, there could be no thing. Family sets the focus of belonging during our first longings. We also suggested that the human body is the house of belonging; it is where we live while we are here. If there were no longing in us, we could subsist in listless indifference. We could be neutral about everything. Because we are always in different states and stages of longing, the ways we belong in the world are always diverse and ever changing. From the ways that longing and belonging criss-cross each other we can identify different styles of belonging. Some continue to belong in the place they arrived on the first journey.

The Native

A native is one who belongs to a place by virtue of birth. The native is from here. The term suggests that somehow your initial belonging to a particular place seeps into your heart in a way that can never be washed out again. This also recognizes that your first years in a place are the time when the main elements of your personality and presence are conditioned by the place, its inhabitants, and the tonality of life and atmosphere of soul that were there. The native is also the one who remains in the place. Others who were born there moved away; the native is faithful to the place and continues the initial belonging. No one knows the feel and memory of a place the way a native does. The one who remains knows the place from the inside and is attuned to the subtle world of longing the native place holds. In past times there was a powerful intimacy between the native and the place; this belonging has been diluted by travel and the voices from outside which have come in through radio, TV, and computers. The belonging has been loosened quite significantly. We are all moving more and more into the middle ground of nowhere in particular. The terrible sameness of the roads we drive has in part abolished place and space. We by-pass place and lose the sense of journeying through space. Consequently, we now find articles and programmes about the particularity and richness of life among indigenous people so fascinating and even exotic. Ironically, together with this general dilution of what is native, there has been the most sinister resurgence of tribalism, for example, in Yugoslavia, Northern Ireland, and Russia. This is the darkest and most destructive expression of native identity. Belonging is defined narrowly and exclusively in terms of land and tribe. Those who embody anything contrary become targets of hate and violence. Such destructive creeds of belonging become poisonous. True belonging is hospitable to difference for it knows that genuine identity can only emerge from the real conversation between self and otherness. There can be no true self without the embrace of the other.

There is always a complex and subtle network of life among the natives of a place. It has a rhythm and balance of its own. To the arrogant outsider, natives seem simple and naïve. This is always a massive over-simplification. It is only when the outsider comes in to live there that the subtlety and depth of the way of life becomes somewhat clearer. Given the immediacy of belonging among the natives, there is usually a whole roster of unsaid and unexpressed life that never appears on the surface, but that secretly anchors the way of life there. The limitation of the native way of life is that the code of belonging is often quite narrow and tight. Individuals who think differently or pursue a different way of life can be very easily identified, targeted, and marginalized. Yet there are treasures preserved by the natives: ancient rhythms of perception and attunement to the world. This way of seeing life and practicing belonging in the world finds unique expression in the language of the place. In the West of Ireland, for instance, the old people are the custodians of Gaeltacht, the Gaelic language. Each one who dies takes a vocabulary to the grave with him or her that will never be replaced. The continual presence of the native underlines the temporary presence of the visitor.

The Visitor

The visitor is one who belongs somewhere else, but is now here in the world of your belonging. The visit is a powerful and ancient theme. Regardless of the frequency of visits, the visitor remains essentially an outsider, an intruder from another area of belonging. We are made somewhat aware of our different identity by the visit. In earlier cultures when communities were more local and separate, the visitor brought news of a different world. Through the stories told of things seen and heard beyond the horizon, the prospect of other worlds became vicariously tangible. In the time of the oral tradition, the visit would have had an effect that would continue to ripple for a long time after. We who are native also become visitors elsewhere: the courtesies of giving and receiving are essential.

In the broad sense, because each of us lives in a body with so much clear space around us, a large portion of our life is awakened and altered by visitations we have. Most of what happens to us in the world comes up along the empty path to the house of belonging called the body. Great thoughts are not simply manufactured by the mind. They occur; they seem to come from elsewhere. Sublime, illuminating, and original thought seems to be inspired; in classical tradition, the visitation of the muse brings the original gift. Our origin in and affinity with the eternal is confirmed by the fact that what seems to come from the distance of Elsewhere turns out to be the most profound expression of our inner nature. The beyond holds the deepest secrets of here. Angels have always been received and understood as eternal visitors. The Christian story begins with such a visit. When the visitation comes from the eternal world, it disrupts the daily order; such a visitation breaks the predictable frame of experience and opens life up to new and more disturbing directions. This visitation can be dark and frightening. It can bring all the hidden vulnerability to the surface and expose a person to a future of loss and emptiness; this is explored in a sparse and penetrating way in Raymond Carver's precise and harrowing short story "A Small Good Thing."

Though the visit is always limited by time, it has a purpose. The visitor comes to see us for a reason. In society, this is often the way a prophet appears. The vision and actions of a prophet visit a great unease on our comfort and complacency. It disturbs us in such a manner that we never regain the ease and amnesia of our old complacency. The prophetic voice disrupts our unreflective belonging and forces us to awaken the awkward questions. When these questions come alive, they retrieve the more humane longings of our nature and force us to disavow our strategies of false satisfaction. For the prophetic spirit, the longing for truth and justice puts every kind of belonging in question.

The visitor and the visitation are ancient motifs. They derive their power from the simple fact that what is most precious to us in the world, namely, our life and presence here, is in the end but a mere visit. Each of us is a temporary visitor to the earth. We spend most of our lives deciphering the purpose and meaning of our visit here. Our time here will end in the embrace of the bleak and irreversible visitor called Death. Meanwhile we live out our longings in the small world of belonging we call our neighbourhood.

The Neighbour

The neighbour is an interesting presence in one's life. No great significance is ever ascribed to the neighbour. They are the people who happen to live adjacent to you. Yet in contrast to others outside the neighbourhood, we feel we somehow have a claim on the courtesy and friendliness of our neighbours. In former times, when people were not such targets of pressure and impression, people were closer to their neighbours. People were poorer, too, and more dependent on each other. In Conamara, there is the phrase "Is fearr comharsa maith ná mailín airgid," i.e., A good neighbour is better than a bag of money. Often, when we need something or someone urgently, our friends and family may be far away. The only ones we have near us are our neighbours. They are the individuals with whom we belong in a local place. In the fragmentation of contemporary life, people live in greater isolation and distance from each other. The old image of the neighbourhood as a group of local individuals who knew each other and met with each other has vanished. A neighbour can be dead for weeks next door and we do not notice now. Our post-modern society is like the world of Leibniz's monadology. Each individual, each home, is an isolated monad with no bridge to the neighbour.

There is also the old phrase "Good fences make good neighbours." Robert Frost in his poem "Mending Wall" subverts this notion: "Something there is that doesn't love a wall." Yet in the old phrase is the idea that a certain kind of neighbour can limit your independence and freedom and invade your privacy. Just because people dwell near you, they have no right to control your life. The ideal neighbourliness means a balance between caring for those near you, but also keeping space free to engage and inhabit your own life. The atmosphere of the neighbourhood should never cripple the longing of the soul to wander.

The Wanderer

The wanderer is one who gives priority to the duties of longing over belonging. No abode is fixed. No one place is allowed finally to corner or claim the wanderer. A new horizon always calls. The wanderer is committed to the adventure of seeing new places and discovering new things. New possibilities are more attractive and intoxicating than the given situation. Freedom is prized highly. The wanderer experiences time and space in a different way than the native or the neighbour who remain faithful to a place. Time is short, and there is so much yet to be experienced. While each place has its own beauty, no particular place can claim to settle the longing in the wanderer's soul. Space and distance are never a barrier. Travel is the adventure. The purpose is never directed towards a specific destination. The journey itself is the ever-changing destination. The wanderer travels light, carries none of the baggage of programmes or agendas, and feels an openness and hospitality to new places and new people. The call of longing is always answered, often to the detriment of achieved belonging. At its extreme, the wanderer can be like a butterfly, having an obsession to explore things with an over-lightness of touch. The journey need not be a real journey, merely a circular route around the same repetitions, each, of course, differently packaged than the last time.

The wanderer has been a great theme in literature and film. An old and innocent, but very subtle, film which explores this theme is *Shane*. He is a wandering cowboy who comes to work for a family—husband, wife, and little boy. He helps them fight their enemies. He keeps to the honour of his task despite the warmth and attraction that is growing between him and the woman. When the difficulties are overcome, he wanders off again. Shane is wounded, a symbol of his awareness that he can never belong in the one place where he felt at home. A great number of Westerns have the hero riding into the sunset at the end. He is the modern version of the knight. He is honourable and courageous and remains completely dedicated to the adventure of the longing, wherever it will take him. No one frame of belonging is large or flexible enough to contain him.

Wandering is a very strong tradition in Ireland. In mythic times, there were fabulous journeys to strange lands; such a journey was known as an immram. In the early centuries Irish monks went into "green exile"; many of them wandered the continent and laid down the basis for medieval civilization. Ireland has also suffered great depletion from the wandering called emigration.

The wanderer travels through a vast array of experience. The word "wander" derives originally from the verb "to wind" and is associated with the German word "wandeln," to change. The wanderer does not find change a threat. Change is an invitation to new possibility. The wanderer is as free as the wind and will get into corners of experience that will escape the settled, fixed person. It is interesting that the word "wander" covers the movement of persons, animals, objects, thoughts, and feelings. Wandering is the natural and indeed native movement of the predominant majority of things in the world. The wind is the great elemental wanderer that roams the universe. In a fascinating passage in the Gospel of John, the nature of spirit is described in terms of the unpredictable dance of the wandering wind:

> The wind blows wherever it pleases;
> You hear its sound,
> But you cannot tell where it
> comes from or where it is going.
> This is how it is with all who are born
> of the Spirit.
> *John 3: 8–9*

The human body is a physical object held down by the force of gravity in a physical world; it is always in some one place. However, the vibrancy of its presence is unmistakable. Thought is a permanent wanderer. No frontier is too far, no depth too deep. The body always belongs in some one place; the ancient and ever-new longing of the soul can never find satisfaction in any one form of belonging. Delmore Schwartz has a poem in which he calls the body "The Heavy Bear who goes with me." It is a poem full of affection for the body, yet impatient with its awkwardness and gravity. The soul is full of wanderlust. When we suppress the longing to wander in the inner landscapes, something dies within us. The soul and the spirit are wanderers; their place of origin and destination remain unknown; they are dedicated to the discovery of what is unknown and strange.

The Stranger

The stranger is an unknown person, one whom one has not met before. The limitation of human individuality means that we know only a few people. Most of the world remains unknown to us. Most people remain strangers. This is one of the shocking things about travel; we can descend from the sky into a different country and people, right into the middle of an ongoing life. We know nothing of the people's names, lives, or place. Yet into the journey of each person there is the occasional intrusion of the stranger. We immediately recognize the stranger as someone we have never encountered. When a stranger approaches, we usually exercise caution and keep him or her at a distance. This is the fascination of encounter. Humans are ancient creatures with millennia of experience in their blood. We are rational animals. The animal side of our nature knows the danger of the intruder, stranger. Every friend was once a total stranger. The stranger can bring blessings and encouragement and can become the most intimate anam-Ċara and companion of our deepest intimacy. New life can come through the encounter with the stranger. Destruction and negativity can also arrive with the intrusion of the stranger. There is always danger in the stranger. Because we sense this, it usually takes a while before we open to let the stranger in. Strangers circle each other for a good while before familiarity begins to build. Each one of us enters the world as a total stranger. No one had ever seen you before. You came without a name and yet you entered fully into the belonging of your life.

It is poignant to remember that even the most intimate anam-Ċara friendship cannot dissolve the strangeness between and within two people. The friend remains partly stranger. It is a naïve acquaintance that presumes that two people can ever know each other completely. Real soul friendship acknowledges the mystery of the other person, which can at times delight and at other times disappoint you. This strangeness keeps the passion and interest alive in a friendship. It is when two friends become predictable with each other that the kinship begins to fade. This is why space and freedom nourish and enrich friendship. Each person remains always partly a stranger to himself as well. Part of the wonder of being a person is the continual discoveries that you find emerging in your own self, nothing cosmically shattering, merely the unfathomable miracle of ordinary being. This is the heart of longing, and what calls ever to new forms of belonging.

It is impossible to be on the earth and to avoid awakening. Everything that happens within and around you calls your heart to awaken. As the density of night gives way to the bright song of the dawn, so your soul continually coaxes you to give way to the light and awaken. Longing is the voice of your soul, it constantly calls you to be fully present in your life: to live to the full the one life given to you. Rilke said to the young poet, "Live everything." You are here on earth now, yet you forget so easily. You travelled a great distance to get here. The dream of your life has been dreamed from eternity. You belong within a great embrace that urges you to have the courage to honour the immensity that sleeps in your heart. When you learn to listen to and trust the wisdom of your soul's longing, you will awaken to the invitation of graced belonging that inhabits the generous depths of your destiny. You will become aware of the miracle of presence within and around you. In the beginning was the dream, and the dream was Providence.

A BLESSING

*Blessed be the longing that brought you here and that
quickens your soul with wonder.*

*May you have the courage to befriend your eternal
longing.*

*May you enjoy the critical and creative companionship of
the question "Who am I?" and may it brighten your
longing.*

*May a secret Providence guide your thought and shelter
your feeling.*

*May your mind inhabit your life with the same sureness
with which your body belongs to the world.*

May the sense of something absent enlarge your life.

May your soul be as free as the ever-new waves of the sea.

May you succumb to the danger of growth.

May you live in the neighbourhood of wonder.

May you belong to love with the wildness of Dance.

*May you know that you are ever embraced in the kind
circle of God.*

2

Presence:

The Flame of Longing

To Realize That You Are Here

There is a lovely, disconcerting moment between sleep and awakening. You have only half emerged from sleep, and for a few seconds you do not know where you are, who you are, or what you are. You are lost between worlds. Then your mind settles, and you recognize the room and you take up your place again in your own life. And you realize that both you and the world have survived the crossing from night to reality. It is a new day, and the world is faithfully there again, offering itself to your longing and imagination, stretching out beyond your room to mountains, seas, the countenances behind which other lives hide. We take our world totally for granted. It is only when we experience the momentary disturbance of being marooned in such an interim that we grasp what a surprise it is to be here and to have the wild companionship of this world. Such disturbances awaken us to the mystery of thereness that we call presence. Often, the first exposure to the one you will love or to a great work of art produces a similar disconcerting confusion.

Presence is alive. You sense and feel presence; it comes towards you and engages you. Landscape has a vast depth and subtlety of presence. The more attentive you are, and the longer you remain in a landscape, the more you will be embraced by its presence. Though you may be completely alone there, you know that you are not on your own. In our relentless quest for human contact, we have forgotten the solace and friendship of Nature. It is interesting in the Irish language how the word for the elements and the word for desire is the same word: dúil. As the term for creation, its accent is on the elemental nature of creation. Dúil suggests a vital elementalism. It also means longing. "Dúil a chur I gceol" means "to get a longing for music." Dúil also holds the sense of expectation and hope. Could it be that dúil originally suggested that human longing was an echo of the elemental vitality of Nature?

You feel the presence in Nature sometimes in great trees that stand like ancient totem spirits night and day, watching over a landscape for hundreds of years. Water also has a soothing and seductive presence that draws us towards it. John Montague writes: "Part order, part wilderness / Water creates its cadenced illusion." Each shape of water—the well, stream, lake, river and ocean—has a distinctive rhythm of presence. Stone, too, has a powerful presence. Michelangelo used to say that sculpture is the art of liberating the shape hidden and submerged in the rock. I went one morning to visit a sculptor friend. He showed me a stone and asked if I saw any hidden form in it. I could not. Then he pointed out the implicit shape of a bird. He said, "For ten years I have been passing that stone on the shore and only this morning did I notice the secret shape of the bird." Whereas human presence is immediate, the presences in landscape are mediate; they are often silent and indirect.

Presence Is Soul-Atmosphere

Presence is the whole atmosphere of a person or thing. Presence is more than the way a person walks, looks, or speaks. It is more than the shape of a tree or the colour of a stone, yet it is a blend of all these aspects. Presence is mainly the atmosphere of spirit that is behind them all and comes through them. This is why no two presences are ever the same. There are landscapes that are deeply still and consoling. Travel a half a mile farther, and you could be in a place that is so brooding and sinister you cannot wait to escape. You can often sense this in people's homes too. Houses now seem to resemble each other more and more. Years ago, as a child, one sensed how different each home was. Each one had a unique aura. When a person came to visit, they seemed to bring in the presence of their home with them. To a child's mind, each neighbour's house was a different cave of presence. The furniture, colours, and décor of each interior were different. In one, you can make yourself at home. In another, a brooding tension or hostility makes you want to leave immediately.

There is a really distinctive and somewhat vulnerable presence to a home in which someone lives alone. A family tends to fill up a house. The sounds of their conversations layer the walls and rooms with the texture of presence. When you come in, you walk into a vibrant web of presence. There are practically no clear spaces in a family home; every corner is packed with echo. In contrast, the home of the solitary person is never completely full. There is clearance and silence here. The silence here belongs around one presence. Regardless of how cosy and welcoming the home may be, there is always a distilled quality of longing in a solitary person's home. Though the person is solitary, the home can often be full of presence and not lonely at all. Yet it is usually a more intimate event to visit such a home. There is none of the distraction and avoidance that meets you in a family home which somehow protects both you and them from exposure. In the solitary home you have a certain access everywhere to the solitude of the inhabitant.

Presence has a depth that lives behind the form or below the surface. There is a well of presence within every thing, but it is usually hidden from the human eye. This comes in different ripples to the surface. No two stages of presence are ever exactly the same. The flow of soul within means the surface is always different. When you know a place well, you can sense this. The fluent nuance of the light alters the presence of the landscape constantly. As the stream of feeling and thinking flows through you, it also alters your presence. Your presence is always in a subtle flow. When you are happy and at peace, your presence is gentle and approachable. When you are worried or anxious, there is a tension in your presence, and it closes and tightens. If we were able to read presence, we could sense what is happening inside a person's mind. Some people have an open presence. They cannot hide anything; you know immediately what is haunting or delighting them. Others are adept actors at putting on a face—to, as T. S. Eliot says, "prepare a face to meet the faces that you meet." The mask is always in place, and it is exceptionally difficult to read what is happening within.

Presence is something you sense and know, but cannot grasp. It engages us, but we can never capture its core; it remains somehow elusive. All the great art forms strive to create living icons of presence. Poets try to cut the line of a poem so that it lives and dances as itself. Poems are some of the most amazing presences in the world. I am always amazed that poems are willing to lie down and sleep inside the flat, closed pages of books. If poems behaved according to their essence, they would be out dancing on the seashore or flying to the heavens or trying to rinse out secrets of the mountains. Reading brings the presence of other times, characters, and cultures into your mind. Reading is an intimate event. When you read a great poem, it reaches deep into regions of your life and memory and reverberates back to the forgotten or invisible regions of your experience. In a great poem, you find lost or silent territories of feeling or thought which were out of your reach. A poem can travel far into your depths to retrieve your neglected longing.

Music as Presence

Art has no interest in generalities. Art wants to create individuals. Music is perhaps the most divine of all the art forms in that it creates an active, living, and moving form that takes us for a while into another world. There is no doubt that music strikes a deep and eternal echo within the human heart. Music resonates in and with us. It is only when you become enraptured in great music that you begin to understand how deeply we are reached and nourished by sound. The rush of our daily lives is dominated by the eye. It is what we see that concerns and calls us. "You wish to see? Listen," advised St. Bernard. Generally, we neglect almost completely the nourishment of listening to good and true sounds. The sound quality of contemporary life is utter dissonance and cacophony. We live in a world of mechanical noise which allows no spaces for silence to come through to enfold us. So much modern music is but a distraught echo of our hollow and mechanical times.

A human life is lived through a physical body. It is no wonder that we are so often tight with stress. We are forever being stoned by dead sounds. It is interesting in terms of architecture that one of the key building materials now is mass concrete. When you strike mass concrete with a hammer, the sound is muffled and dead and swallows itself. When you strike a stone, an echo leaps from it; the stone is like an anvil; the music of the stone sings out. The sounds of our times have little inner music; all you hear is muffled hunger. When great music quickens your heart, brings tears to your eyes, or takes you away, then you know that in its deepest hearth the soul is musical. The soul is sonorous, echoing the eternal music of the spheres.

It would be a lovely gift to yourself to expose your soul to great music. Have a critical look at your music habits. Do you actually listen to any music at all? What do you listen to? Is the music that you hear too small for your growing soul? It is sad that classical music does not have a larger audience. We all need the wonder and magic of Mozart, Beethoven, Wagner, and Brahms. I remember a cartoon in the *Süddeutsche Zeitung*. It was a simple, vacant sketch of a desert. Overhead was the caption "Eine Landschaft ohne Mozart," i.e., a landscape without Mozart. Even if you never prayed or visited a temple or church, you could come into vast presences of the Divine through the simple, mindful activity of bathing your soul in the wonderful tides of classical music. The friendship with this music is slow at the beginning. Like any great friendship, the more you let yourself into it, the deeper you belong. It calms the soul, awakens the heart, and enriches your sensibility in a delightful way. It somehow manages to harbour in a simplicity of surface the greatest complexity of feeling and thought. Great music opens doorways into eternal presence. It educates and refines your listening; you begin to sense your own eternity in the echoes of your soul. Music is the perfect sister of silence. Georg Solti, the great conductor, said shortly before his death that he was becoming ever more fascinated with the silence at the heart of music and the depth structure it had. Music excavates the kingdom of silence until the eternal sound echoes in us; it is one of the most beautiful presences that humans have brought to the earth. It is one of the most powerful presences in which the ancient and the eternal human longing comes to voice. Nietzsche said, "The relationship between music and life is not only that of one language to another; it is also the relationship of the perfect world of listening to the whole world of seeing."

The Silence of Sculpture

Sculpture attempts the same presence. The pure silence of a piece by Barbara Hepworth can catch the quiet symmetry at the heart of things. Giacometti creates such poignant shapes, long slender figures who seem to be thinning out into the nothingness of the air and the gallery. It is almost as if they are inhabited by some mystical humility which urges them to let go. I remember once visiting an exhibition in the museum in Cologne. There was one special room for a piece by Josef Beuys, called *The End of the Twentieth Century*. It consisted of huge blocks of stone piled in a scattered way on each other. Each column had a hole at one end. It was as if the stones had waited for millennia for the arrival and adventure of human presence to bring voice, warmth, and belonging to the earth. Human presence had indeed come. But something awful had gone wrong. Humans had destroyed themselves and all that was left now was huge stone columns used and abandoned. Beuys had so clearly anticipated the huge sadness that would issue from the placing and context of these stones. Sculpture is a powerful and wistful form of presence. There is an old anecdote that when Michelangelo was finished carving the sitting Moses, he was so enthralled with the figure's presence that he tapped him on the knee with his chisel and said, "Moses, get up."

Within a fixed frame, the artistic imagination strives to

create or release living presence. The human imagination loves suggestion rather than exhaustive description of a thing. Often, for instance, one dimension of a thing can suggest the whole presence that is not there or available now. From the tone of a friend's voice on the phone, your imagination can fill in the physical presence perfectly. Imagination strives to create real presence. Imagination is rarely drawn towards what is complacent or fixed. It loves to explore the edges where cohesion is breaking apart, and where new things are emerging from difficulty and darkness. The imagination never presents merely the idea or the feeling, but reaches deep enough into the experience to find the root where they are already one. As beautiful and inspiring as art might be, it can never reach the power of presence naturally expressed in a baby's smile or the sinister glower that can cross an old woman's eyes. Human presence is different from everything else in the world. To fields, stones, mountains, and trees we must be amazing creatures, utterly strange and incomprehensible. Because we ourselves are human presence, we are blind to its miracle.

No concept, image, or symbol can ever gather or hold down a presence. Indeed, the very existence of words, music, thoughts, and art are the voices of longing which ripple forth from the shimmering depths of presence in us and in creation. Presence is longing reaching at once outwards and inwards.

The Sanctuary of Human Presence

D. H. Lawrence's poems treat of the presence of nature: natural objects and creatures are not self-centred or self-pitying; they claim no privilege and do not intrude. It is the nature of humans to be present in a way that impinges on and engages others. Human presence is never neutral. It always has an effect. Human presence strikes a resonance. Colloquially, we refer to the chemistry of someone's presence. When two people discover each other, the way they look at and talk to each other indicates that they are enfolding each other in a circle of presence. Their style of presence evokes an affinity and calls them towards a voyage of discovery with each other. The echo of their outer presence calls them nearer and nearer so that they can begin to reveal the depth of inner presence which illuminates their physical presence. The opposite experience is also common. Two people meet and find that each other's presence pushes them away from each other. Outer presence has its own compass. Chemistry has a secret and powerful logic. We can never predict or plan whether we will move towards or away from an other's presence. This is something that the occasion and the encounter will decide; it is a happening with its own freedom.

The human body longs for presence. The very structuring and shape of the body makes it a living sanctuary of presence. When a thing is closed, we only encounter its outer shell. The human body can never close off in such a hermetical way. The body is one of the most open and manifest presences in the world. Even from a person who is shy and always withdraws, presence still manages to seep forth. The human body is a language that cannot remain silent. The countenance is an intense and luminous icon of presence. Nowhere else in the world are you encountered and engaged as totally as by a human person. The human face is a miniature village of presence. Every dimension of the face expresses presence: the lines from which it is drawn, the curvature of the mouth, the shape of the face, the dome of the head and especially the eyes. All the aspects of the face combine to bring one individual life to expression. The face is the icon where all the atmosphere, feeling, and thought of an individual life assemble visually.

The days and nights a person has lived seep into presence in the countenance. It is interesting that the Latin root of the word face is "facies," meaning the shape or form of the head, which is derived from the verb "facere," which means "to make." This background confirms the artistic and active force of the face. Neither a surface nor a cover, the face is a doorway to the soul. When you gaze into someone's face, a pathway opens, resonant with his or her life and memory. You glimpse what life has made or unmade, woven or unravelled in that life. Each face fronts a different world. The philosopher Maurice Merleau-Ponty said, "My body is the awareness of the gaze of the other." We are animated through the presence of the other. Every face is a window outwards and inwards on a unique life. Of course, in dance and in theatrical activity, the whole body becomes expressive. Because others can see us, our lives never remain merely ours alone. The openness of the face shows that we participate in the lives of others. Presence to each other is the door to all belonging. And nowhere in the universe is longing so powerfully present as in the human countenance. From here issues all desire for dwelling and community.

The Witness of Hands

The whole structure of the human body anticipates and expects the presence of others. Hands reach out to embrace the world. Human hands are powerful images. Hands painted the roof on the Sistine Chapel and the heavenly women on the wall of Sigeria, wrote the *Paradiso*, sculpted the *David;* in Auschwitz, hands rose to bless tormentors. Hands reach out to touch and caress the lover. Hands build walls, sow gardens, and direct symphonies. Hands wield knives, pull triggers, and press switches that bring terminal darkness. Hands write stories that deface people, strip lives bare. The whole history of our presence on earth could be gleaned from the witness and actions of hands. One of the great thresholds in human civilization was the development of tools with which we changed and civilized the landscape. The use of simple tools still meant personal contact with Nature. In these times, we have crossed another threshold where the tool is replaced by the mechanical instrument. The instrument is a means of exercising a function. With the development of instrumentalization, so much of our work and engagement with the world is no longer hands-on. Rather, our hands press the key and the instrument expedites the action. Instrumentalization saves labour but at the cost of direct contact with the world.

The instrumentalization of contemporary life pushes us ever further away from Nature. Even farmers do not really get their hands dirty anymore. Years ago, when you looked at a farmer's hands, they were like miniature lexicons of the landscape. The hands were worn and roughened through contact with soil and stone. Often rib lines of clay insinuated themselves into the lines of the skin. It was a powerful image of living hands reminding us that those hands were originally and would again be clay. People dressed in their Sunday best to go to Mass. Serving Mass, you would see perfectly dressed men come to the altar for Holy Communion. They would stand reverently and offer a pair of withered earthened palms on which the white host would glisten: the bread of life on hands of clay. This is a vignette from a vanishing world. Generally, when we lose individual contact with Nature and with each other, we gradually lose our depth and diversity of presence. The world of function, instrument, and image is a limbo where no presence lives, where no face is identifiable, where everything flattens into the one panel of sameness.

Styles of Presence:
The Encouraging Presence Helps You to
Awaken Your Gift

There are people whose presence is encouraging. One of the most beautiful gifts in the world is the gift of encouragement. When someone encourages you, that person helps you over a threshold you might otherwise never have crossed on your own. There are times of great uncertainty in every life. Left alone at such a time, you feel dishevelment and confusion like gravity. When a friend comes with words of encouragement, a light and lightness visit you and you begin to find the stairs and the door out of the dark. The sense of encouragement you feel from the friend is not simply her words or gestures; it is rather her whole presence enfolding you and helping you find the concealed door. The encouraging presence manages to understand you and put herself in your shoes. There is no judgement but words of relief and release.

Encouragement also helps you to engage and trust your own possibility and potential. Sometimes you are unable to see the special gift that you bring to the world. No gift is ever given for your private use. To follow your gift is a calling to a wonderful adventure of discovery. Some of the deepest longing in you is the voice of your gift. The gift calls you to embrace it, not to be afraid of it. The only way to honour the unmerited presence of the gift in your life is to attend to the gift; this is also a most difficult path to walk. Each gift is different; there is no plan or programme you can get ready-made from someone else. The gift alone knows where its path leads. It calls you to courage and humility. If you hear its voice in your heart, you simply have to follow it. Otherwise your life could be dragged into the valley of disappointment. People who truly follow their gift find that it can often strip their lives and yet invest them with a sense of enrichment and fulfilment that nothing else could bring. Those who renege on or repress their gift are unwittingly sowing the seeds of regret.

The Blurred Presence

Some people have a blurred presence. For some reason, so many thoughts and bands of feeling criss-cross simultaneously in their personalities that you can never, finally, decide where you are with them. Their presence is distracted and confused. There is no line or contour you can finally follow. Such presences are usually self absorbed and have neither clarity nor a sense of clearance around them to enable them to attend or engage with anyone else. When such a person is manager or chairperson of a group or company, there is neither vision nor an effective or clear resolution of anything.

The Angry Presence

Anger is a great flame of presence. It is difficult to mistake or ignore any angry presence. Usually anger is like fire. It starts with a spark and then multiplies in a rapid exponential rhythm. Anger wants to break out; it stops us in our tracks. Much of the time we avoid conflict; we put up with things. We let things go. When the flame of anger rises, it confronts things. Anger shouts, "Stop!" It can be a great force for change. It is so encouraging to hear the voice of righteous anger raised. It names and confronts injustice. It brings clearly to light whatever is wrong and makes it clear to the perpetrators of injustice what they are doing. It is very interesting to notice how politically incorrect anger now is. Especially in these times, there are so many issues that should warrant great anger. The psychologist James Hillmann remarks in his devastatingly incisive way that psychotherapy has managed to convert anger into anxiety. If one becomes angry on television, one immediately loses the trust of the audience. Whatever common denominator of propriety television exercises, it seems that an angry presence, even when it is fully justified, still only manages to evoke sympathy for the target of the anger and the diminution of the presence of the angered one. Perhaps this only confirms even more trenchantly that television manages to depict only image and never real presence. Anger disrupts the fluent sequence of images and makes awareness awkward.

There are some people who seem to manage almost permanent anger. Every time you meet them, there is something new drawing their anger. Such people never relent. They are victims of a fire that started somewhere further back, but continues to flare up on every new ground they enter. There are also people who are constantly nice; they are always pleasing and accommodating. They never lose their composure; they give nothing away. Yet, if you really watch them, you will begin to detect a quiet fury behind the mask of niceness. It would be wonderful for them if even once they could unleash the fury with no concern for the situation in which they find themselves. It would limber up their personalities, and they would experience the immense relief of realizing that they did not need to desperately court approval in the first place.

Certain individuals use their anger as a brooding hostility to control those around them. There is a wonderful portrayal of this in John McGahern's novel *Amongst Women*. Moran, the father in a household of women, can use his silent anger as a controlling force that infests the home with a permanent undercurrent of tension. His wife is the mediating presence who adverts to this ever-present hostility and ensures that Daddy is not disturbed. Related to this is the depressive presence. Sometimes the old definition of depression as inverted anger is accurate. The natural anger that should flame forth into the world is turned inwards on the self and used as a force of self-punishment. The outer presence is weary and passive, but deep underneath somewhere a searing flame crackles in the self.

When you really inhabit your anger, you enter into your power as a person. This should not be a permanent necessity. If you are in a situation where you are being controlled or bullied, the expression of your anger can liberate you. It is frightening that we often secretly believe that those who have power over us have right on their side, and our duty is to comply. No one can oppress you without some anger awakening in you, even covertly. If you listen to that anger, it will call you to recognize your right to an integrity of presence. And it will bring you to act and clearly show your strength. It is astounding how each day we give away so much of our power to systems and people who are totally unworthy of it. Ultimately anger points towards life. When your anger flames, it targets the falsity of expectation or tightness of belonging that is being inflicted on you. Anger breaks you free, suddenly.

The Charismatic Presence

You really become aware of the force and light of human presence when you are in the company of a charismatic person. In theology, "charisma" means "divinely conferred favour." A charismatic presence is one that inspires people. It has a natural balance between the personality and the vision that the person represents. In some way, the luminosity in the person is an aura that tangibly reaches out and affects others. In German one speaks of "eine grosse Ausstrahlung," i.e., a great streaming forth of radiance. The charismatic person does have a radiance that stirs us. It is given to some people to be carriers of huge spirit. This is not something they have sought out or earned. It is not something that they have worked up in themselves. It seems to belong deeply in their nature. I remember once speaking to a friend about a family we both knew who had such spirit and he said, "If you put one of them in a house on her own, you would fill it." Charisma reminds us that there is no system or frame large enough to hold the secret immensity that is in each person.

The truly charismatic presence is also to be distinguished from the overblown personality who fills a room with talk and bustle, but manages to create more heat than light. When silence and poise anchor the charismatic presence, there is a lovely balance between what the person is affecting outside and his or her own self-belonging and self-possession. If this anchorage is not maintained, then such a presence is in danger of burning itself out. It is the art of belonging to one's soul that keeps one's presence aflame. From this belonging comes the light of inspiration and vision, which cannot be manufactured, only received. Without such belonging, the charismatic presence can, in extreme cases, become toxic. It can let in dark, dark forces and inflame people with hatred, as in the case of fundamentalism and fascism, or numb them into passivity, as happens in cults.

The Anxious Presence

There are anxious times in every life. These are times of trembling. Your confidence and security evaporates. What lies ahead of you seems brooding and threatening. Because we live in space, anything can approach and assail us. Because we live in time, there is always an interim period between us and what is coming. When we grow anxious, we fill up that interim with every imaginable disaster. Our fantasy turns wild and dark. Then when the dreaded event comes, it is never as bad as we have imagined and we are hugely relieved. We find again our natural poise. Some people make a habit of anxiousness. Somehow, they have slipped into a mode of permanent worry. When they enter a room, they bring an aura of anxiousness that darkens the company and installs a certain gloom. If the others present attempt to continue their liveliness of presence, the anxious presence withdraws deeper into itself and looms in the room like an accusation. Such people may have great lives, but they feel little of their lives' joy or happiness. It is so difficult for such people to find any inner distance from their anxiousness. To them, it is serious and ultimate. There is no humour or any sense of irony. Trying to force themselves out of it often only enforces it. Sometimes paying too much attention to it only confirms it as a condition for them. It is lovely to see a person liberate himself from this. Somehow it dawns on a person that it is not a condition at all, rather this anxiousness is something he does to himself. With this recognition already a huge breakthrough is achieved. When a person explores further and asks why he needs to punish himself in this way, he is already on his way to peace. He stops punishing himself and gradually the occasional smile begins to transform the anxious countenance. And laughter may not be far away!

Dignity of Presence

There is great beauty in dignity; it is a special quality of presence. It is lovely to behold people who inhabit their own dignity. The human body is its own language. Every gesture you make speaks about who you are. The way you hold yourself, how you walk, sit, speak, and touch things tells of your quality of soul. Some people have a clear dignity of carriage and composure. You sense their self-respect and the ease with which they are at home in their own presence. There is no forcing of presence; they do not drive themselves outwards to impress or ingratiate themselves. Other people squander their dignity completely. They live a half-mile outside themselves, their personalities sprung in search of notice and affirmation. Your presence inevitably reveals what you think of yourself. If you do not hold yourself in esteem, it is unlikely that others will respect you either.

The beauty of dignity is its truth. When you were sent to the world you were given great freedom. This is a gift we forget. Regardless of how you appear to others, you are free to view yourself with affection, understanding, and respect. Although you depend on the affection and love of others to awaken your love for yourself, your sense of self should not depend on outside affirmation. When you have a worthy sense of your self, this communicates itself in your physical presence and personality. Outer dignity is gracious and honourable; it is the mirror of inner dignity. No one else can confer dignity on you; it is something that comes from within. You cannot fake it or acquire it as you would an accent. You can only receive the gift of dignity from your own heart. When you learn to embrace your self with a sense of appreciation and affection, you begin to glimpse the goodness and light that is in you, and gradually you will realize that you are worthy of respect from yourself. When you recognize your limits, but still embrace your life with affection and graciousness, the sense of inner dignity begins to grow. You become freer and less dependent on the affirmation of outer voices and less troubled by the negativity of others. Now you know that no one has the right to tarnish the image that you have of yourself.

There is such a feeling of shame when you let yourself down, when you have acted beneath your dignity. There is something demeaning about having done something that is "infra dignitatem." You would give anything to return to the point two minutes before the event and act differently. Having dignity of presence is not to be equated with being nice, always good, or behaving conventionally. You can be as free as the wind in your views, beliefs, and actions; you could be angry and awkward at times and still hold your dignity. Neither is dignity equivalent to stiffness or arrogant aloofness of personality. Dignity allows an immense pliability and diversity of presence, but still holds the sense of worthiness and the honour of a larger horizon of grace and graciousness. Even in compromising and demeaning situations, you can still hold your sense of dignity. At such times your sense of dignity will keep a space of tranquillity about you. In the Third World, one is often struck by the immense dignity of the poor. Even hunger and oppression cannot rob them of this grace of spirit. If you do not give it away, no event, situation, or person can take your dignity away from you. The different styles of presence reveal how we belong to ourselves.

The Architecture of Belonging

A Canadian who recently visited Ireland for the first time remarked on landing at Shannon Airport how the patchwork of fields had human proportion. Our world is indeed addicted to the vast expanse, be it the World Wide Web or globalization. With this relentless extension, we are losing our sense of the humane proportion. When a thing becomes over-extended, it loses its individuality and presence and the power to speak to us. The landscape in the West of Ireland partly owes its intensity and diversity of presence to the proportion of its fields. Each field has its own unique shape and personality. When the walls frame a piece of land, they bring all that is in that field into sharp and individual relief: the stones, the bushes, and the gradient of the field. Patrick Kavanagh speaks of "the undying difference in the corner of a field." The corner is always where a wall is most intense. The walls focus the field as an individual countenance in the landscape. It is no wonder many of the fields have their own names and stories.

Where there is neither frame nor frontier, it is difficult to feel any presence. This is our human difficulty with air. It is invisible and always the same blank nothingness. The sky is a massive expanse but it is rarely the same blue all over; it is brindled with cloud and colour and framed by the horizon. The human mind loves proportion and texture. Though we are largely unaware of it, we always need a frame around an experience in order to feel and live it. When you reflect on all the things you have known and experienced, you begin to see how each of them had its own different frame. Think of the time you met your partner and fell in love. This event happened at a certain time, in a certain place, and at a very particular phase in your life. At any other time, it could not have happened in this way. In the landscape of memory there are many fields. Each experience belongs in its own field. This is what hurts and saddens us so profoundly about death. When we lose people to death, they literally disappear. They vanish into thin air and become invisible to us. Our hearts reach towards them, but their new presence has no frame and is now no longer to be located in any one place that we can know or visit. Our voices call to them, yet no echo returns.

All of human experience comes to expression in some kind of form or frame. It is literally impossible to have an experience that did not have a form. The frame focuses individuality and gathers presence. Without this frame, neither identity nor belonging would ever be possible. Belonging presumes warmth and intimacy. You cannot belong in a vast, nameless space. There is no belonging in the air except for birds who ride its currents. Belonging is equally difficult in the ocean; the vast expanse of water is anonymous. It has no face, and only sailors who know it well can identify a particular place in its endless sameness. Where there is anonymity, there can be no real belonging. Of the four elements, the earth is the one with the greatest stable presence and thereness. Clay loves shape and texture. Of all the elements, the earth forms naturally into individual shapes, each of which is different. It is no wonder that the human body, being made of clay, is capable of such longing and belonging. The human self is intimacy. When we choose to give our hearts to or belong with someone, we do it only when we find a like echo in the intimacy of the other. Belonging seeks out affinity that has a definite form and frame. We feel we can trust that which has its own contour and individual autonomy of shape. This trust enables belonging.

The structures of our world bring the architecture of belonging to expression. In order to *be*, we need to *belong*. At work or among people, your social mask is on. When you come home, you are back where you belong, in your safe, sheltering space. Outside in the world you have to temper your longing and obey convention. When you come back home, you can relax and be yourself. This recognition is caught in the old phrase "A man's home is his castle." At an exhibition in London some years ago, there was a minimalist Zen painting suggestive of great presence and shelter. Over the painting was the caption "All the holy man needs is a shelter over his head." The shelter of home liberates creativity and spirituality. When a person has lived in institutional spaces, there is great joy in privacy and celebration in the shelter of belonging. In a world where privacy is being eradicated, it is wonderful that we still have the shelter of our own homes, though modern technology has punctured that privacy.

All belonging is an extension of the first and closest belonging of living in your own body. The body is a home which shelters you. All other forms of belonging continue this first belonging. You can see this continuity of belonging in the rooms you inhabit, the places you live, the office, the church, the shop, the pub, etc. Each one of these spaces presents a different style of presence in the diverse architecture of belonging through which our lives move. A different level of belonging is offered and required in each of these spaces. Different longings are met and mirrored in each of these different spaces. You always live in a space that frames your belonging but is yet unable to fully reflect your longing. This ambivalence gives such vitality and passion to human presence.

In the Heart, the Ache of Longing

The human heart is never still. There is a divine restlessness in each of us which creates a continual state of longing. You are never quite at one with yourself, and the self is never fixed. There are always new thoughts and experiences emerging in your life; some moments delight and surprise you, others bring you onto shaky ground. On the outside, your body looks the same. Your behaviour, work, home, and circle of friends remain consistent and predictable. Yet behind this outer façade, another life is going on in you. The mind and heart are wanderers who are always tempted by new horizons. Your life belongs in a visible, outer consistency; your inner life is nomadic. Hegel says, "just this unrest that is the Self." Your longing frequently takes you on inner voyages that no one would ever guess. Longing is the deepest and most ancient voice in the human soul. It is the secret source of all presence, and the driving force of all creativity and imagination: longing keeps the door open and calls towards us the gifts and blessings which our lives dream.

Longing belongs to the word family associated with the word "long"; it suggests either a spatial measurement or a temporal duration. The crucial point here is that longing is a quality of desire which distance or duration evokes. In other words, your longing reaches out into the distance to unite you with whatever or whomsoever your heart desires. Longing awakens when there is a feeling that someone or something is away from you. It is interesting that the word "desire" comes from the Latin "desiderare," which originally meant "to cease to see." This suggested a sense of absence and the desire to seek and find the absent one. Another possible root of "desire" is "de-sidus," "away from a star." When you are in a state of desire, you are away from your star. Your heart yearns for the light and luminosity that are now absent. While we are in the world, a large area of the heart is always in exile. This is why we are suffused with longing. Deep down, we desire to come back into the intimate unity of belonging.

Celebration: When the Moment Blossoms

Celebration is one of the most intense and delightful forms of human presence. It is lovely to be able to celebrate. Some people never celebrate anything. They have no time. Others are too serious ever to think of celebrating. Some feel there is nothing to celebrate. Such people are prisoners who slog away in a secure and predictable routine. There are few surprises, and no surprise is allowed to interfere with the onerous burden of endurance and commitment. There is no time out for play or devilment. Other people are wonderful at celebrating. Even a small event can be an excuse for a celebration. There is a sense of joy and happiness in celebration. It is interesting that sadness generally drives us towards solitude, whereas joy draws us together in celebration. Nothing does your heart so much good as real celebration. Laughter loosens all the tension in you. When you dance and sing, your soul lifts and the lovely light of the eternal lifts you to a new lightness. Hegel said something fascinating about the True as a passionate festival: "The True is thus the Bacchanalian revel in which no member is not drunk; yet because each member collapses as soon as he drops out, the revel is just as much transparent as simple repose."

When we celebrate, we joyfully acknowledge and recognize the presence of some person, thing, or achievement that delights us. The desire to celebrate is the longing to enter more deeply into the mystery of actuality. Longing is no longer directed away towards an anticipated future. Now, the present moment has blossomed. You really want what you have. You know the blessings and gifts that are around you. Celebration is an attentive and gracious joy of presence. When you celebrate, you are taking time to recognize, to open your eyes and behold in your life the quiet miracles and gifts that seek no attention; yet each day they nourish, shelter, and animate your life. The art of belonging in, with, and to your self is what gives life and light to your presence; it brings a radiance to your countenance and a poise to your carriage. When your heart is content, your life can always find the path inwards to this deep stillness in you. Rilke said this beautifully: "Hier zu sein ist so viel," i.e., To be here is so much. Real celebration is the opposite of contemporary consumerism. In fact, consumerism gradually kills both the desire and the capacity to celebrate. The turbo motor within the consumerist spirit ensures that enough is never, ever enough. The mind becomes slow and heavy; the effort to think differently is too demanding; the least stir in that direction already has us out of breath. Our minds have become obese.

Functionalism Kills Presence

Some forms of technology extend human presence over great distance and bring the absent one nearer; the telephone and fax machine do this. Most technology, however, attempts to explain life in terms of function. Increasingly, when we approach something new our first question is never about the surprise of the thing but about how it functions. Our culture is saturated with information, which stubbornly refuses to come alive with understanding. The more we become immersed in technology, the more difficult it is to be patient with the natural unevenness and unpredictability of living. We learn to close ourselves off, and we think of our souls and minds no longer as presence but more in terms of apparatus and function. Functionalist thinking impoverishes presence. The functionalist mind is committed to maintenance and efficiency. The priority is that things continue to work. You can often experience this in your professional life. You are called to the director's office for a chat. Whether you are to be promoted or demoted, you feel you are not being seen. What is at stake is what the system either can get out of you or no longer wants from you. If you have staked your identity on belonging to that system, you are now in deep trouble. There are so many disappointed people within companies and corporations and public-service jobs, people who were once idealistic, but then reached the threshold of recognition where they discovered they were being treated as mere functionaries. They then lost confidence and belief in themselves.

Without Reverence There Is No Sense of Presence

Functionalism is lethal when it is not balanced by a sense of reverence. Without reverence, there is no sense of presence or wonder. Functionalism eats into this necessary respect for otherness, which makes us human. The functionalist mind is skilled in the art of using people and Nature for its own projects and achievements. In contrast, the reverential mind is respectful of the presence and difference of each person and thing. This does not imply that the reverential mind stagnates in passive attention towards life. It is well able to engage and tussle with the world, but it continues to relate to life with a sense of mystery and respect. To engage life in a reverential way is to maintain a sense of proportion and balance. You acknowledge that there is a depth of presence in every person that should never be reduced in order to satisfy your own selfishness and greed. You cannot have a personal integrity of presence without recognizing and revering the presence of others. There is some strange, hidden symmetry in the soul. When you diminish another person, you diminish your self. When you diminish your self, you diminish others.

There is something deeply sacred about every presence. When we become blind to this, we violate Nature and turn our beautiful world into a wasteland. We treat people as if they were disposable objects. We lament today the absence of God and the demise of the sacred. Yet it is we ourselves who have killed God. The world today is just as full of sacred presence as it was centuries ago. With the hardening of our minds we are no longer able to feel and sense the ever-present sacred the way our ancestors did. Our arrogance and greed have killed the gods. Unknown to us, the suppression of Divine Presence exacts a terrible price, because Nature and person lose their inner divinity when the gods depart. Past generations were often victims of a bleak, monolithic god who suppressed all creativity; we recognize the authority of no god and much of our creativity is monstrous. Dostoyevsky said, "If God does not exist, everything is permitted." All the horizons become flattened and the wells dry up. We no longer walk the earth with wonder. We have purchased the fatal ticket. Instead of being guests of the earth, we are now crowded passengers on the runaway train of progress and productivity; the windows are darkened and we can no longer see out. The gadgets and games in each compartment are quite fascinating. There is constant theatre. Public relations experts offer sensational help in manicuring the image and searching out the best sound-bite. Even if we wanted to alight, no one seems to be able to stop the train.

We desperately need to retrieve our capacity for reverence. Each day that is given to you is full of the shy graciousness of divine tenderness. It is a lovely practice at night to spend a little while revisiting the invisible sanctuaries of your lived day. Each day is a secret story woven around the radiant heart of wonder. We let our days fall away like empty shells and miss all the treasure.

The Ascetical Presence:
The Wisdom to Subtract from the Feast

Functionalism wants to acquire and control; its hunger is endless. The reverential mind can let things be and celebrate a person's presence or a thing's beauty without wanting something from them. There is an ascetical rhythm to experience. It is content to endure its own emptiness and does not need to rush to fill the emptiness with the latest distraction. It is interesting that asceticism has always been a key practice in the great religious traditions. In its most intense form, the ascetical mind was very bleak and engaged in a radical denial of self and the world. Its more balanced expression recognizes and respects the otherness and the beauty of the world and endeavours to transfigure the desire to define oneself through possessions, achievements, and power. Much of contemporary life suffers from a vast over-saturation. We have so much that we are unable to acknowledge or enjoy it. There is the obscenity of banks buying Van Gogh paintings as products and storing them in their dark vaults where no eye can enjoy them.

We would benefit greatly were we able to develop a more ascetic approach to our lives. As with all manner of spiritual discipline, we gain most when we are willing freely to choose what is difficult. To include the ascetic as a vital dimension in our daily life would deeply enrich us. It would gain us a sense of space. It would help us make clearances in the exponential growth of banality, sensation, and exteriority that leaves us so distracted and overwhelmed. It is interesting that much of the modern fascination with mysticism is more self-indulgent than ascetic. We like to filter out the appealing insights or ideas and often choose to forget the ascetic demands of the mystics. Yet it is only through inner clearance of the ascetical that the insights can take root and grow in the clay of our lives. The writings of John of the Cross have the severance of asceticism at their core. The practice of ascetical longing clarifies all belonging.

> To reach satisfaction in all
> Desire its possession in nothing.
> To come to possess all
> Desire the possession of nothing.
> To arrive at being all
> Desire to be nothing.

To come to the knowledge of all
Desire the knowledge of nothing. . . .
To come to be what you are not
You must go by a way in which you are not.

When you practise even some small asceticism, your experience gains a new sense of focus. Consumerist culture is not simply an outer frame that surrounds our lives. It is deeper and more penetrating than that. In fact it is a way of thinking that seeps into our minds and becomes a powerful inner compass. Consumerism and its greed are an awful perversion of our longing; they damage our very ability to experience things. They clutter our lives with things we do not need and subvert our sense of priority. They reduce everything to its functionalist common denominator. In contrast, the ascetical way clarifies our perception. It helps us to see clearly and sift the substance from the chaff. The fruit of even limited asceticism is clarity and discernment; you begin to recognize as chaff much of what you had held for the grain of nourishment.

Consumerism leaves us marooned in a cul-de-sac of demented longing, helpless targets of its relentless multiplication. The ascetical approach is selective and subtracts from the feast of what is offered in order to enjoy, explore, and celebrate. The functionalist mind only multiplies everything. It fills its own house to the brim. Within its creed of acquisition, it becomes a helpless victim of the insidious multiplication of things until there is such a false fullness that the natural light of life cannot get in anymore. Milton says in Book 8 of *Paradise Lost*, "But man by number is to manifest / His single imperfection . . ." In the dreary liturgies of this creed, asceticism is anathematized or treated as treason. There is a driven desperation at the heart of functionalism. Deep down, it is a craven desire for identity and poise, but it is also a desperate flight from oneself. At its root, it is a fear of nothing-ness. It panics in the face of the creative and generous uncertainty at the heart of life. Any ascetical practice is dif-ficult; you learn to walk a little on the path of self-denial. You could build into the rhythm of your week some little practice: it could mean fasting from food on a particular day; risking more regular and clearer meeting with your solitude; coming out from under the protection of your entrenched opinions or beliefs; visiting a prison, hospital, or old people's home once a fortnight or once a month. The intention of an ascetical discipline is not to turn you into a spiritual warrior, but to free you for compassion and love towards others and towards yourself.

We Cannot Live Without the Infinite

The functional mind fears infinity. It chooses to ignore the stirrings of the infinite in the soul and will not recognize the infinite present in Nature or person. Yet we cannot live with-out some form of the infinite. St. Augustine said, " Thou hast created us for Thy self O Lord and our hearts are restless until they rest in thee." The longing is ancient; it comes from Elsewhere. Our longing always stretches towards a further frontier. It is in our nature to seek the infinite. Consequently, the functionalist mind constructs its own infinite out of things, possessions, achievements, stimulants, and distrac-tions. It is fixed on the treadmill of multiplication. This kind of addiction is portrayed with uncanny precision by Jorge Luis Borges in his story "The Book of Sand": A man buys a book that is infinite and he becomes a prisoner of the book. This is the cold anonymous infinite; it is without care, tender-ness, mercy, or mystery. It seems to awaken a longing that is repetitive and utterly obsessed with the single-destination kind of life. The wonder of human life is the generous diversity of presences that dwell in the house of the soul. While all of our inner presences belong together in the one intimacy, each presence is a different longing for a different destination. The cold infinite numbs our richness of longing and bundles all our longings until they make a magnetic projectile that draws our one life dementedly towards the palace of pale satisfaction. In contrast to the living and life-giving infinite, Hegel characterized this as "die schlechte Unendlichkeit," i.e., bad infinity.

Some of the most sinister work of the cold infinite is apparent in the field of genetic engineering. Genetic intervention and manipulation allow unquestioned intrusion into the very identity of plant, animal, and even human species. The world continues each day; we get up, go to work, and put our hearts into the lives we live. Meanwhile, the researchers work away secretly in laboratories we know nothing about. These powerful, anonymous, skilled strangers are literally reinventing creation, adding new and altered species to the earth. They are altering life in a frightening way, and we are only faintly aware that what they call great developments are taking place. Suddenly, then, an ordinary-looking sheep appears on our television screens one evening. She bears the coquettish name Dolly. No other sheep in the world knows anything about her. She has never seen another sheep. It is astounding how those who control sinister change know how to parade their first product with such sickly innocence. Faust's dilemma is now ours. We have sold our souls for knowledge that is a dangerous intrusion into realms where we have no right to trespass. The brilliance of the functionalist imagination is its technical ability to invent objects to perform new functions. This ability has been central to the origin, evolution, and definition of human society. We have learned to tame and harness the forces of Nature. Now, at the end of this millennium, the functionalist mind is exerting an exclusive monopoly and sinister control over our lives. We invented the machine, but now the high priests of the machine are reinventing us.

An infinite that ignores the sacred becomes monstrous. The sense of proportion disappears. In its most sinister sense anything is possible. Consumerism is the new religion. It is practised by increasing numbers of people in the Western world. Quantity is the new divinity; more and more products are offered. The more you have, the greater your status. The power of this divinity is its ability to reach you anywhere. The "good news" of what it offers you is permanently coming towards you. Its messages flow right into your home through television. Advertising is its liturgy. Such advertisements sell themselves before they sell the product. There is no surplus with which the mind can conjure in advertisements. Everything is exactly divisible by the purposes of those who write copy. The fact that skill is involved does not make advertising into an art form, any more than criminals who display skill and even courage, deserve our admiration. Advertising is schooling in false desire.

We could never become consumers if we had no desire. It is poignant that despite maturity and judgement there remain visceral appetites within your heart that crave immediate satisfaction. Once awakened to a certain intensity, appetite races towards the object of desire. Your ability to discern or distance yourself from this drive becomes redundant. The adult returns almost to a child-like single-mindedness. In this sense, consumerist attitude is an obsessive and uncritical passion. It has a powerful and sophisticated ability to deconstruct all resistance. This new divinity is never abstract and does not insist on any major moral obedience. It touches our longing in a very concrete way. It ensures that it always targets the pocket as well as the heart. This is done with consummate skill so that we inevitably find ourselves magnetically attracted to the advertised icon, buy it, and bring it home. The advertisement is a tiny thought package inserted deftly into the mind; once it opens and expands, its control over us is immense. At a broader cultural level, it is astounding to watch it unravel the complex network of the folk world. Within a few years, this virus can penetrate to the very heart of an intricate way of life that had taken hundreds of years of history to construct. Before long, a distinctive and unique way of life is rifled, and the inhabitants exiled and drawn into the net of consumerist culture.

The Blessings of Desire

Desire is one of the key forces in the origin, evolution, and definition of identity. Blindly, but yet instinctively, desire brought you out of the invisible world, sowed you in the womb, and guided your way through a gallery of forms until you emerged as a baby. Instinctively, in the innocence of childhood, desire still directs your feelings and thoughts towards fulfilment. It leads you to explore new frontiers. When the innocence of childhood breaks and your consciousness becomes divided, your desire divides too. The belonging of childhood breaks; you feel confused and alone in a way you never were in childhood. New longings are surfacing, and you can find little sense of belonging. Part of your desire becomes focused on what you want to do with your life. This is the task of realizing your life's dream. Your desire crystallizes in questions like: What do I want to do with my life? Where do I want to work? Whom do I want to marry or do I want to marry? This is a complex and difficult time.

Deep down you desire the freedom to live the life you would love. Yet life itself will rarely give you exactly what you desire and seldom offers it to you in the form you would long for. Consequently, you learn the art of compromise. You learn to do with what you have. Destiny often deals us unexpected cards. Perhaps you have your dream profession, live in a lovely area, and yet the person with whom you live has never managed to reach you. Often you look out at her/him from someplace deep within and sadly acknowledge that, despite the dignity and endurance of your daily affection and care for each other, she/he will never want to travel that landscape to meet you. Or it could be the case that you find that you cannot give love at all; this is a worse hell than not receiving love. In relationship, the initial passion often settles in such a manner that you instinctively agree to meet on a certain level; other regions are to remain undisturbed. Inevitably in life, we end up walking one path. This demands choice and selection; we harness and limit the call of desire. Yet to live with a sense of balance, creativity, and integrity so much depends on how and what we choose.

To Keep the Contours of Choice Porous

Though choice deepens and incarnates a way of life, your soul and imagination have an immensity and diversity that can neither be reduced to nor accommodated in your chosen path. If you neglect your own immensity, your life-path itself becomes repressive and unnatural. It cannot unfurl in its own natural rhythm. You have to push your way through; your life becomes over-deliberate. Every action and movement has to be forcibly chosen. You try to keep yourself together. You do not feel that you have taken a wrong path. No. This is the way life is. One cannot drift endlessly. Eventually some direction must be taken. That is all you have done. Yet you feel disproportionately disappointed; it is as if you have given up something that was unfairly demanded of you. Eventually it becomes easier. You have made the compromise that everyone seems to have to make at a certain point. You do not have to force yourself as you did at the beginning. Gradually something seems to close off within you and habit takes over so smoothly. Now it all happens automatically. You have achieved cohesion and stability in your life, but you have paid an awful price—the death of your longing and the loss of the future you long for.

"Purity of Heart Is to Will One Thing."

A life's journey is made up of continual daily choices. But there are moments of profound choosing, when a partner, a life-direction, or a new way of being in the world is chosen. This can be a wonderful time of focus and re-direction. When such a moment of choosing is genuine, it is usually preceded by a time of gestation and gathering. Many different strands of your past experience begin to weave together until gradually the new direction announces itself. Its voice is sure with the inevitability of the truth. When your life-decisions emerge in this way from the matrix of your experience, they warrant your trust and commitment. When you can choose in this way, you move gracefully within the deeper rhythm of your soul. The geography of your destiny is always clearer to the eye of your soul than to the intentions and the needs of your surface mind. Wordsworth says in "The Prelude," "Soul, that art the eternity of thought." The eye of the soul can see in all directions. When you truly listen to the voice of your soul, you awaken your kinship with the eternal urgency that longs to lead you home. The deepest call to a creative life comes from within your own interiority. It may be awakened or occasioned by a person or situation outside you, yet the surest voice arises from your own secret depth. The surest choosing grows out of the natural soil of experience. The Buddhists say, "When the apple is ripe, it falls of itself from the Tree."

When we come to moments of profound choosing, we need to be careful about how and where we draw the lines of our choice. Even though a choice sets the fundamental direction of your life, it should not hermetically seal you off from the rest of life. The outer lines of choice should remain porous. Though we always end up having to choose, choice itself remains a mystery, utterly opaque, no matter how much we deliberate. Frost's poem "The Road Not Taken" shows how, after the event, we achieve clarity and self-importance in dramatizing choices already made. But the choice we made is, was, and remains mysterious. We are fashioned from the earth, are clay shapes in human form. We are children of Nature, where borders are seldom sealed. Underneath our walls and city streets, left to itself, the earth is still one ever-changing field. In order for life to flow, frontiers must remain porous. Nowhere is this more evident than the outer frontier of the human body, our skin. Skin is porous and in a constant interflow with nature. Were it to seal itself off in some hermetic act, it would kill the body. Similarly, the outer lines of a clear choice or life-path should also remain porous in order to allow our other unchosen lives to continue to bless us.

Great Choices Need the Shelter of Blessing

Such moments of choosing are also moments of great vulnerability. Often, there seems to be a dark side to destiny; it gathers to conspire against the freshly formed choice or chosen direction. The act of making a profound choice lifts one out of the level shelter of the crowd. There is the Daoist saying "The wind in the forest always hits the tallest trees." A choice creates clearance. In this new space, the unknown has clear sights on the individual. No obstacles blur the target. Literary tragedy offers a profound exploration of this vulnerability. With passion, the tragic hero makes a choice. Unknown to him, he stumbles against some divine law. The choice that opened the glimpse of a wonderful journey and possibility squeezes and tightens now like a noose around the protagonist's neck. The terrible consequences of the passionately chosen path begin to collapse underneath the hero and destroy him and his world. The transfiguration in tragedy is the hero's recognition of the secret order that he unintentionally violated.

When the garden of your unchosen lives has enough space to breathe beneath your chosen path, your life enjoys a vitality and a sense of creative tension. Rilke refers to this as "the repository of unlived things." You know that you have not compromised the immensity that you carry, and in which you participate. You have not avoided the call of commitment; yet you hold your loyalty to your chosen path in such a way as to be true to the blessings and dangers of life's passionate sacramentality. No life is single. Around and beneath each life is the living presence of these adjacencies. Often, it is not the fact of our choosing that is vital, but rather the way we hold that choice. In so far as we can, we should ensure that our chosen path is not a flight from complexity. If we opt for complacency, we exclude ourselves from the adventure of being human. Where all danger is neutralized, nothing can ever grow. To keep the borders of choice porous demands critical vigilance and affective hospitality. To live in such a way invites risk and engages complexity. Life cannot be neatly compartmentalized. Once the psyche is engaged with such invitation and courage, it is no longer possible to practise tidy psychological housekeeping. To keep one's views and convictions permeable is to risk the intake of new possibility, which can lead to awkward change. Yet the integrity of growth demands such courage and vulnerability from us; otherwise the tissues of our sensibility atrophy and we become trapped behind the same predictable mask of behaviour.

To Be Faithful to Your Longing

To live in such a hospitable way brings many challenges. In marriage or with a life's partner, it demands trust and flexibility in the commitment. Many relationships die quietly soon after the initial commitment. They lose their passion and adventure. The relationship becomes an arrangement. This often happens because the couple renege on a plurality of other friendships as central to their lives. Even though you have one anam-ċara, one to whom you are committed, one who reaches you where no one else can or will, this person cannot become the absolute mirror for your life. To expect any one individual to satisfy your life-longing is a completely unjust demand. No one could live up to that expectation. The self is not singular. There are many selves within the one individual. Different friends awaken and reach different selves within you. Different gifts and different challenges come through your different friendships. To hold the borders of your commitment open allows you to give and receive from others without necessarily endangering the sacredness of your anam-ċara bond. In fact, it can enrich and deepen the primordial and permanent intimacy between you. To live with this porousness can at times lead to ambivalence, but with discernment and integrity that need not become destructive. This art of living is vital in the workplace. This porousness often allows the alternative light to come through so that you do not have a blind faith in the system. You can still work committedly and creatively and yet recognize the surrounding functionalism and refrain from giving yourself totally and making yourself permanently vulnerable.

The Addiction of Distraction

When you choose someone or some way of life, you invest your heart. Choice becomes an invitation to commitment. When you commit, you deepen presence. Though your choice narrows the range of possibility now open to you, it increases the intensity of the chosen possibility. New dimensions of the chosen path reveal themselves; a new path opens inwards to depth and outwards to new horizons. Your choice has freed your longing from dispersing itself over a whole range of surface. When we avoid choice we often become victims of distraction. We flit like the butterfly from one flower to the next, delightfully seduced by its perfume and colour. We remain secretly addicted to the temporary satisfaction and pleasure of immediacy. Kierkegaard divided the life-journey into stages, and he saw that the aesthetic stage was the wanderer whose longing is magnetized on the endless array of novelties. We celebrate the surface unwilling to become acquainted with the depths where the darkness plies its slow and patient transfigurations. The colour and excitement of the surface, though delightful, are ultimately deceptive; they keep us from recognizing the habit of our repetitions and the boredom and poverty that sleep there. When we choose a definite path or partner, we leave the endless array of beckoning surface. We go below the façade of repetition and risk the danger of encounter, challenge, and responsibility. When you choose with discernment, integrity, and passion, you submit yourself to the slow and unglamorous miracle of change.

Irony and Recognition

When the hero in a tragedy acts out of great passion and longing, he is often blind to the choice he is awakening. He participates in a sequence of actions without ever dreaming where it is actually leading him. Often it may be clear to others, but not to him. When one acts greatly, one engenders great vulnerability. True recognition is withheld. The ground of realization prepares itself slowly. You are so close to what you are involved in that you literally cannot see it. This can often happen in relationships. The film *Fatal Attraction* portrayed a man who was guided totally by sexual passion and was blind to the nature of the person with whom he had become involved. It can also happen in a life over-committed to work. The workaholic is doing everything right to provide for the family, but is blind to the fact that he is already losing his family because of his obsession with work. They never see him; they and he are quietly becoming strangers to each other. When we spoil our children, we deprive them of learning the art of discipline and the recognition of boundaries. We think we are showing them love and support. Ironically, we are preparing great difficulties for them. Irony continues so long as you do not see. Then, when you suddenly do, you see through the whole sequence at once. You realize how the consequences have been building the whole time, unknown to you. Such recognition breaks your blindness; it also shows you clearly your own part in the story and your responsibility for what happened. It reveals that you have been obscurely complicit in your own downfall. Irony is the shy sister of such recognition.

It is vital that one's spiritual quest be accompanied by a sense of irony. To have a sense of irony ensures humility. Even in your moments of purest, honest intention, there is a sense in which you do not know and can never know what it is that you are actually doing. There is an opaque backdrop to even the clearest action. In everything we do and say, we risk encounter with the unknown. Often its ways are not our ways, and only at the end do we see the deeper meaning of our actions. Certain longings want tenancy of your heart; when you succumb to these, you betray your deeper, eternal longing. You need to remain open, yet maintain discernment and critical vigilance. Critical openness is true hospitality and receptivity.

Longing Keeps Your Sense of Life Kindled

The value of such openness is that it permits a crucial distance between you and the activity of your life in the world. It keeps a certain inner solitude clear, so that you remain aware of a primordial longing of life rising in you. Longing in this sense is not a search for gratification or pleasure. This longing is the primal presence of your own vitality. It is the sense of life in you which makes you feel alive. Psychology, philosophy, or religion rarely refer to the "sense of life." They concern themselves with the outer meaning of the world, the inner meaning of the soul, and the threshold where the two meet. This search for meaning is as ancient as the awakening of the first question; it is as new and urgent as the question that is troubling you now. Without a sense of meaning, life becomes absurd and surrealistic. In our times Camus, Sartre, Beckett, and Kafka have explored the possibilities and consequences of taking any human action amid the unpredictable chaos of life.

When your sense of meaning collapses or is violated, it becomes exceptionally difficult to remain creative or even to continue believing in anything. In the Siberian Gulag, prisoners were forced victims of absurdity. They were forced to do tasks that involved hard labour in the freezing cold. Regardless of how minimal and slight a task might be, the human mind always desires that the task have some significance. The Gulag prisoners were often forced to move hundreds of tons of stones from a pile to another location some miles away. Each day, in the freezing cold, each prisoner filled his wheelbarrow and slowly wheeled barrow after barrow of rock to the other location. You can imagine their sense of satisfaction as over the weeks the new rock pile began to grow from the transported stone. Every stone was earned. On the very day that all the stones were transferred, the guards made the prisoners begin to bring the stones back again to reconstruct the original pile in the same place. This forced absurdity would eat into the coherence and break the secret belonging of any mind.

Each Person Incarnates Longing

Our quest for meaning, though often unacknowledged, is what secretly sustains our passion and guides our instinct and action. Our need to find meaning is urged upon us by our sense of life. Normally, when we look at people, whether at work, on the street, or in our homes, we inevitably think of them in practical terms. We experience other people very concretely. We notice the way they look, the role they play, the clothes they wear, the habits they have, and especially the styles of their personalities.

Yet when you distance yourself from the particularities of individual lives, you begin to realize that no human person is here on earth accidentally or neutrally. Each person is a living world of longing. You are here not simply because you were sent here. You are here because you long to be here. A person is an incarnation of longing. Behind your image, role, personality, and deeper than your thoughts, there is a pulse of desire that sustains you in the world. All your thoughts, feelings, and actions arise from a secret source within you which desires life. This is where your sense of life is rooted. Your sense of life expresses itself in your convictions, intentions, and passions; it precedes them. Your sense of life is pre-reflective, yet passionate and powerful. This secret presence of longing helps you endure the routine of the daily round; it emerges strongly when difficulty entangles you, or when suffering strips away your networks of connection with the world. Your sense of life is not something you can invent or force with your mind. It is the wisdom of your clay and is eternally acquainted with awakening. As you discover the faithfulness of life within you, your sense of life transfigures your fear and assures you that you are more deeply rooted than you realize. It frees you for the adventure of solitude.

To Find Your True Home Within Your Life

Each one of us is alone in the world. It takes great courage to meet the full force of your aloneness. Most of the activity in society is subconsciously designed to quell the voice crying in the wilderness within you. The mystic Thomas à Kempis said that when you go out into the world, you return having lost some of yourself. Until you learn to inhabit your aloneness, the lonely distraction and noise of society will seduce you into false belonging, with which you will only become empty and weary. When you face your aloneness, something begins to happen. Gradually, the sense of bleakness changes into a sense of true belonging. This is a slow and open-ended transition but it is utterly vital in order to come into rhythm with your own individuality. In a sense this is the endless task of finding your true home within your life. It is not narcissistic, for as soon as you rest in the house of your own heart, doors and windows begin to open outwards to the world. No longer on the run from your aloneness, your connections with others become real and creative. You no longer need to covertly scrape affirmation from others or from projects outside yourself. This is slow work; it takes years to bring your mind home.

The human mind is an amazing gift. It delights in the activity of exploring, gathering, and relating things. Whereas stones or trees never seem bothered by their particular uniqueness, each human mind is powerfully conscious of its own difference; it has an intimate and unbreakable relationship with its own difference. This is what makes human individuality journey out of itself to explore and engage others; but it is also what makes each of us so deeply aware of our aloneness. In contrast to the rest of Nature, the human mind makes us feel alone, aware of the distances we will never be able to cross. The mind cannot resist exploration, because it always sees the world mirrored in itself. The huge longing of the human mind is to discover ever larger shelters of belonging.

The Eros of Thought

Your mind is the double mirror of the outer world and of your inner world. It is always actively making pictures of things. If you lost your mind, you would lose your world as well. Your mind is so precious and vulnerable precisely because it holds your world. Thoughts are the furniture of the mind. They are the echoes and pictures that hold your world together. This is the fascinating adventure of perception. When you become aware of your thoughts and your particular style of thinking, you begin to see why your world is shaped the way it is. It is an exciting and frightening moment to realize your responsibility for your own thoughts. Then you know that you also have the freedom to think differently. Rather than having to travel always along a predetermined track of thought, you now begin to realize the excitement of thinking in new directions and in different rhythms. You see that thinking has something eternal in it. In the Western tradition, thought has been understood as the place within the human person where we are most intimately connected with divinity. Thought is the place of revelation. The dance of thoughts is endless. In his essay on John Donne, T. S. Eliot suggests that a thought to him was an experience as immediate as the scent of a flower.

Thought is a profound form of longing. Much of the thought that cripples us is dried out, dead thought. There is no warmth of longing alive in it. Thought that loses touch with feeling is lethal. This separation is the fracture from which fascism and holocaust emerge. Knowledge is intimacy. This is most evident in the activity of friendship. When the longing awakens between you and a stranger, you want to know that person—to come close. Closeness without knowing can be either a fascination and reverence for mystery or the prostitution of longing. Spiritual longing is what first draws you close to a friend. This desire refines and deepens itself in coming to know him or her. Friendship is one of the most beautiful places in which longing reaches initial fulfilment and is then further deepened, refined, and transfigured. You can also see the longing of thought in the fascination of ideas. When you find yourself in a cul-de-sac in your life and you feel lost and trapped, a new insight or awareness can come to you, enabling you to free yourself.

Our Longing Is an Echo of the Divine Longing

Thought crosses fascinating thresholds when it engages mystery. Mystery cannot be unravelled by thought, yet the most interesting thinking always illuminates some lineaments of mystery. It opens our minds to a depth of presence that cannot be rifled by even our brightest or most vigorous ideas. Mystery keeps its secret to itself. With its reserve, it invites us ever nearer to the hearth of truth and belonging. Mystery kindles our longing and draws us out of complacency into ever more refined and appropriate belonging. A life that has closed off mystery has deadened itself. Perhaps this is why modern discourse so often sounds inane; it is a forsaken language in which thought has lost its kinship with mystery. When this inner conversation is broken, the sense of mystery dies. When we lose the guidance of mystery, our culture becomes flat. At the end of these flat fields of thought, there is no horizon, merely piles of negativity, an apocalyptic doom that darkens all hope.

Thought is the form of the mind's desire. It is in our thinking that the depth of our longing comes to expression. This longing can never be fulfilled by any one person, project, or thing. The secret immensity of the soul is the longing for the divine. This is not simply a haunted desire for an absent, distant divine presence that is totally different from us. Our longing is passionate and endless because the divine calls us home to presence. Our longing is an echo of the divine longing for us. Our longing is the living imprint of divine desire. This desire lives in each of us in that ineffable space in the heart where nothing else can satisfy or still us. This is what gives us that vital gift we have called "the sense of life."

The wonder of presence is the majesty of what it so subtly conceals. Real presence is eternity become radiant. This is why the "sense of life" in us has such power and vitality. Our deepest longing is like a restless artist who tirelessly seeks to make our presence real in order that the mystery we harbour may become known to us. The glory of human presence is the divine longing fully alive.

A BLESSING

May you awaken to the mystery of being here and enter
    the quiet immensity of your own presence.

May you have joy and peace in the temple of your senses.

May you receive great encouragement when new frontiers
    beckon.

May you respond to the call of your gift and find the
    courage to follow its path.

May the flame of anger free you from falsity.

May warmth of heart keep your presence aflame and may
    anxiety never linger about you.

May your outer dignity mirror an inner dignity of soul.

May you take time to celebrate the quiet miracles that
    seek no attention.

May you be consoled in the secret symmetry of your soul.

May you experience each day as a sacred gift woven
    around the heart of wonder.

3

Prisons We Choose to Live In

The Beauty of Wild Distance

Outside there is great distance. When you walk out into the
landscape the fields stretch away towards the horizon. At
dawn, the light unveils the vast spread of nature. Gnarled
stones hold nests of fossils from a time so distant we cannot
even imagine it. At night, the stars reflect light from the infi-
nite distance of the cosmos. When you experience this dis-
tance stretching away from the shore of your body, it can
make you feel minuscule. Pascal said, "The eternal silence of
these infinite spaces frightens me." There is a magnificent
freedom in Nature; no frontier could ever frame her infinity.
There is a natural wildness in the earth. You sense this par-
ticularly in wild places that have never been tamed by
human domestication. There are places where the ocean
praises the steady shore in a continual hymn of wave. There
are fresh, cold streams pouring through mountain corners in
a rhythm that never anticipated the gaze of a human eye.
Animals never interfere with the wildness of the earth. They
attune themselves to the longing of the earth and move
within it as if it were a home rhythm. Animals have no dis-
tance from the earth. They have no plan or programme in

relation to it. They live naturally in its landscapes, always present completely to where they are. There is an apt way in which the animal who always lives in the "now" of time can fit so perfectly into the "where" of landscape. The time and mind of the animal rest wherever it is. The poet Wendell Berry says, "I come into the peace of wild things. . . . / . . . For a time / I rest in the grace of the world, and am free."

The House Keeps the Universe Out

The human person is the creature that changes the wildness of the earth to suit the intentions of his own agenda. Gerard Manley Hopkins argues against disturbing Nature: "Long live the weeds and the wilderness yet." *Homo sapiens* is the one species that has deliberately altered the earth. One of the first ways this happened was by clearing trees and land to build homes. Humans wanted to come in from the great immensities of Nature and the heavens. Homes provided shelter against marauding animals. They also provided shelters of belonging. Perhaps the awakening of infinity in the mind demanded relief from the cosmos in the refuge of simple belonging. At another level, the home represents a certain limitation. It frames off the privacy of your life from the outside world. As cities expand octopus-like into the countryside, it is sad to see beautiful fields serrated with replica housing developments. An old neighbour of mine who rarely visited the city until recently was heard to remark as he looked at all the housing developments, "The houses are all the same. How would a person find his way home in the evening?" A few minutes later the logic of his own musing had the solution: "I bet you they are all numbered."

A house can become a little self-enclosed world. Sheltered there, we learn to forget the wild, magnificent universe in which we live. When we domesticate our minds and hearts, we reduce our lives. We disinherit ourselves as children of the universe. Almost without knowing it, we slip inside ready-made roles and routines which then set the frames of our possibilities and permissions. Our longing becomes streamlined. We acquire sets of convictions in relation to politics, religion, and work. We parrot these back and forth at each other, as if they were absolute insights. Yet for the most part these frames of belief function as self-constructed barriers, fragile clichés pulled around our lives to keep out the mystery. The game of society helps us to forget the unknown and subversive presence of the human person. The control and ordering of society is amazing: we comply so totally with its unwritten rules. In a city at morning, you see the lines of traffic and the rows of faces all on their way to work. We show up. We behave ourselves. We obey fashion and taste. Meanwhile, almost unknown to ourselves, we are standing on wild earth at a crossroads in time where anything can come towards us. Yet we behave as if we carry the world and were the executives of a great plan. Everywhere around us mystery never sleeps. The same deep nature is within us. Each person is an incredibly sophisticated, subtle, and open-ended work of art. We live at the heart of our own intimacy, yet we are strangers to its endless nature.

Our Fear of Freedom: The Refuge of False Belonging

On the outside a person may seem contented and free, but the inner landscape may be a secret prison. Why do so many of us reduce and domesticate our one journey through this universe? Why do we long for the invisible walls to keep us in and keep mystery out? We have a real fear of freedom. In general, everyone is apparently in favour of freedom. We fight for it and we praise it. In the practice of our lives, however, we usually keep back from freedom. We find it awkward and disturbing. Freedom challenges us to awaken and realize all the possibilities that sleep in the clay of our hearts. Dostoyevsky's legend of the Grand Inquisitor in *The Brothers Karamazov* is a haunting reflection on the idea of freedom. In the story Jesus comes back to sixteenth-century Seville during the Spanish Inquisition. He is put in prison, and the Cardinal Inquisitor comes to interview Jesus, but he remains silent. The Cardinal complains to Jesus in a fascinating monologue: "Why did you have to come back and interfere with our work?" He suggests that Jesus made a fatal mistake in overestimating humans. We are not capable of using the freedom that he attributed to and expected of us. The Cardinal says that the Church "corrected" his work. Instead of the invitation to liberation and creativity, the Church chooses to offer the people "miracle, mystery and authority." This is what people like and need. People are not capable of freedom.

The Cage of Frightened Identity

In the inner landscape of the soul is a nourishing and melodious voice of freedom always calling you. It encourages you to enlarge your frames of belonging—not to settle for a false shelter that does not serve your potential. There is no cage for the soul. Each of us should travel inwards from the surface constraints and visit the wild places within us. There are no small rooms there. Each of us needs the nourishment and healing of these inner clearances. One of the most crippling prisons is the prison of reduced identity. The way we treat our own identity is often Procrustean. In Greek legend, Procrustes was a robber who stretched his victims until they fitted the length of his bed. Each one of us is inevitably involved in deciphering who we actually are. No other can answer that question for you. "Who are you?" is a surface question which has a vast, intricate rootage. Who are you behind your mask, your role? Who are you behind your words? Who are you when you are alone with yourself? In the middle of the night, when you awake, who are you then? When dawn rescues you from the rainforest of the night, who are you before you slip back safely beneath the mask and the name by which you are known during the day? It is one of the unnoticed achievements of daily life to keep the wild complexity of your real identity so well hidden that most people never suspect the worlds that collide in your heart. Friendship and love should be the safe regions where your unknown selves can come out to play. Instead of holding your friend or beloved limited within the neat cage of frightened identity, love should liberate both of you to celebrate the festival of complexity within you. We remain so hesitant and frightened to enjoy the beauty of our own divinity.

There are no manuals for the construction of the individual you would like to become. You are the only one who can decide this and take up the lifetime of work that it demands. This is such a wonderful privilege and such an exciting adventure. To grow into the person that your deepest longing desires is a great blessing. If you can find a creative harmony between your soul and your life, you will have found something infinitely precious. You may not be able to do much about the great problems of the world or to change the situation you are in, but if you can awaken the eternal beauty and light of your soul, you will bring light wherever you go. The gift of life is given to us for ourselves and also to bring peace, courage, and compassion to others.

The Fixed Image Atrophies Longing

We are no sooner out of the womb than we must begin this precarious unfolding and shaping of who we are. If we have bad or destructive times in childhood, we begin to fix on a survival identity to cover over and to compensate for what happens to us. If we were never encouraged to be ourselves, we begin to construct an identity that will gain us either attention or approval. When we set out to construct our lives according to a fixed image, we damage ourselves. The image becomes the desperate focus of all our longing. There are no frames for the soul. In truth, we are called, in so far as we can, to live without an image of ourselves, or at least to keep the images we have free and open. When you sense the immensity of the unknown within you, any image you have built of yourself gradually loses its promise. Your name, your face, your address only suggest the threshold of your identity. Somehow you are always secretly aware of this. Sometimes, you find yourself listening to someone telling you what you should do or describing what is going on inside you, and you whisper to yourself that they have not the foggiest idea who you actually are.

The Swiss writer Max Frisch describes something of the mystery of friendship in one of his diaries: "It is remarkable that in relation to the one we love we are least able to declare how he is. We simply love him. This is exactly what love is. The wonder of love is that it holds us in the flow of that which is alive; it maintains us in the readiness to follow this person in all his possible unfoldings. We know that every person feels transfigured and unfolded when we love him. And also for the one who loves, everything continues in the same unfolding, the things that are nearest and the things that are long familiar. We begin to see things as if for the first time. Love frees us from every image. That is the excitement and adventure and tension: we will never be finished with the one that we love as long as we love him and because we love him" (author's translation). As it continues to unfold, a loving relationship fosters the adventure of belonging. It also becomes a mirror for our thoughts and emotions: we can look at life from another's point of view and expand our horizons of imagination and perception; it rescues us from false limitation.

It may be more helpful to consider yourself in terms of symbol rather than image. A symbol is never completely in the light. It holds a vital line into the rootage in the dark. It has many faces. Paul Ricoeur says, "A symbol invites thought." The symbol does not nail thought to half-truth. A symbol is alive; it constantly nudges thought towards new windows of seeing. Because it is alive, it mirrors most faithfully the subtle changes that are always happening in your soul. Though our outer lives retain a certain similarity—our faces, behaviour, friends, work, remain the same—there is an endless ebb and flow of newness inside you. This is the paradox of being a human. Looking at your body, thoughts, and feelings in a symbolic way enables you to inhabit more fully your presence and its freedoms. There is hospitality and space in a symbol for your depth and paradox. The self is not an object or a fixed point of reference. It is a diverse inner landscape too rich to be grasped in any one concept. There is a plurality of divine echoes within you. The *Tao Te Ching* says wryly, "The Great Symbol is out of shape."

To Become Free Is Everything

Sometimes ideas hold us down; they become heavy anchors that hold the bark of identity fixated in shallow, dead water. In the Western tradition, the idea of the sinfulness and self-ishness of the self has trapped many lovely people all their lives in a false, inner civil war. Fearful of valuing themselves in any way, they have shunned their own light and mystery. Their inner world remained permanently off limits. People were given to believe that they were naturally bad and sinful. They let this toxic idea into their minds and it gradually poisoned their whole way of seeing themselves. Sin was around every corner, and in any case, probable damnation waited at the end of the road. People were unwittingly drafted into blaspheming against their own nature. You could not let yourself go. Any longing to claim your nature or to pursue your wildness would lead to ruin. This corrupted the innocence of people's sensual life and broke the fluency of their souls. Rather than walking the path with the encouraging companionship of your protecting angel beside you and the passionate creativity of the Holy Spirit at your deepest core, you were made to feel like a convict trapped between guilt and fear. It is one of the awful sins committed against people. So many good people were internally colonized with a poisonous ideology that had nothing to do with the kind gentleness and tender sympathy of God.

Despite our being subjugated by negative belief, there remains a deep longing in every person for self-discovery. No one can remain continually unmoved by the surprising things that rise to the surface of one's life. It is a great moment when you break out of the prison of negative self-criticism and develop a sense of the inner adventure of the soul. Suddenly everything seems to become possible. You feel new and young. As you step through the dead threshold, you can hear the old structures of self-hate and self-torment collapsing behind you. Now you know that your life is yours and that good things are going to happen to you. At a Gospel Mass in New Orleans recently, the preacher invited each one of us to turn to our neighbour and say, "Something good is going to happen to you." It made me realize that there are such beautiful bouquets of words that we never offer each other. For days afterwards, I could see the chubby face and hear the gravel voice of the little boy beside me saying, "Somethin' good's gonna happen to You." His words became a kind of inner mantra that blessed me for days.

We were created to be free; within you there is deep freedom. This freedom will not intrude; it will not hammer at the door of your life and force you to embrace it. The greater presences within us do not act in this way. Their invitation is inevitably subtle and gracious. In order to inherit your freedom, you need to go towards it. You have to claim your own freedom before it becomes yours. This is neither arrogant nor selfish; it is simply moving towards the gift that was prepared for you from ancient times. As a German thinker said, "Frei sein ist nichts, / frei werden ist alles," i.e., To be free is nothing, to become free is everything. Albert Camus's story "The Adulterous Woman" is a fine portrait of a woman who has fled from herself into the prison of a relationship with a man who is vacillating, demanding, and lost. One night, during a listless and utterly frustrating business trip with him, she leaves the bedroom and goes out into the desert: "Then with unbearable gentleness the water of the night began to fill Janine, drowned the cold, rose gradually from the hidden core of her being and overflowed in wave after wave, rising up even to her mouth full of moans. The next moment, the whole sky stretched over her, fallen on her back on the cold earth." With sensuous and spiritual intimacy, Nature comes to find and free her by calling her suppressed nature alive.

Rousseau said, "Man was born free, yet everywhere I look, I see him in chains." Each of us has a reservoir of unknown freedom, yet our fear holds us back. The worst chains are not the chains which others would have you wear. The chains with which you manacle yourself cut deepest and hold you longest. In a certain sense, no one outside you can imprison you. They can only turn you into a prisoner, if you assent and put on the chains they offer. There are no psychological police. Only you can step over that threshold into the prison of image, the prison of expectation, or the prison of anxiety.

The Mental Prison

A mental prison can be as bad as a physical prison. When you are trapped in a mental prison, the crippling idea or feeling robs you of all joy and freedom. You can see and feel little else. Your mind becomes a small room without light. You turn the wild mystery of your own mind into a shabby, negative little room; the windows are blocked, and there is no door. The mental prison is devastatingly lonely. It is a sorrowful place, because ultimately it is you who locks yourself up within a demented idea or feeling.

It is a helpless place to be trapped; all outside life lessens. There is a distance between you and everything else. It is difficult for anyone to reach you. You come to believe that the shape of the prison is the shape of reality. It is so difficult to leave the mental prison precisely because you cannot see beyond your pain. In other words, you are completely blind to the fact that it is you who construct it and decide to stay locked in there; this punishment is mainly self-punishment. Inevitably, you tend to blame others and hold them responsible for whatever hurt put you away. It is only when you become aware of your own longing to be free that you realize how you let what happened to you take away your power and freedom. You were so hurt that you were no longer able to distinguish your life from the hurt. It took you over completely. You acted in complicity with the hurt and turned against yourself.

We Take upon Ourselves
the Images
Made for Us

It is astounding how we take on the violence that is directed towards us. When someone attacks you, it is practically certain that internally you will attack yourself. It would be great to have enough confidence in your self, and enough freedom and inner poise, that when hostility comes towards you, you could let it pass right over your shoulder. Someone assaults you verbally, points out your weaknesses and failures, testifies to the fact that the very sight of you is enough to make him want to reincarnate on the spot, and expresses the sincerest compassion with those who have to endure your blighted presence on a more frequent basis. Wouldn't it be lovely on such an occasion to be able to look that person in the eye and say from your heart, "I am sorry that it disturbs you so much, but you know, right now I am just feeling so good. I am sorry that you are feeling that miserable. Can I get you a cup of coffee or anything?" What usually happens is you are hurt and begin to use the ammunition that has been just delivered against yourself. Such confrontation can burrow into you for weeks afterwards.

No one outside can open the door to release you from inner prison. The key is actually on the inside. It takes a long time to find the door and turn the key to come out onto the pastures where the wildflowers grow and the air is fresh and full. We are children of Nature. Thoughts should stir like the wind through the rich spring branches, and lift you, opening you towards new horizons, and not confine you to the stale, dead air of shabby inner rooms. The New Testament tells how people often begged Jesus to cure them. Sometimes these were people who had lived inside the prison of illness for years. In his gentle yet incisive way, he often turned the question inwards and asked, "Do you want to be healed?" This is a great question to ask yourself when you notice that the changes you long for are not happening. Maybe you do not want to be free. Something in the inner confinement confirms something in you which you are not yet ready to let go. The mind does not need to endure any internal police or prison guards holding you confined. You can be as free as your longing desires.

The Prison of Guilt

It is awful to feel guilty. Your mind and Spirit become haunted. You keep on returning to some action or event in the past. You acted dishonourably in some way. Perhaps it was some scalpel of a sentence that cut into someone's life or severed a friendship. Or something you did to someone that was wrong and has shadowed that person's life ever since. Perhaps it was something you did in ignorance or blindness; you only glimpsed the consequences later, but by then it was too late. You can also carry a burden of guilt not because of an action, but because of your non-action at a crucial juncture. If you had had the vision or courage to say or do something, then someone else might have been spared great pain. Once you began to see what your failure to act actually allowed, you feel guilty and ashamed.

There is hardly any life that is not shadowed in some place by guilt. There is always some little corner of even the most immaculate cupboard where there is the stain, if not the splinter, of a hidden skeleton. No one lives a perfect life; there are places where we have been weak, ignorant, and blind and the results have been damaging and destructive. The person who never made a mistake never made anything. We would be ashamed and humiliated if these failures were paraded before the public. Every life has some more or less burdensome secret. When you visit the corner in your heart where the secret lives, the guilt comes alive. When your burden of guilt is truthful to what actually happened and to your part and responsibility in it, then the burden is appropriate. This is a very important condition, and one that is difficult to judge. Sometimes we feel guilty about things in the past that should hold no guilt for us. Because we feel bad about something, we exaggerate our part in it and retrospectively ascribe more power and freedom to ourselves than we actually had in the actual situation.

Guilt in itself is useless. It belongs to the past, and the past is over and gone. Regardless of how guilty you feel, you cannot return to that time, enter the situation, and act as honourably as you now wish you had then. One of the great developments in modern culture is the way we have emancipated ourselves from the gnawing feeling of guilt that tormented past generations. When the God and the system were harsh, and culture was more uniform, good and innocent people felt scrupulously guilty about nothing. Now we are at the other extreme, where people in our rapid consumerist culture have lost all ability to feel guilt. When there is no capacity for warranted and proportionate guilt, some terrible deadening of human sensibility has taken place. When we treat a person wrongly or badly, when we hurt or damage someone, when we allow awful things to happen around us or in our name and we remain silent, when we buy goods that are products of the slavery and oppression of the poor, when we support institutions and policies that blight the hidden lives of those who have no voice, we definitely should feel a haunting guilt that should eat into our complacency and render our belonging uneasy.

When personal guilt in relation to a past event becomes a continuous cloud over your life, you are locked in a mental prison. You have become your own jailer. Although you should not erase your responsibility for the past, when you make the past your jailer, you destroy your future. It is such a great moment of liberation when you learn to forgive yourself, let the burden go, and walk out into a new path of promise and possibility. Self-compassion is a wonderful gift to give yourself. You should never reduce the mystery and expanse of your presence to a haunted fixation with something you did or did not do. To learn the art of integrating your faults is to begin a journey of healing on which you will regain your poise and find new creativity. Your soul is more immense than any one moment or event in your past. When you allow guilt to fester and reduce you like this, it has little to do with guilt. The guilt is only an uncomfortable but convenient excuse for your fear of growth.

The Prison of Shame

Shame is one of the most distressing and humiliating emotions. When you feel ashamed, your dignity is torn and compromised. Shame is a powerful emotion; it somehow penetrates to the core of your soul. There is inevitably a strong social dimension to shame. You feel ashamed because you have acted dishonourably in some way. In some cultures, the very danger of incurring shame seemed to keep people from stepping out of line. When someone did, the tribe cohered into one accusing eye glaring at the offender in disgust and judgement. Such a person was inevitably pushed out to the margins of isolation and horrific emotional reprobation. Shame is a force intended to put one outside all belonging. More often than not, such one-sided conformity and its conventions of judgement are factitious and secretly corrupt. The one who does the forbidden thing becomes the focus for all the anger of those who would love to have done it too, but are afraid of the exclusion and shame.

Conventions that can wield the stick of shame are immensely powerful. It is tragic how much women have endured under such conventions. Thousands of women were burned at the stake on suspicion of being witches. Wouldn't it be lovely to see a religious leader visit one of these sites and go down on his knees to ask forgiveness from the women of the world for what was done to their sisters in the name of his religion.

Other women were denigrated for being pregnant. The act of bringing a child into the world is how woman works at the creative heart of the Divine; this sacred work became for millions of women a devastating occasion of shame for them and their children. Their characters and reputations were blackened and they were driven out of belonging. The Irish poet and painter Patricia Burke has contributed hugely to the acknowledgement and healing of this wound in Irish culture in her wonderful and devastating play *Eclipsed*.

We rarely think of the esteem and reputation we enjoy until we are in danger of losing it. This esteem allows us an independent and free space among people. There is no negative intrusion. We can get on with our lives. When you are shamed, the space around you is eviscerated. Now your every move draws negative attention. Hostility and disgust are flung at you. It is impossible from outside even to imagine the humiliation that shame brings. All the natural shelter and support around your presence is taken from you. All the natural imagination with which others have considered the different aspects of your presence stops. Everything about you is telescoped into the single view of this one shameful thing. Everything else is forgotten. A kind of psychological murdering is done. The mystery of your life is reduced to that one thing. You become "a thing of shame." Shame dehumanizes a person.

In ancient Ireland, words had incredible power. Invocations and curses could set massive events in motion. It is not surprising that poets at that time had great status. It was said that a bard could write an "aor," a satire about a person that would cause "boils of shame" to rise on his skin. Shame could not effect its punishment without language. The language of shame is lethal. Its words carry no hesitation or doubt. There is no graciousness or light in the language of shame. It is a language spoken without compassion or respect. The word of shame is put on you in a way reminiscent of how farmers used to brand cattle. The brand is to mark you out. You are now owned by your "shameful" deed.

Imagine how shame imprisons those who are on the target list of convention. Imagine the years of silent torment so many gay people have endured, unable to tell their secret. Then, when they declare they are gay, the hostility that rises to assail them. Think of the victims of racism. lovely people who are humiliated and tagged for hostility. The simple fact of their physical presence is sufficient to have a barrage of aggression unleashed on them. The intention of racism is to shame its victims into becoming non-persons.

Beyond its social dimension, shame also has a devastating personal complexity. When a person is sexually abused or raped, she often feels great shame at what happened to her. The strategy of such violence is to make the victim feel guilty and even responsible for what has happened. Sometimes this personal shame makes the victim silent and passive; consequently, the crime never becomes public. In some instances the threat of social shame further strengthens the decision to stay silent. Part of the essential work in healing such lonely wounding is to help the person to see her own innocence and goodness and thus unmask the absolutely unwarranted violence of such intrusion and attack. When a person begins to see this, she often begins to awaken the force of anger within her in relation to what has happened to her. The fire of anger can be magnificent in burning off the false garments of shame.

The Prison of Belief

There is nothing in the universe as intimate as the Divine. When the image of the Divine we inherit is negative, it can do untold damage. When your God is a harsh judge, he forces your life to become a watched and haunted hunt for salvation. Like a sinister Argus, this God has eyes everywhere. He sees everything and forgets nothing. Such images of the Divine cripple us. If salvation and healing do not come lyrically as gifts, they are nothing. Belief should liberate your life. Anything that turns belief into torment hardly merits the term "salvation." The reduction of the wild eternity of your one life to a harsh divine project is a blasphemy against the call of your soul. People who inhabit the tormented prison of negative deity have awful lives. Tragically, they are partly responsible for keeping themselves locked in there; religion supplied the building material and they took up the task of their own self-incarceration. The spirit of a person is as intimate as his or her sexuality. When a person is theologically or spiritually abused, the pain can shadow the whole life. Spiritual abuse sticks like tar in the core of the mind. When you stay in the inner jail of harsh deity, all the fun, humour, and irony go out of your life. Such a God has a fierce grip; he awakens everything fearful and negative in you and whispers to you that this is who you really are. Your presence becomes atrophied. Your face turns into a brittle, mask-like surface. You have become prisoner and warder in one.

When you turn your natural longing for the Divine into a prison, then everything in you will continue to ache. The prison subverts your longing and makes it toxic. Watched by a negative God, you learn to watch your self with the same harshness. You look out on life and see only sin. Your language becomes over-finished and cold. Others sense behind your eyes the ache of forsakenness that does not even know where to begin searching for itself.

The Wildness of Celtic Spirituality

The world of Celtic spirituality never had such walls. It was not a world of clear boundaries; persons and things were never placed in bleak isolation from each other. Everything was connected and there was a lovely sense of the fluent flow of presences in and out of each other. The physical world was experienced as the shoreline of an invisible world which flowed underneath it and whose music reverberated upwards. In a certain sense, the Celts understood a parallel fluency in the inner world of the mind. The inner world was no prison. It was a moving theatre of thoughts, visions, and feelings. The Celtic universe was the homeland of the inspirational and the unexpected. This means that the interim region between one person and another, and between the person and Nature, was not empty. Post-modern culture is so lonely, partly because we see nothing in this interim region. Our way of thinking is addicted to what we can see and control. Perception creates the mental prison. The surrounding culture inevitably informs the perception. Part of the wisdom of the Celtic imagination was the tendency to keep realities free and fluent; the Celts avoided the clinical certainties which cause separation and isolation. Such loneliness would have been alien to the Celts. They saw themselves as guests in a living, breathing universe. They had great respect for the tenuous regions between the worlds and between the times. The in-between world was also the world of in-between times: between sowing and reaping, pregnancy and birth, intention and action, the end of one season and the beginning of another. The presences who watched over this world were known as the fairies.

The Lightness and Imagination of the Fairy World

To the contemporary mind any acknowledgment of the fairy world sounds naïve. Yet at a metaphoric level, recognition of the fairy world is recognition of the subtle presences that inhabit the interim places in experience, the edges of time and space impenetrable to the human eye. Our clear-cut vision imprisons us. The fairies were especially at home in the air element. There is nothing as free as the wind. In modern Ireland there is still a sense of their presence. Often at evening one sees a fog low in the fields. Usually fog is first on the mountains and then it comes down. In the gathering dusk, this other fog collects in white streamers and clouds over the fields. It is almost as if a vaporous white wood suddenly stands suspended over the grass. All outlines are blurred; the interim kingdom becomes visible in a presence that is neither object nor light nor darkness. The ancient name for this presence still lingers. It is called "an ceo draíochta," the fairy fog. On a still, clear day a few years ago, a friend and I were visiting an old "cillín," a children's graveyard, between two mountains. Suddenly, out of nowhere a powerful gust of a breeze threw itself out all over the cillín, bent the bushes low, and just as abruptly vanished back into the seamless stillness of the day. It was as if all the sighs of the lost children had unravelled for a moment from the quiet ground and had come in a massive whoosh into our world. This is called the fairy breeze, "an Sí Gaoth."

There are many stories in the Irish tradition of musicians who learned some of our most beautiful tunes from the fairies, for example, the tune "Port na bpúcái." This music often has a haunting beauty that seems to be inspired from beyond the limits of the human. A famous old fiddle player in County Clare always played a special tune and claimed that the tune came in a visitation from the other world. The fairies might use a person's home while the whole family were in bed asleep. Humans were often brought into the fairy world. The fairies were invisible, but if they allowed it, you could see them.

There is a lovely old story from the West of Ireland about a midwife who was called to tend a fairy woman who was giving birth. When the child was born, the fairies gave her some ointment to rub on the baby. By accident, the woman rubbed her own eye with the ointment. When her work was finished, the fairies took her home. Some time afterwards, the woman was at the market. Suddenly, she recognized one of the men at the market as one of the people from the fairy dwelling. When she spoke to him, he realized that she could see him because of the ointment that had touched her eye. He was very angry to be visible to her. It was said that he put his finger in her eye and blinded her. The invisible world is full of presences. They like to keep to themselves under the protection of invisibility. Through accident a mortal receives the unintended gift of seeing the invisible; it turns out to be an intrusion that has to be punished and the gift revoked.

There are many fantastic anecdotes about the fairies. Long ago, there was a man who lived near us who often went with the fairies. One night they went over to one of the islands with the intention of substituting a fairy child for a newborn there. The fairies and the man were up in the rafters of the house. Someone sneezed down below, and the man uttered a loud blessing. The fairies dropped him, and he fell onto the floor below among the people, who recognized at once that he had been there with the fairies. They chased him and he ran for the shore of the island. Catching an old plough, he uttered an invocation: "Molaim do léim a sheanbhéim céachta. Tabhair abhaile mé." I.e., I praise your leap old beam of plough. Take me home. With that, he gave a mighty leap over the ocean and landed home.

The fairy world was not subservient to the normal laws of causality which regulate time and space. Their world had a lightness and playfulness. The fairy world was not merely adjacent to the mortal world, it seemed to suffuse it. Such a vital and fluent sense of the world never permitted the notion of the Divine to become a sinister, crippling prison. The Celtic world was not a world of stolid fixation. It was a wild, rhythmic world where the unexpected and the unknown were constantly flowing in on human presence and perception and enlarging them. When perception and culture are open to the possibility of surprise and visitation, it is more difficult for individuals to lock themselves away in mental prisons of forsaken thought and feeling. It is interesting to reflect that the Celts were not taken with the construction of great architecture. They loved the vitality and magic of open spaces. Celtic spirituality is an outdoor spirituality. Living outside must make for a very different rhythm of mind!

Your Vision Is Your Home

Thought is one of the most powerful forces in the universe. The way you see things makes them what they are. We never meet life innocently. We always take in life through the grid of thought we use. Our thoughts filter experience all the time. The beauty of philosophy is the way it shows us the nature of the layers of thought which always stand invisibly between us and everything we see. Even your meetings with yourself happen in and by means of thinking. The study of philosophy helps you to see how you think. Philosophy has no doctrines; it is an activity of disclosure and illumination. One of the great tasks in life is to find a way of thinking which is honest and original and yet right for your style of individuality. The shape of each soul is different. It takes a lifetime of slow work to find a rhythm of thinking which reflects and articulates the uniqueness of your soul.

More often than not, we have picked up the habits of thinking of those around us. These thought-habits are not yours; they can damage the way you see the world and make you doubt your own instinct and sense of life. When you become aware that your thinking has a life of its own, you will never make a prison of your own perception. Your vision is your home. A closed vision always wants to make a small room out of whatever it sees. Thinking that limits you denies you life. In order to deconstruct the inner prison, the first step is learning to see that it is a prison. You can move in the direction of this discovery by reflecting on the places where your life feels limited and tight. To recognize the crippling feeling of being limited is already to have begun moving beyond it. Heidegger said, "To recognize a frontier is already to have gone beyond it." Life continues to remain faithful to us. If we move even the smallest step out of our limitation, life comes to embrace us and lead us out into the pastures of possibility.

The German philosopher Ernst Bloch has the following epitaph on his gravestone in Tübingen: "Denken heisst überschreiten," i.e., To think is to go beyond. Thinking that deserves the name never attempts to make a cage for mystery. Reverential thought breaks down the thought-cages that domesticate mystery. This thinking is disturbing but liberating. This is the kind of thinking at the heart of prayer, namely, the liberation of the Divine from the small prisons of our fear and control. To liberate the Divine is to liberate oneself. Each person is so vulnerable in the way he or she sees things. You are so close to your own way of thinking that you are probably unaware of its power and control over how you experience everything, including yourself. This is the importance of drama as a literary form; it provides you with the opportunity to know yourself at one remove, so to speak, without threatening you with self-annihilation. Your thinking can be damaged. You may sense this but put it down to how life is. You remain unaware of your freedom to change how you think. When your thinking is locked in false certainty or negativity, it puts so many interesting and vital areas of life out of your reach. You live impoverished and hungry in the midst of your own abundance.

The Haunted Room in the Mind

In Ireland there are many stories of haunted houses. There may be a room in which one senses a presence or hears footsteps or a strange voice. Such haunted places remain uninhabited. People are afraid to go there. The place is forsaken and left to deepen ever further into the shadow of itself. The way you think about your life can turn your soul into a haunted room. You are afraid to risk going in there anymore. Your fantasy peoples this room of the heart with sad presences which ultimately become disturbing and sinister. The haunted room in the mind installs a lonesomeness at the heart of your life. It would be devastating in the autumn of your life to look back and recognize that you had created a series of haunted rooms in your heart. Fear and negativity are immense forces which constantly tussle with us. They long to turn the mansions of the soul into a totally haunted house. These are the living conditions for which fear and negativity long, and in which they thrive. We were sent here to live life to the full. When you manage to be generous in your passion and vulnerability, life always comes to bless you. Had you but the courage to acknowledge the haunted inner room, turn the key, and enter, you would encounter nothing strange or sinister there. You would meet some vital self of yours that you had banished during a time of pain or difficulty. Sometimes, when life squeezes you into lonely crevices, you may have to decide between survival or breaking apart. At such times, you can be harsh with yourself and settle to be someone other than who you really long to be. At such a time, you can do nothing else; you have to survive. But your soul always remains faithful to your longing to become who you really are. The banished self from an earlier time of life remains within you waiting to be released and integrated. The soul has its own logic of loyalty and concealment. Ironically, it is usually in its most awkward rooms that the special blessings and healing are locked away. Your thinking can also freeze and falsify the flow of your life's continuity to make you a prisoner of routine and judgement.

The Shelter of Continuity

Continuity is one of the great mysteries of life; it is essential to identity. When you look at the waves on the shore, one after the other, they unfold in perfect pleated sequence. From the break of dawn, the day arises until the height of noon and then gradually falls to gather in the coloured shadow-basket of twilight. The seasons, too, follow the melody of forward unfolding. One of the most beautiful images of continuity and sequence is the river. Always in motion towards the ocean, it continues to look the same. As Heraclitus said, "You cannot step twice into the same river." In a matter of seconds, both you and the river are different. The river is the ideal of continuity. It preserves the fluency of continual change and yet holds the one form. The river is so interesting because it offers a creative metaphor of the way the mind flows in and through experience. Your life is made up of a sequence of days. Each day brings something new and different. The secret of time's intention and generosity depends on how your days follow each other. Every yesterday prepares you for today. What today brings could not have reached you yesterday or a hundred days ago. Time is more careful in its sequence than we often notice. Time ripens according to its hidden rhythm. In its heart, time is eternal longing.

Regardless of how you look back on your life, you cannot force it out of the order in which it has unfolded. You cannot de-sequence your life. The structure of your life holds together. That is the unnoticed miracle of memory; it is the intimate mirror of the continuity of your experience and presence. While you sleep, your memory continues to gather and store up every moment. If your memory had forsaken you moments before you awoke this morning, you would not recognize your family. And when you looked in the mirror, the face of a stranger would look back at you. If your memory were wiped, your world would evaporate. Continuity is difficult to grasp, because it is hidden and subtle. In a sense, we are powerless ever to break continuity. Even the severest and most shocking change insists on its belonging to the moments that preceded it. Then, even that shocking change in its turn builds the next bridge to the future. We try to understand and control continuity by calling it causality. We claim that every event has a cause. We attempt to understand the parts of the sequence in a clear and linear way. The difficulty here is our tendency to jump to conclusions about how one time or thing grows out of another in our lives. When we make the connections too easy for ourselves, we let the mystery, like sand, slip through the openings.

Certainty Freezes the Mind

I love the radical novelty of the Scottish philosopher David Hume, who proclaimed on looking inside his own mind that he could see no sign of a self anywhere. Neither could he see any such thing as a cause. Hume's theory is bold and provocative; like all the most interesting philosophical theories, it brings great difficulties. It is refreshing that he torpedoed the notion of causality. We do have a deadening desire to reduce the mystery of continuity to a chain of causality. We bind our lives up in solid chains of forced connections that block and fixate us. This silences the voices within us that are always urging us to change and become free. Our sense of uncertainty and our need for security nail our world down. We pretend that we live in a ready-made house of belonging. We walk through its halls, open its doors, and shelter inside its walls as if it were a fixed house and not the invention and creation of our own thinking and imagination, a flimsy nest of belonging swinging on a light branch that tempts the unknown storms. Each one of us, like the birds, is an artist of the invisible. Like them, we leave no traces on the invisible air.

Each time we go out, the world is open and free; it offers itself so graciously to our hearts, to create something new and wholesome from it each day. It is such a travesty of possibility and freedom to think we have no choice, that things are the way they are and that the one street, the one destination, the one role is all that is allotted to us. That we are lucky with so little. Certainty is a subtle destroyer.

We confine our mystery within the prison of routine and repetition. One of the most deadening forces of all is repetition. Your response to the invitation and edge of your life becomes reduced to a series of automatic reflexes. For example, you are so used to getting up in the morning and observing the morning rituals of washing and dressing. You are still somewhat sleepy, your mind is thinking of things you have to do in the day that lies ahead. You go through these first gestures of the morning often without even noticing that you are doing them. This is a disturbing little image, because it suggests that you live so much of your one life with the same automatic blindness of adaptation. After a while, unknown to you, a wall has grown between you and the native force of your experiences. You go through things only half aware that they are actually happening to you. This subtle conditioning becomes so effortless that you are only half present in your life. Sometimes you are lucky and destiny wakes you up abruptly, you stumble and trip into love, or some arrow of suffering pierces your armour. These routines of repetition are often most evident in your work. You somehow manage enough concentration to get the motions right, so that hardly anybody suspects that you really live Elsewhere or that you have got badly lost in some bland Nowhere. It also often happens in our emotional life with the person with whom we live. Time and again, we find ourselves back at the same point in the circle of repetition with each other. The same difficulty repeats itself in an uncanny echo of the past.

Habit is a strong invisible prison. Habits are styles of feeling, perception, or action that have now become second nature to us. A habit is a sure cell of predictability; it can close you off from the unknown, the new, and the unexpected. You were sent to the earth to become a receiver of the unknown. From ancient times, these gifts were prepared for you; now they come towards you across eternal distances. Their destination is the altar of your heart. When you allow your life to move primarily along the tracks of habit, the creative side of your life diminishes. There is an old story from Russia about a prince who lived with a large retinue in a huge palace. One of the key rules in palace life was that no one could sleep two consecutive nights in the same room. The prince insisted on this constant changing about to keep alive their sense of being pilgrims here on earth. The true pilgrim is always at a new threshold.

The Danger of the Name

Language is one of the most fascinating presences in the world. The emergence of language and use of language are a unique human achievement. Words become the mirrors of reality. Imagine if the veil of language fell away totally from us tomorrow. We would not be able to think, understand, or communicate. Consciousness would be wiped clean. Words are the unnoticed treasure houses of discovery and meaning. Wittgenstein said, "The limits of my language are the limits of my world." Without language, the world would fade away from us. Words keep things present. Language has a secret life, an undercurrent murmuring away, audible in rhymes and rhythms, ambiguities and assonances. Most official uses of language are hostile to this undercurrent. The poetic use of language honours these possibilities, keeps them alive, and sometimes reanimates the "ordinary" language we speak without thinking. Yet often our language is over-finished and cripplingly tight. Language is a great power. When something flows into the shore of your life, one of your first responses is the attempt to name it. A name should never trap a thing. In the Jewish tradition, for instance, if you knew the name of a thing, you had an inkling of its secret and mystery. The name was a doorway of reverence. When you name a dimension of your experience, one of your qualities or difficulties, or some presence within you, you give it an identity. It then responds to you according to the tone of its name. We need to exercise great care and respect when we come to name something. We always need to find a name that is worthy and spacious.

When we name things in a small way, we cripple them. Often our way of naming things is driven by our addiction to what is obviously visible. Celtic spirituality is awakening so powerfully now because it illuminates the fact that the visible is only one little edge of things. The visible is only the shoreline of the magnificent ocean of the invisible. The invisible is not empty, but is textured and tense with presences. These presences cannot be named; they can only be sensed, not seen. Names are powerful. Sometimes in folk culture people are quite "pisréogach," or superstitious, about telling their own name. This is illustrated by a story I heard from a priest who was appointed to a rural area. During his first months there, he visited the whole parish. One day, he noticed an old man digging a garden. He said hello and the man came up, rested his arms on the wall, and held a most interesting and quite personal conversation with the new priest. As the conversation was about to end, the priest asked him his name. The old man glowered at him and said, "That is something I never told any one in my life" and went back to dig his garden.

Many of the places in our lives at which our growth has arrested are places where we have carried out negative baptisms. We have put the wrong names on many of our most important experiences. We have often caricatured and shown disrespect to some of our most faithful desires. We have kept some of our most beautiful longings as prisoners in our hearts, falsely imprisoned simply because of mistaken identity. Pablo Neruda has a poem called "Too Many Names":

> Mondays are meshed with Tuesdays
> And the week with the whole year.
> Time cannot be cut
> With your exhausted scissors,
> And all the names of the day
> Are washed out in the waters of night.
> No one can claim the name of Pedro,
> Nobody is Rosa or Maria,
> All of us are dust or sand,

> All of us are rain under rain.
> They have spoken to me of Venezuelas,
> Of Chiles and Paraguays;
> I have no idea what they are saying.
> I know only the skin of the earth
> And I know of it is without a name. . . .

The wildness of the invisible world is nameless. It has no name. A first step towards reawakening respect for your inner life may be to become aware of the private collage of dead names you have for your inner life. Often, the experiences of wilderness can return us to the nameless wildness within. Sometime, go away to a wild place on your own. Leave your name and the grid of intentions and projects and images which mark you out as citizen Z. Leave it all, and let yourself just slip back into the rhythms of your intimate wildness. You will be surprised at the lost terrains, wells, and mountains that you will rediscover, territories which have been buried under well-meant but dead names. To go beyond confinement is to rediscover yourself.

The Limit as Invitation to the Beyond

The prisons we choose to live in are closely connected to our experience of limit and frontier. We often remain passively within our inner prisons, because we believe the limitations are fixed and given. It is strange how being caught makes you lose the sense of the outside and the beyond. You become trapped on one side of a wall. After a while you learn to see only what cages you; you begin to forget other views and possibilities. It is the lonely struggle of the prisoner to continue to remember that he belongs to life and not to limitation. Limitation is, of course, real and factual, but it is meant to be temporary. A limit is meant to call you beyond itself towards the next new field of experience. We usually view limitation not as a calling to growth, but as confinement and impossibility. Something begins to change when we can see exactly where the walls of limitation stand in our lives. A strong poem by Cavafy, "Walls," describes how the walls that lock us in are secretly built. You hear nothing and you notice nothing.

> When they were building the walls,
> How could I not have noticed?
> But I never heard the builders,
> Not a sound,
> Imperceptibly they closed me off
> From the outside world.

Cavafy articulates something that happens to all of us. Your complicity with other people's images and expectations of you allows them to box you in completely. It takes a long time to recognize how some key people on your life's journey exercise so much control over your mind, behaviour, and actions. Through the image they project onto you or through the expectations they have of you, they claim you. Most of this is subtle and works in the domain of the implicit and unstated subtext; it is, of course, all the more powerful for not being direct and obvious. When you become conscious of these powerful builders and their work of housing you in, something within you refuses to comply; you begin to send back the building materials. There is no planning permission here, thanks for the kindness! Such projection and expectation is based on their fear and the need to control. Expectation is resentment waiting to happen. In contrast, friendship liberates you.

The Delicate Art of Freeing Yourself

Real friendship is a powerful presence in helping you to see the prisons within which you live. From inside your own life, it is so difficult to gain enough distance to look back on yourself and see the outer shape of your life. This discernment is often easier for your friend than it would be for you. Real friends will never come with a battering ram to demolish the prison in which they see you. They know that it could be too soon. You are not yet ready to leave. They also know that until you see for yourself how and where you are caught, you cannot become free. If they destroy this prison cell, you will inevitably build a new one from the old material. True friendship attunes itself in care to the rhythm of your soul. In conversation and affection, your friend will only attempt something very modest, namely, to remove one pebble from the wall. When that pencil of light shines in on your darkness, it arouses your longing to become free. It reminds you of the freshness and fragrance of another life that you had learned to forget in your cell. This dot of light empowers you, and then, brick by brick, you will remove the walls you had placed between the light and yourself. True friendship trusts the soul to find the light, to loosen one pebble in the wall and open the way to freedom. Massive inner structures begin to loosen and break when the first pencil-thin beam of recognition hits us.

Often others may judge you to be in a prison, whereas in actual fact you were never more free and creative. True knowing goes beyond projection, impression, and expectation. There is a whole moral question here regarding the nature and timing of disclosure and intervention. If you show someone bluntly that he is caught in a prison, you make him aware of his confinement. If the person is incapable of liberating himself, you have left him with a heavier burden.

There is a telling story of a British anthropologist who came to a village in India where the natives wove the most beautiful shawls. The art of weaving was highly prized there. The workers wove the shawls amidst conversation with each other about local events and old stories. Weaving was their secret skill, and its methods had become like second nature. The anthropologist observed them for weeks. Then one morning, he came there and told them that he had worked out exactly how they did it. He made explicit the implicit skill they exercised. He showed them the secret of their artistry. In that disclosure, he robbed their artistry of all its magic. With that he changed them from surprised artists of emergent beauty into helpless, impoverished workers. This story could stand as a metaphor for the massive transformation in the modern world. The natural and ancient creativity of soul is being replaced by the miserable little arithmetic of know-how.

Creativity is rich with unexpected possibility. Know-how is mere fragmented mechanics which lacks tradition, context, and surprise. Analysis is always subsequent to and parasitic on creativity. Our culture is becoming crowded with analysts, and much of what passes for creativity is merely clever know-how. When creativity dries up, the analysts turn on themselves and begin to empty out the inner world; this has contributed to the terrible loss of soul in our culture. It is wise to recall that "analysis" comes from the Greek word "ana-luein," which means to break something complex into its simple elements. When the embrace and depth of creativity are absent, analysis becomes destruction. It can break things apart, but there is nothing now to put them back together again. Nature always maintains this balance between breakage and new life.

The True Shelter of the Porous Wall

Among the most delightful features in the West of Ireland landscape are the stone walls. These walls frame off the fields from each other. They bestow personality and shape on the fields. These walls are more like frontiers than hermetic boundaries. When you see a wall on the mountain, you see the different styles of openings between the stones. Each wall is a series of different windows of light. Rabbits, hares, and foxes have favourite windows in these walls through which they always cross. Each wall is frontier and simultaneously a labyrinth of invisibility. Often, as children, if we were herding cattle on the mountain, we would shelter during showers by these walls. When we looked out from one of these windows between the stones, we would see the whole landscape beneath us in a new way; everything was framed differently. These walls, called "foiseach" in Irish, are also often shelters for all kinds of growth: grasses, plants, briars. They became home to a whole subculture of insects, bees, birds, and animals. Because of the shelter and kindness of the walls, you would often find the sweetest grasses there. Sheep and cattle were never slow to find out the sweetest grass. Wouldn't it be interesting if instead of hermetically sealed barriers, the areas of beginning and ending in our hearts and lives could be such rich and latticed frontiers? They would be windows to look out on alternative possibilities; in other words, the freshness of other styles of being and thinking could still be somehow present even if they were not directly adjacent or even engaged. The natural shelter that grows on both sides of such frontiers would be left alone, to grow according to its own instinct. The most trustable shelter around the human mind and heart is the one that grows naturally there.

Every life has its own natural shelter belt. So often our

severity with ourselves cuts that to shreds. Then we wonder why we feel so naked and unsheltered when the storm comes. The wisdom of folk culture always recognizes that when the storm of suffering rages one should not go out there into single combat with it. Rather, one should lie in and shelter close to the wall until the storm has abated. There is a lovely humility in the idea of lying low and sheltering. It recognizes that the storm comes from the penumbral unknown; it has a mind and direction of its own, and the vulnerable individual can but shelter until the time of tranquillity returns. The modern tendency to safari into subjectivity to find the cause of everything was alien to the folk mind.

To Roll the Stone off the Heart

The Christian story is about the subversive transformation of all barriers that confine or imprison. Jesus never advocated a life that confined itself within safe, complacent walls. He always called people into the beyond: "I have come that you may have life and have it more abundantly." The Resurrection is frightening because it is a call to live a life without the walls of crippling definition or false protection. The huge stone over Christ's tomb was rolled away. The cave of dying was ventilated and freed. It is a powerful image of smashing open the inner prison. The confined, the exiled, the neglected are visited by the healing and luminosity of a great liberation.

On a farm, the season of greatest change is springtime. Everything is in the flourish of growth. You often notice where a large flat rock has fallen onto the grass. All around the rock is growth. Beneath the rock, the grass has turned yellow and sour. In every life, there are some places where we have allowed great slabs of burden to remain fallen on our heart. These slabs have turned much of our inner world sour and killed many of the possibilities which once called us: the possibilities of play, of making holidays, of seeing something new and unexpected in our lives, of going to new places within and without, of living life to the full. When these slabs are pulled off our hearts, we can move freely again and breathe and feel alive. Wouldn't it bring such calmness and freedom to your life, if your thoughts about yourself, your feelings, and your prayer could become a window which would look inward on the presence of the Divine?

If You Cannot Forgive, You Are Still in Jail

In an article in the *New York Times* shortly before he died Joseph Brodsky wrote about prison literature. In prison you have limited space and unlimited time. This is the exact context in which your mind could unravel. You can do terrible things to your mind. It is so lonely that you cannot be protected from your self. It would bring relief to give your tormenting self a holiday away from your life so that you could find peace. At such times, you are a prisoner of your worst self. Prisoners have to be very careful about minding their inner world. One should pray for those in prison that though they have lost the outside world, the mystery of the inner world might open for them.

When you have unlimited time with yourself, the danger is that you would tear yourself apart. Nietzsche said, "In a time of peace the warlike person attacks himself." This happens also of course to communities; they go to war with themselves in the absence of enemies. This danger is, however, a permanent companionship of some lives. There are people this morning whose lives were never better. There is peace around them. Objectively, their conditions are very good, yet they are totally tormented. They have scraped away the last vestiges of shelter from their souls. There is nothing significantly wrong here. It is just that these demented people have designated their minds to become their tormentors. Their hostility is now focused on everything about themselves. They have become prisoner and torturer in one.

Forgiveness is one of the really difficult things in life. The logic of receiving hurt seems to run in the direction of never forgetting either the hurt or the hurter. When you forgive, some deeper, divine generosity takes you over. When you can forgive, then you are free. When you cannot forgive, you are a prisoner of the hurt done to you. If you are really disappointed in someone and you become embittered, you become incarcerated inside that feeling. Only the grace of forgiveness can break the straight logic of hurt and embitterment. It gives you a way out, because it places the conflict on a completely different level. In a strange way, it keeps the whole conflict human. You begin to see and understand the conditions, circumstances, or weakness that made the other person act as she did.

I remember once, during the former Communist dictatorship in Czechoslovakia, reading an interview with a leading Czech dissident. The authorities often arrested and jailed him. He was asked in the interview how he kept his poise. He said he never allowed himself to forget during interrogation that his interrogators were human like himself. He said that were he to caricature them as monsters he would have lost his freedom and shelter in the situation. To keep it human helped him stay human, too.

A friend from the former East Germany spent a lot of time in jail there. The Communist regime saw him as a subversive who kept raising awkward questions about the system. He says that one of the first things he had to learn in jail was not to resent the prison guards. If he had, he could not have endured the jail. He was friendly with them, insofar as that was possible, and never allowed his mind to focus destructively on them. Walking this emotional tightrope, he managed to keep his balance and freedom during his years of imprisonment. Years afterwards, when he was out of jail, he happened to meet one of his former fellow prisoners. They talked of their years in jail. This man began to tell him of the hatred he still harboured for the prison guards, and told my friend what he would do to them if he ever met any of them. My friend said to him, "The sad thing about what you are saying is that it shows that you are still in prison." If you cannot forgive you are still in jail. When you forgive those who have wronged you, you free yourself from prison. You take from your own heart the hook that has dragged you along behind those people across fields of years.

Why are we so reluctant to leave our inner prisons? There is the security of the confinement and limitation that we know. We are often willing to endure the searing sense of forsakenness and distance which limitation brings rather than risking the step out into the field of the unknown. It used to be common that longtime prisoners when released often gravitated back towards the jail; the daylight hurt their eyes, and it was so long since they had had to live in the outside world. This reluctance is captured powerfully in Pär Lagerkvist's novel *Barabbas*, in which he imagines Barabbas being released from jail. His future life is poignantly haunted by the shadow of the young man who was crucified in place of him. "Windows," a poem by the Greek poet Constantine Cavafy, describes living inside hungry days in confinement: "I wander round and round / trying to find the windows. . . ." Without the grace and encouragement of the eternal, we would be forever confined.

Our Secret Companions and Liberators

If the human person were alone, it would be exceptionally difficult to liberate oneself from such inner prisons. In the Celtic tradition, there was a strong sense that each of us has an invisible companion who walks the road of life with us. I imagine that our secret companions in the invisible world are the angels. One of the poverties of modern life is the loss of belief in such presences. The Christian tradition says that when you were sent here to the earth, a special angel was chosen to accompany your every step, breath, thought, and feeling. This is your guardian angel who is right beside you, as near as your skin. The Irish poet Denis Devlin says, "It is inside our life the angel happens." The imagination of the tradition understands that your angel has a special responsibility for your life, to watch over you and to keep a circle of light around you, lest any negativity damage you in any way. When we reflect on this, we can imagine the depth of presence the angel is. Your angel is as ancient as eternity itself and has memory that is older than the earth. Your angel was there when the eternal artist began to dream you. Your angel is wedded to the dream and possibility of your life, and wishes to keep your life from becoming fixated in any inner prison.

Your angel is aware of the secret life that sleeps in your soul. Without you even knowing it, your angel is always at work for you. It is possible to sense this if you consider for a moment the key thresholds in your life. You may feel that you should contact an old friend or someone you had not seen for a while. You set out to do this, and you discover that the friend really needs you. The visit could never have been more opportune. There are also the times when someone comes into your mind, and the next thing they are at your door or on the phone. This is the secret world of association and inspiration which can never be explained. Artists could never create without the inspiration the angel brings. It is the gift of the angel to watch over that threshold where your invisible world comes to visible form. Any art, belief, or spirituality that lacks inspiration is ultimately dry and mechanical. Something inspired has the surprise, vitality, and warmth of the eternal in it. The Irish word for angel is "aingeal." This was also the word for a burnt-out cinder taken from the fire. It was often given to children going out in the night to protect them. It was said to represent an angel. The word "aingeal" shows how our Celtic tradition fused a spirituality of the elements with that of the angels.

I imagine that the angels are spirits of light and playfulness. They are often depicted as playing musical instruments. They have none of the seriousness or narrowness that often accompanies dead religion. Angels are specially present around young children. In the West of Ireland, people always recognized that the angels were near children. Fresh from the eternal world, babies are often said to be able to see their own angels. To know that you have a strong and individual spiritual companion is great encouragement not to linger for false shelter in unnecessary prisons. In your angel, you have as much shelter as you need. You are not on your own. If you could see your path with the eyes of your soul, you would see that it is a luminous path and that there are two of you walking together; you are not alone. When loneliness or helplessness overcomes you, it is time to call on your angel for help and courage. This is the tender region of the heart for which your angel is especially competent and helpful. There are lovely prayers the Celts said to their angels:

SOUL-SHRINE

Thou angel of God who hast charge of me
From the fragrant Father of mercifulness,
The gentle encompassing of the Sacred Heart
To make round my soul-shrine this night,
Oh, round my soul-shrine this night.

Ward from me every distress and danger,
Encompass my course over the ocean of truth,
I pray thee, place thy pure light before me,
O bright beauteous angel on this very night,
Bright beauteous angel on this very night.

Be Thyself the guiding star above me,
Illume Thou to me every reef and shoal,
Pilot my barque on the crest of the wave,
To the restful haven of the waveless sea,
Oh, the restful haven of the waveless sea.

Carmina Gadelica, translated by
Alexander Carmichael

The Angel of Attraction and Inspiration

The angel keeps a circle of light around your life, and your angel is particularly active in the region of friendship and relationship. One of the mysteries of friendship is the attraction between two people. Where does it come from? What animates this attraction? How do two people meet? How do they manage to be in the same place at that particular moment so that the whole adventure of longing and belonging can come awake between them? Had they missed that moment, would they have remained strangers? Or would some other moment have gathered them towards this beginning? There is a whole arena of secret preparation and gathering here that we cannot penetrate with our analytical or conscious minds; perhaps this is the domain of angelic creativity. Perhaps the attraction between two people is not accidental; could it be that their ancient angels know how much they have to bring each other and without this their lives cannot become true? The angels are artists in the subtle chemistry of Spirit. If you are in difficulty in your friendship, it is wise to go to your mutual angels for the gifts and blessings that you both need. Because your friendship is now paralysed you cannot give anything to each other. When the metallic distance of pain cripples the sacred space between you and the one you love, it is wise to ask the spirits of light and inspiration to make a path for you towards each other.

The angels awaken the sacred melodies of inspiration and brightness and beauty in the soul. A friendship with one's angel is a choice for each of us. If we do not open this up, the angel continues to work for us anyway. To make this explicit is to come into a new depth and sense of presence. It releases you from the grey walls of the inner prisons where life gets lost and stale. In a certain sense, your angel is the voice and presence of ancient divine longing within you. This urges you forth from all false belonging until you come into the divine rhythm where longing and belonging are one.

The Angel as Artist of Your Transfiguration

In our post-modern, consumerist culture, anything is marketable. With the yawning abyss of spiritual hunger opening, any little relic of the sacred is for sale. There is a huge market for things of the Spirit that can be easily digested. The angels are now in fashion. They are talked about in the idiom of magic and apparition. It is important to recall that the sacred has both a silence and a secrecy about it. Divine intimacy has a crucial reserve and shyness. Your friendship with your angel is ancient. It is intimate in a way that concerns the very essence of your identity and destiny. A person should never reduce the mystery of his invisible world to the clichéd descriptions of external banter. The very nature of angelic presence is totally alien to this garish, neon attention. Perhaps such empty and undignified talk drives away our invisible companions. It disrespects their reverential and eternal shyness. In the Celtic world, there was a lyrical and natural sense of these divine presences without any of the garishness or voyeurism of the disappointed contemporary mind.

When you begin to awaken to your incredible freedom, the walls of your inner prisons gradually become the thresholds of your new life, your new place of growth. The old walls can become the thresholds of new belonging which is hospitable to the depths and directions of longing within you. Your angel can liberate your soul from the false, tight spaces where fear, limitation, negativity, bitterness, and disappointment hold you. The angel is the inner artist of transfiguration, adept at opening and structuring new configurations of Spirit where longing and belonging live in the most creative tension with each other. Your angel can see your invisible world and knows where you have been imprisoned, where the lost and forsaken parts of your life are locked away. Your angel is the custodian of your deep and ancient memory. In this way, nourishment, courage, and strength are brought from the harvest of your memory to meet the hungry places in your present time. Your angel works in and through your imagination. The divine imagination offers you all the gifts that you need and particularly those blessings for the broken areas of contradiction, suffering, and pain. You could ask your angel to go to the places of nourishment to assuage your present hunger and thirst.

Some lovely poems by Kathleen Raine link the images of angel, birth, and renewal.

Dear angel of my birth,
All my life's loss,
Gold of fallen flowers,
Shells after ebbing wave
Gathered on lonely shores
With secret toil of love,
Deathless in memory save
The treasures of my grave.

Your angel is the spirit of renewal and transfiguration. Celtic mythology had a wonderful sense of novelty. There was no such thing as a prison in the Celtic mind. You could see that so powerfully in the way that things continued to change shape and take on other different forms. There was no fixed boundary between the visible and the invisible. Without warning or preparation, things could appear suddenly out of the invisible air. This happens often in the Irish epic *The Táin*. A presence coagulates itself, comes out, and is standing there giving advice or warning or prophesy. The Celts inhabited a rich imaginative landscape. At the heart of Celtic spirituality is the fire, force, and tenderness of the Celtic imagination. All spirituality derives from the quality and power of the imagination. The beauty of Celtic spirituality is the imagination behind it, which had no boundaries. The essence of a thing or person was never confined in any prison of definition or image. Celtic spirituality is an invitation to a wonderful freedom. The recovery and awakening of the invisible world is as wild and free as the immeasurable riches of the earth.

W. H. Auden in his poem "In Memory of W. B. Yeats" has the following beautiful verse:

In the deserts of the heart
Let the healing fountains start,
In the prison of his days
Teach the free man how to praise.

In prayer, your angel can help you to praise and sing the song of freedom from your heart. Your angelic presence can convert a dead world into a new world of mystery, potential, and promise. The British poet Philip Larkin wrote a poem called "First Sight," about lambs born in the snow. On a farm it is exciting to see new lambs finding the world during their first few hours here. Larkin's poem describes the snow-covered landscapes into which these new lambs arrive. They see and know nothing except snow. They have landed in a white world; before them every hill and bush is white. Larkin then suggests the absolute novelty that is still concealed. Waiting for them is

> Earth's immeasurable surprise,
> They could not grasp it if they knew,
> What so soon will wake and grow
> Utterly unlike the snow.

This poem marks and articulates an unnoticed and surprising threshold of recognition. Similarly, outside the walls of the inner prison in which you are now locked, there is the gift of the earth's immeasurable surprise awaiting to bless and enlarge your Spirit. You were born for life, you were born for eternal life. No fear or false conviction should confine you in any crippled emotional or thought-space that is unworthy of the springtime that sleeps so lightly in the clay of your heart. Winter always precedes spring and is often a time of suffering. In the prisons we build for ourselves, our belonging becomes crippled and our longing haunted. When we suffer, our sense of belonging is broken.

A BLESSING

May you listen to your longing to be free.
May the frames of your belonging be large enough
for the dreams of your soul.
May you arise each day with a voice of blessing
whispering in your heart that something good is going
to happen to you.
May you find a harmony between your soul and your life.
May the mansion of your soul never become a haunted
place.
May you know the eternal longing which lives at the heart
of time.
May there be kindness in your gaze when you look within.
May you never place walls between the light and yourself.
May your angel free you from the prisons of guilt,
fear, disappointment, and despair.
May you allow the wild beauty of the invisible world to
gather you, mind you, and embrace you in belonging.

4

Suffering as the Dark Valley of Broken Belonging

Our Secret Kinship with the Darkness

Regardless of how lucky, blessed, or privileged one might be, there is no person that is not called at some time to walk through the bleak valley of suffering. This is a path without hope, without shelter, and without light. When suffering comes into your life, it brings great loneliness and isolation. Your life becomes haunted; your belonging breaks. Suffering and pain can assail us with such ferocity, because darkness is so near us; within this darkness, our longing is numbed and calls out for release and healing.

Though you live and work in the light, you were conceived and shaped in darkness. Darkness is one of our closest companions. It can never really surprise us; something within us knows the darkness more deeply than it knows the light. The dark is older than the light. In the beginning was the darkness. The first light was born out of the dark. All through evolution the light grew and refined itself, until, finally, a new lamp was lit with the human mind. Before electricity came to rural areas, the candle and the lamp brightened the home at night. There was one special lamp with a mirror fitted behind it to magnify the light. If you looked into the light at an angle, you could catch a heart-shaped light reflected in the mirror. It was as if the light wished to see itself. Of all previous brightness in creation, this was the new secret of the light of the mind: it was a light that could see itself. The mind brought a new quality of light, which could acknowledge and unveil mystery and create mysteries of its own.

Its eternity of patience rewarded, infinity discovered at last its true mirror in the human soul. For the first time, there was someone who could see the depths and reflect the glimpses. In a certain sense, all human action, thought, and creativity make mirrors for life to behold itself. Yet the closer our acquaintance with the mystery, the more the mystery deepens. Brightness only reinforces the opaque soul of the darkness. We forget so easily that all our feelings, thoughts, and brightness of mind are born in darkness. Thoughts are sparks of illumination within the dark silence and stillness of our bodies. We have an inner kinship with darkness that nothing can dissolve. This protects us from allowing too much outside light into the secret centre of our minds. The immensity and slow beauty of the inner life need the shelter of the dark in order to grow and find their appropriate forms.

Light Has Many Faces—the Dark Has One

There is a touching innocence in the mystery of the human self. Even after thousands of years of experience and reflection, we still remain a mystery to ourselves. In the so-called ordinary person, there is something deeply unpredictable and unfathomable. We have never been able to definitively decipher the secret of our nature. Of course, every secret delights in the dark and fears the light. Regardless of how you might force the neon light of analysis on your self, it can never penetrate. It remains on the surface and creates tantalizing but ultimately empty images. Even when you approach your self tenderly with the candle of receptive and reverential seeing, all you achieve is a glimpse. There is something in the sacred darkness of the mind that does not trust the facility and quickness of light. Darkness resists the name. Darkness knows the regions which the name can never reach or hold or dream. The dark must smile at the proud pretence of words to hold networks of identity and meaning, but the dark knows only too well the fragile surface on which words stand. Darkness keeps its secrets. Light is diverse and plural: sunlight, moonlight, dusk, dawn, and twilight. The dark has only one name. There is something deep in us which implicitly recognizes the primacy and wonder of the dark. Perhaps this is why we instinctively insist on avoiding and ignoring its mysteries.

The human eye loves the light. Feasts of colour and varieties of shape continually draw towards the shore of its vision. Movement excites and attracts the eye. So much of our understanding of ourselves and the world finds expression in metaphors of vision: awareness, seeing, clarity, illumination, and light. To become aware is to see the light. It is interesting that, outside of poetry, there is little corresponding geography of differentiation or appreciation of darkness. Darkness is the end of light. We are confronted by the unknown. Though we peer deeply into its anonymity, we can see little. We speak of darkness as the domain of mystery. Darkness resists the eye. It is where all our vision and seeing becomes qualified and revised. Marina Tsvetayeva wrote an amazing long poem called "Insomnia" in which she recognizes the ancient presence of the night:

Black as—the centre of an eye, the centre, a blackness
That sucks at light. I love your vigilance.

Night, first mother of songs, give me the voice to sing of you
In those fingers lies the bridle of the four winds.

Crying out, offering words of homage to you. I am
Only a shell where the ocean is still sounding.

But I have looked too long into human eyes.
Reduce me now to ashes—Night, like a black sun.

Translated by Elaine Feinstein

The Bright Night of the Earth

Yet the eye can become accustomed to the dark. Country
people know this well. When a city person moves to a rural
region, she is often overwhelmed by the darkness of the
night. Houses shine out like beacons, but all roads and fields
are buried in pitch darkness. She discovers how brightly and
magically the night sky shines through. With no light pollu-
tion, the stars and moon perforate the night with such lucid
brightenings. When you leave a lighted room and go out into
the night, you are almost totally lost and blind at first. Then,
as your eyes grow more accustomed to the night, the out-
lines of things begin to loom more clearly; shadowed pres-
ences become visible. There is an inner depth and texture to
darkness that we never notice until we have to negotiate the
absence of light.

It is no wonder then that Nature supplies the most appro-
priate metaphors for the spiritual life of the mind. The
fecundity of such metaphors is their capacity to disclose the
slow creativity of the dark. The darkness is the cradle of

growth. Everything that grows has to succumb to darkness first. All death is a return to darkness. When you sow seeds, you commit them to the dark. It must be a shock for seeds to find themselves engulfed in the black smother of clay. They are helpless and cannot resist the intricate dissolution which the earth will practise on them. The seed has no defence; it must give way, abandoning itself to the new weave of life that will thread forth from its own dissolving. A new plant will gradually rise, observing the ancient symmetry of growth: root farther into darkness and rise towards the sun. When the new plant breaks the surface of the ground, it is a gift of the hidden wisdom of the clay. She knows the mystery of growth. This wisdom finds such solid expression in trees.

The Tree as Artist of Belonging

There is something so sure and dignified in a tree's presence. The Celts had a refined sense of the worthy wonder of trees. For them many trees were sacred. Near their holy wells there was often either an ash or oak tree. The Yugoslavian poet Ivan Lalić captures the secrets of wisdom and guidance that direct the tree's growth. In his poem "What Any Tree Can Tell You," he follows the patience of the tree as it navigates the dark. The tree knows how to avoid the stone and knows where to seek the water:

> . . . should it not act so,
> to foster its own loss, its branches will be stunted,
> its upward effort hunched. . . .
> Translated by Francis Jones

The tree rises from the dark. It circles around the "heart of darkness" from which it reaches towards the light. A tree is a perfect presence. It is somehow able to engage and integrate its own dissolution. The tree is wise in knowing how to foster its own loss. It does not become haunted by the loss nor addicted to it. The tree shelters and minds the loss. Out of this comes the quiet dignity and poise of a tree's presence. Trees stand beautifully on the clay. They stand with dignity. A life that wishes to honour its own possibility has to learn too how to integrate the suffering of dark and bleak times into a dignity of presence. Letting go of old forms of life, a tree practises hospitality towards new forms of life. It balances the perennial energies of winter and spring within its own living bark. The tree is wise in the art of belonging. The tree teaches us how to journey. Too frequently our inner journeys have no depth. We move forward feverishly into new situations and experiences which neither nourish nor challenge us, because we have left our deeper selves behind. It is no wonder that the addiction to superficial novelty leaves us invariably empty and weary. Much of our experience is literally superficial; it slips deftly from surface to surface. It lacks rootage. The tree can reach towards the light, endure wind, rain, and storm, precisely because it is rooted. Each of its branches is ultimately anchored in a reliable depth of clay. The wisdom of the tree balances the path inwards with the pathway outwards.

When we put down our roots into the ground, we choose from life's bounty, we need to exercise a tender caution about where the roots should go. One of the vital criteria of personal integrity is whether you belong to your own life or not. When you belong in yourself, you have poise and freedom. Even when the storm of suffering or confusion rages, it will not unhouse you. Even in the maelstrom of turbulence, some place within you will still anchor you faithfully. These inner roots will enable you later to understand and integrate the suffering that has visited. True belonging can integrate the phases of exile.

The Suffering of Self-Exile

Many people sense a yawning emptiness at the centre of their lives. This secretly terrifies them. They become afraid that if they engage the emptiness, they will lose all control over their life and identity. This fear drives them towards permanent flight from any possibility of real self-encounter. They keep conversations always on safe ground. Often they are the humorous figures who constantly joke and will not allow any question through their protection shields. They labour valiantly to be accepted by others, but no one, not even they themselves, ever gets near them. A phalanx of language and movement keeps them hidden. It is as if their every word and gesture strain desperately into the safe middle distance. Yet they long all the while to enter the door of their own hearts, but fear has hidden the key. This is a neglected and unattended region of suffering, the secret suffering of the permanently self-exiled. They are always circling within inches of home, yet they seem never to be able to get there. They are somehow forlorn, and their presence is dislocated. The suffering here is the exile from true inner belonging, the voice of forlorn longing. It is as if a secret limbo has opened in that region between a person's intimate heart and all his actions and connections in the outer world. In the intense whirr of dislocation and fragmentation which assails modern consciousness, this limbo has become ever more extensive. There is a consuming loneliness which separates more and more individuals from each other and from their own inner life.

Post-modern culture is deeply lonely. This loneliness derives in large part from the intense drive to avoid suffering and pain and the repudiation of commitment. People relentlessly attempt to calm their inner turbulence by all manner of therapy and spirituality. They seek refuge in each new programme or method as if it offered final resolution. Yet so many of these programmes have no earth beneath the seductive surface. They can offer no growth, nor enable a person to identify the pain at the root of identity. Such external tamperings never manage to reach or embrace the inner loss which is a natural part of being a human person. Every heart has to manage the emptiness of its own dark. Carl Jung suggested that neurosis was unmet suffering. This dialogue with your inner loss is slow and painful. Yet to avoid or sidestep this necessary pain only brings a slow, seeping sense of loneliness that continues to shadow and haunt your life. The Romanian philosopher E. M. Cioran said: "Suffering is the cause of consciousness. (Dostoyevsky) Men belong to two categories: those who have understood this, and the others."

Why Are You So Vulnerable?

Why is the individual so easily a target of suffering and pain? Why are we so exposed and vulnerable? First, we are vulnerable because each of us is housed in a body. This little clay tent is a sacramental place. The body is in constant conversation with creation; it allows us through our senses to smell the roses, to see the waves and stars, and to read forever the hieroglyphics of the human countenance. The body is also very unsheltered. You are surrounded by infinite space without physical shelter. This is why from the very beginning humans have sought secure belonging in caves and then in houses. The desire for strong physical shelters mirrors and reveals how space is open, and anything can approach the temple of your life from any side. Home offers shelter from the threat of contingency. Yet home, too, is vulnerable. No walls are strong enough to keep the destructive visitations abroad. The human body is a fragile home.

Second, you are vulnerable because you are an individual.

To be an individual is to be different. Each individual is separate. There is a dark logic to experience which often seems to target individuality. Suffering is suffering because it is an anonymous and destructive force. It has a darkness which vision cannot penetrate. Suffering happens when this bleak and opaque anonymity invades your individuality. A dark force of pain surrounds the unique signature of your presence. Suffering would be more manageable if its pain were restricted merely to the surface of one's life or at least to some one corner of one's individuality. Some religious theories suggest that suffering belongs only to the area of the non-self. If this were true, it would lessen the fever of pain that suffering brings. Alas, one's individuality is not constructed in such convenient compartments. Your heart, mind, and body are a unity, each place within you intimately one with every other. Pain in one part of the body affects every other. Your nervous system is the miracle that makes of all the different parts one living and feeling presence. There is something about pain and suffering that is pervasive. It suffuses your full presence.

Third, we are vulnerable because we live in time. We cannot control time. The tides of time can throw absolutely anything up on the shore of your life. It is amazing how successfully we repress the recognition of our total vulnerability. We have learned to forget that any moment can bring an abrupt and irreversible change of destiny. As you are reading this, there are people who woke up happy this morning and are now receiving news that will utterly change their lives. Suddenly, death is a gathering presence. Others are coming under the blade of disappointment. Forever more, they will remember this day as the day that divided their life in two. The time before will be looked back on as a time of unrealized contentment, the time after as the time of carrying a new loss that turned meadows of possibility into a desert.

Fourth, we are vulnerable because of the destiny that is given to each of us. Each person who walks through this world is called at some time to carry some of the weight of pain that assails the world. To help carry some of this pain a little farther for others is a precious calling, though it is a lonely, sad, and isolating time in one's life. Yet often, when the suffering has lightened, you may glimpse some of the good that it brought. We are all deeply connected with each other. In some strange way, we all belong with each other in the unfolding and articulation of the one human story. Each of us is secretly active in weaving the tapestry of Spirit. When you see a Persian tapestry, it looks beautiful. Yet underneath, the tapestry is a mesh of various rough threads. Perhaps this is part of our difficulty in understanding the sore weave of pain that often sears our life. In terms of understanding, we remain at the back and see only the raw weave. Perhaps there is something beautiful being woven, but we are unable in this life to see much of the hidden aesthetic of pain.

The Pain of Exposure

Vulnerability is an infinitely precious thing. There is nothing as lonely as that which has become hardened. When your heart hardens, your life has become numb. Yeats says, "Too long a sacrifice can make a stone of the heart." Though vulnerability leaves one open to pain, one should somehow still be ultimately glad of vulnerability. Part of our origin lies in the Darwinian kingdom of species competition and adaptation. Some instinct within us knows that we must be careful about exposure. We cannot let the heart be too easily seen, or we will get hurt. Everyone gets hurt. The extreme response to hurt is to close the heart. Yet to make yourself invulnerable is to lose something very precious. You put yourself outside the arena of risk where possibility and growth are alive. Vulnerability risks hurt, disappointment, and failure. Yet it remains a vital opening to change and to truth. We should not see our vulnerability as something we need to hide or get over. The slow and difficult work of living out your vulnerability holds you in the flow of life. It is great when we can learn to behold our vulnerability as one of the most important gates of blessing into the inner world. In giving love we are most human and most vulnerable.

The Loss of Spontaneity

In the Bible practically all the real points of novelty, change, and growth are related to points of vulnerability. When you are vulnerable, you are exposed externally; what comes towards you can really hurt you. When you are in harmony, you can take untold pressure. You can carry many burdens with grace. When you suffer, your sense of rhythm deserts you. Perhaps it is only then that you become aware of how deeply your life is normally blessed by unnoticed spontaneity. A natural spontaneity always holds you in the dance of your soul. When that spontaneity dries up, you fall out of the embrace and onto the rough gravel of deliberateness. You can no longer depend on your natural presence. When you really suffer, you learn the awful necessity of deliberateness. Even the smallest act must be willed, and it costs you disproportionate energy. It is the last straw that breaks the camel's back. I heard this as a child, and it always struck me as quite incredible that one more straw could have such a destructive effect on the strong back of the camel. The last straw was surely no heavier than all the prior straws. It was the fact of the camel's vulnerability and the cumulative weight of all the prior straws that were so destructive. When you carry a great weight of pain, you can be knocked over by a feather.

Cut off from your spontaneity, it is extremely difficult to stand at all on your own ground. It takes a constant renewal of energy to hold yourself to your own routine. After a day of suffering, you are totally exhausted and empty, and most probably you cannot look forward to the ease of sleep either. The serpents of anxiety never sleep; they poison the innocence of the night.

The Point of Equilibrium

It is lonely to carry a burden. A burden is always heavy. If you learn how to carry it, you can lessen its weight and awkwardness. It takes time to learn this; you must experience the weight of the burden, and then you discover its secret. At home we had a garden up in the mountains. There was no water in the garden, and the well was quite distant. To keep blight away the potatoes had to be sprayed with bluestone. The water had to be carried in buckets to fill the barrel of spray. If you had only one bucket to carry, it was very awkward. Though two buckets of water were heavier, they were far easier to carry. The burden was heavier but each side balanced the other and could be endured in the long distance over rough ground. Similarly with the burden of suffering. When in patience and prayer we painstakingly manage to discover the point of equilibrium within our burdens, we are able to carry them more easily.

People who do physical labour know the secret of balanced endurance. One summer I worked as part of a construction crew in Connecticut. I was working with Swedish and Norwegian carpenters. My job was to carry long heavy planks of timber over to the new houses and then pull them up on to the roof so that the carpenters had them ready to hand. I will never forget my first day. It was pure slavery. Fifty times I promised myself silently that they would not see me tomorrow. However, by evening, I was beginning to manage the art of carrying huge planks twenty or thirty feet long on my shoulder. Once I learned to judge where the point of equilibrium at the centre of the plank was, I could carry the weight more easily. If you do not learn how to carry it, even a small burden can tread you into the ground. Only by listening to the burden that has come to you will you be able to discover its secret structure. No one else can help you here. This is something that you must find out for yourself. Each burden is different. You alone know what it is like from underneath. While you are suffering, you live each day in the harsh and bruising presence of your burden. You know its inner configuration. No burden is uniform, it is made up of many different strands and materials. If you attend to it, the point of equilibrium will gradually reveal itself.

When You Stand in the Place of Pain, You Are No One

Suffering is frightening. It unhouses and dislocates you. Suffering is the arrival of darkness from an angle you never expected. There are different kinds of darkness. There is the night when the darkness is evenly brushed. The sky is studded with the crystal light of stars and the moon casts mint light over the fields. Though you are in the darkness, your ways are guided by a gentle light. This is not the darkness of deep suffering. When real suffering comes, the light goes out completely. There is nothing but a forsaken darkness, frightening in its density and anonymity. The human face is the icon of creation. In this countenance creation becomes intimate. Here you are engaged by immediate presence. There is something in suffering that resents the human face. Suffering resents the shelter of intimacy. The dark squall of suffering dismantles belonging and darkens the mind. It rips the fragile net of meaning to shreds. Like a dark tide, it comes in a torrent over every shoreline of your inner world. Nothing can hold it back. When you endure such a night, you never forget it.

When you stand in the place of pain, you are no one. A poignant line from Virgil's *Aeneid* describes one of the heroes found dead in anonymous circumstances: "corpe sine nomine," i.e., a body without a name. Belonging is shredded. You are visited and claimed by a nothingness which has neither contour nor texture. Suffering is the harrowing and acidic force of anonymity. You are utterly unhoused. Now you know where Nowhere is. No one can reach you. Suffering seems to be a force of primal regression. It almost wipes away your signature as an individual and reduces you to faceless clay. Suffering is raw, relentless otherness coming alive around you and inside you.

Suffering's Slow Teachings

When suffering comes, we feel panic and fear. Frightened, we want to hide. You want to climb up on to some high ledge to escape the dismemberment of this acidic tide. Yet the strange thing is: the more you resist, the longer it stays. The more intensely you endeavour to depart the ground of pain, the more firmly you remain fixed there. It is difficult to be gentle with yourself when you are suffering. Gentleness helps you to stop resisting the pain that is visiting you. When you stop resisting suffering, something else begins to happen. You begin slowly to allow your suffering to follow its own logic. The assumption here is that suffering does not visit you gratuitously. There is in suffering some hidden shadowed light. Destiny has a perspective on us and our pathway that we can never fully glimpse; it alone knows why suffering comes.

Suffering has its own reasoning. It wants to teach us something. When you stop resisting its dark work, you are open to learning what it wants to show you. Often, we learn most deeply and receive profoundly from the black, lonely tide of pain. We often see in Nature how pruning strengthens. Fruit trees look so wounded after being pruned, yet the limitation of this cutting forces the tree to fill and flourish. Similarly with drills of potatoes when they are raised, earth is banked up around them and seems to smother them. Yet as the days go by the stalks grow stronger. Suffering can often become a time of pruning. Though it is sore and cuts into us, later we may become aware that this dark suffering was secretly a liturgy of light and growth. Wordsworth suggests that "suffering . . . shares the nature of infinity."

It is lonely to acknowledge that often only suffering can teach us certain things. There is subtle beauty in the faces of those who have suffered. The light that suffering leaves is a precious light. One often meets people who have had the companionship of suffering for forty or fifty years. It is humbling to see how someone can actually build a real friendship with suffering. Often these people are confined to bed. They are forsaken there. Yet I often think that such people are secret artists of the Spirit. Perhaps their endurance is quietly refining the world and bringing light to the neglected and despairing. The call to suffering can be a call to bring healing to the world and to carry light to forsaken territories. The way you behold your pain is utterly vital in its integration and transfiguration. When you begin to sense how it may be creative in the unseen world, this can help the sense of purpose and meaning to unfold. Gradually your sense of its deeper meaning begins to bring out the concealed dignity of suffering.

There is a belief nowadays that true growth can only happen when all the optimum conditions prevail. If a person has had a difficult childhood or has been hurt, there is a presumption that his life is eternally shadowed and his growth severely limited. Someone once asked a wonderful actress from which well she drew her creativity and how it was that she never got lost in the Hollywood glitter. She said, "All my life I have had the blessing of an extremely hard childhood behind me." This is not to wish difficulty on anyone or naïvely to praise it, yet if we can embrace difficulty, great fruits can grow from it. The lovely things that happen bless us and confirm us in who we are. It is through difficulty and opposition that we define ourselves. The mind needs something against which it can profile and discover itself. Opposition forces our abilities to awaken; it tests the temper and substance of who we are. Difficulty is a severe looking-glass; yet in it we often glimpse sterling aspects of our soul that we would otherwise never have seen or even have known we possessed. Not that what happens to us is in the end decisive, but rather how we embrace and integrate it. Often, the most wonderful gifts arrive in shabby packaging.

In terms of history, every people goes through terrible times of suffering. Irish history carries a great weight of pain. It is difficult to come to terms with such lonely cultural memory. The theologian J. B. Metz speaks of the "dangerous memory" of suffering. There is a tendency now in revisionist history to explain the past in terms of movements and trends of the contemporary time. This is inevitably reductionist. The suffering of the people is forgotten; they become faceless, mere ciphers of a trend or dynamic of history. To sanitize history is to blaspheme against memory. Equally, to become obsessed with the past is to paralyse the future.

The Sense of Meaning Vanishes

The devastation of suffering eclipses the sense of meaning. As Cordelia says at the end of *King Lear*, "We are not the first who with best meaning have incurred the worst." People who are sent on to the dark ground of suffering know how all the normal certainties collapse. Painstakingly, you have to begin again to reconstruct some minimal shelter for your burdened heart and your cleft soul. Pain breaks your innocence. It shatters your trust in the world you knew. Now you know how destructive and lonesome life can become. No one shouts for joy when she feels the ground of pain opening beneath her and exclaims, "God, I know exactly why this came now. Is it not wonderful that I am totally miserable? I will carry this for a few weeks. Afterwards, I will be happier than I have ever been." If you can do that, then it is not suffering at all, or else you have actually broken through to sainthood!

Suffering seems to be a frightening totality. When it comes, it puts you in the place of unknowing. All the old knowing of the conscious mind becomes redundant. The leave-taking of your surface knowing often allows the deeper knowing within you to emerge. The experience of suffering can free a person to be in the world in a completely fresh and vital way. The intention of suffering may be to break the shell of ego with which each of us deftly surrounds ourselves. That we spin a cocoon around ourselves is completely understandable. We are so small and fragile. The universe is too big for us. Our inner worlds are too immense. The possibilities are endless and the dangers too frightening. Even if you had kind parents and a magic childhood, there are still places in your heart that have grown hard in the rough and tumble of experience. There are few people walking through the world without the shell of ego. Suffering makes an incision in that shell and breaks it open, so that a new hidden life within can actually emerge.

Farm life often shows how shells give way to reveal new life. We had hens at home. They would hatch every year. As a child, I always found it fascinating to see the eggs when the little chicks were ready to come out of the shell. At that time, you would hear the tiniest twitter of knocking against the wall of the shell from within. Then ever so slowly, the new little wet chick would force its way out and gradually break the shell that was its womb until then, so that it could come out into the new world which awaited it. Similarly, suffering helps us break the shell of ego from within, enabling us to release a new dimension of ourselves which is now too large and too bright for the small darkness in which it has been growing; it could no longer breathe and live. Real suffering breaks open the smallness within you and liberates you into larger and more hospitable places in life. It enlarges your belonging.

"When Sorrows Come, They Come Not Single Spies, but in Battalions."

Suffering always brings a myriad of questions we cannot answer: Why me? What did I do to deserve this? Why was what was so precious in my life so abruptly taken from me? Will I be able to survive this at all? How will I live from now on? When you are standing in the place of pain, none of these questions can be answered. Suffering often resembles fire. The flames of pain sear and burn you. The metaphor of the flame is illuminating because suffering often exhibits the exponential rapidity of flames; the pain can suddenly multiply within you. Like fire, suffering is a swift and powerful force. There is no distance between the spark and the flame. There is a hunger and passion in fire which totally take over, transforming something that was solid and stable into powdered ashes. Often the flame of pain can have a cleansing effect and burn away the dross that has accumulated around your life. It is difficult to accept that what you are losing is what is used, what you no longer need. The Daoist tradition has a wonderful understanding that in the human body and Spirit there is always a wintertime, when something is dying and falling away. There is always simultaneously a spring-time, when something new is coming to life. When you allow your soul to work on that threshold where the old can fall away and the new arrive, you come into rhythm with your destiny.

The New Window Is Open

Suffering is the sister of your future possibility. Suffering can open a window in the closed wall of your life and allow you to glimpse the new pastures of creativity on which you are called to walk and wander. But this window often opens only when the suffering begins to recede. While you are going through the dark valley, it is almost impossible to understand what is happening to you. The light that suffer-ing brings is always a gift that it leaves as it departs. While you are in pain, you can see and understand nothing. The flame of suffering burns away our certainties; it also burns out the falsity within us. Each of us lives with a certain set of illusions that are very dear to us. We use these illusions as consoling lenses through which we view the world. An illu-sion is always a false lens; it can never show us the truth or reality of a situation. Suffering cleanses us of the falsities that have accumulated in our hearts. So often our minds are like magpies. We pick up and take on everything that glitters, even though it may have no substance. In a magpie's nest, one finds random collections of colourful but useless debris. The fire of suffering cleanses completely the falsities to which our longing has attached itself. This liberates us from the emptiness of false belonging and allows us to belong in a real and truthful way in our lives again. Truth is difficult to reach and endure, but it is always the doorway to new freedom and life. As Shakespeare says in *Othello*, "This sorrow's heavenly / It strikes where it doth love."

How Is the Hard-Earned Harvest Divided?

One of the most haunting questions is, How are the fruits of suffering divided? This question touches on the old question of the one and the many. Though there are billions of people in the world, we are all part of the one individuality. We are all one. Each of us is intimately linked with every other person. Though most of the others are strangers to us, who knows the secret effect that we have on each other? "No one lives for himself alone," the Bible says. The pathways of causality and continuity are hidden in the world of soul. Perhaps the visitation of suffering in your life is bringing healing and light to the heart of someone far away, whom you will never know or meet. When lonely suffering is courageously embraced and integrated, it brings new light and shelter to our world and to the human family. This is the invisible work of the Great Spirit, who divides and distributes the precious harvest of suffering. Gifts and possibilities unexpectedly arrive on the tables of those in despair and torment. This perspective brings some consoling meaning to the isolation of pain. When the flames of suffering sear you, you are not suffering for yourself alone. Though you feel like a nobody and you are locked into a grey nowhere, you were perhaps ironically never nearer to the heart of human intimacy. When we receive the courage to stand gracefully in the place of pain, we mediate for others the gifts that help heal their torment. Through the fog of forsakenness, a new shoreline of belonging becomes clear.

A haunting poem by Fernando Pessoa captures the searing uncertainty of pain.

I KNOW, I ALONE

I know, I alone
How much it hurts, this heart
With no faith nor law
Nor melody nor thought.
Only I, only I,
And none of this can I say
Because feeling is like the sky—
Seen, nothing in it to see.

The Mystery of Transfiguration

Part of the beauty of Christianity is the utter realism with which it engages suffering. At the heart of Christianity is suffering embraced and transfigured. There is a depth of meaning to the term "transfiguration." It means so much more than mere change. When a thing "changes," there is the suggestion that it is no longer itself. A thing "transfigured" is more fully itself than ever, and more: it is irradiated with beauty, whether it is a vase painted by Cézanne or a turn of phrase that comes to new life in a great poem. Often you see this in a simple gesture—a great actor can utterly transfigure such a gesture. Often in the films of Kieslowski the camera moves from the biography of the drama to focus on an old person, possibly a beggar, shuffling laboriously along a street. In the context, the moment becomes a deft window into an unknown and unrecognized world. At its most sublime intensity, transfiguration is utter vision; no one can stay long on the Mountain of Transfiguration, but if you have ever been there, you cannot suppress this seeing without damaging yourself. For thousands of years, the Cross has been a symbol of the transfiguration of pain. It is a powerful, touching, and sacred symbol. In ancient times, the cross was a sign of shame. People were crucified as criminals.

The glory, light, and healing of Christianity earn their way through the fire-path of great suffering. This is the profound tension; here light and dark, suffering and healing are sistered. The fire-path of suffering is the final gathering-place of all the ideas and intentions of Jesus.

Jesus is a fascinating man. The book I would give anything to read has never been written; it would be the autobiography of Jesus. What was his life really like? What did he dream of? What happened on the day when it finally dawned on him that he was from the heart of the Divine? What did he do for the rest of that afternoon? Jesus had a beautiful mind and a wonderful imagination. He was deeply creative; he was a carpenter and a poet. His practice of compassion was subversive. He never judged anyone. I always imagine that Jesus had beautiful eyes. All upon whom he gazed must have felt the infinite gentleness of the Divine suffusing their hearts. T. S. Eliot speaks of some "infinitely gentle . . . infinitely suffering thing." Something about Jesus' presence offered people a new life. Religion has often forgotten this and fashioned an image of God which only brings fear and guilt on us. Given the defensive and self-perpetuating tendency of all institutions, it is doubtful that any system could ever embody Jesus' infinite gentleness and subversive perception.

There is hardly any other figure in the Western tradition who has been so thoroughly domesticated as Jesus. He was a free spirit who had a lovely wildness in him. Every time religious institutions of the time tried to box him in, he danced away from their threats and trick questions effortlessly. It is enthralling that there are twenty-six or twenty-seven years of his life about which we know nothing. Only in the last few years of his life did he begin to present himself as God. It would be fascinating to have the possibility of excavating the inner landscapes of his solitude to see what was dawning on him. How such tender and wild light was brightening in the clay of his heart. There must have been great disturbance and excitement in his mind in those days of such inner quickening. His decision to take it on, to let his life and individuality be driven by this, must have had the inevitability of destiny. Could he glimpse the lonely consequences this choice would have? He would take upon his young body, gentle face, and unique mind the pain, loneliness, and suffering of the world. He would become a thing with no beauty— a thing that would bring sadness to every eye that looked upon it. He would become the suffering servant of life's most merciless negativity—and thus achieve a beauty beyond conventional understanding to which poets, artists, and mystics have responded for two millennia.

He would come into this destiny not as a victim or accidental martyr. No. Through choice he gathered into the circle of his heart the pain of the world. This is horribly evident in his inner torture and fear in Gethsemane. Something awful happened in that garden. He sweated blood there. He was overcome with doubt. Everything was taken from him. Here the anguished scream of human desolation reached out for divine consolation. And from the severe silence of the heavens, no sheltering echo returned. This is what the Cross is: that bleak, empty place where no certainty can ever settle. His friends betrayed and abandoned him. Christ explores the endless heart of loss with such gentle and vulnerable courage.

Behind the Dark a Subtle Brightening

The Stations of the Cross are poignant places of pathos. They are a series of icons which show how pain focuses in human life. The Cross is a unique axis in time. It is where time and timelessness intersect. All past, present, and future pain were physically carried up the Hill of Calvary in this Cross. This darkness is carried up the hill so that it could face the new dawn of Resurrection and become transfigured. In essence, the Cross and the Resurrection are one thing. They are not subsequent to each other. The Resurrection is the inner light hidden at the heart of darkness in the Cross. On Easter morning, this light explodes onto the world. This is the mystery of the Eucharist. The Eucharist is a fascinating place; it embraces Calvary and Resurrection within the one circle. In Christian terms, there is no way to light or glory except through the sore ground under the dark weight of the Cross.

The Cross is a lonely forsaken symbol. Good Friday is always deeply lonesome. There is an eerie and disturbing sadness at the heart of this day. On Good Friday, the pain of the world is returning to the Cross, awaiting transfiguration again. The Cross is an ancient symbol. Expressed lyrically, there is cruciform structure to every pain, difficulty, and sadness. In this sense, the Cross is not an external object that belongs far away on a hill in Jerusalem. Rather, the shape of the Cross is internal to the human heart. Every heart has a cruciform shape. When you look at the different conflicts in your life, you find that they are placed where the contradictions cross each other. At the nerve of contradiction, you have the centre of the Cross, the nail of pain where two intimate but conflicting realities criss-cross. To view the standing Cross is to see how it embraces all directions. The vertical beam reaches from the lowest depth of clay to the highest zenith of divinity, the horizontal beam stretches the breadth of the world. The promise to each of us is that we will never be called to walk the lonely path of suffering without seeing the footprints ahead of us which lead eventually over the brow of the hill where Resurrection awaits us.

Behind the darkness of suffering, a subtle brightening often manifests itself. Two lines in a poem by Philippe

Jaccottet echo this: "Love, like fire, can only reveal its bright-
ness / on the failure and the beauty of burnt wood." There is
consolation and transfiguration here. The fires of suffering
are disclosures of love. It is the nature of the lover to suffer.
The marks and wounds that suffering leave on us are even-
tually places of beauty. This is the deep beauty of soul where
limitation and damage, rather than remaining forces that
cripple, are revealed as transfiguration.

Sweet Honey from Old Failures

Suffering makes us deeply aware of our own inability. It
takes away our power; we lose control. The light of our eyes
can see nothing. Now it is only the inner light in the eye of
the soul that can help you to travel this sudden, foreign land-
scape. Here we slowly come to a new understanding of fail-
ure. We do not like to fail. We are uncomfortable in looking
back on our old failures. Yet failure is often the place where
suffering has left the most special gifts. I remember some
time ago speaking to a friend who was celebrating his fiftieth
birthday. He told me that this milestone made him reflect
deeply on his life. He was surprised and excited on looking
back at his life to discover that much of what he had under-
stood as the successes in his life did not hold their substance
under more critical reflection. As against that, what he had
always termed his failures now began to seem ever more
interesting and substantial. The places of failure had been the
real points of change and growth.

This is often true in our own experience. Sometimes a
person puts his heart and soul into his career. He makes huge
sacrifices, putting his family in second place. Then, when the
key position becomes available, someone else walks into it.
At the crucial moment, through no fault of his own, he has
failed, and the opening will not come again. Initially, this is a

devastating experience. Finding understanding and support in the bosom of his family, he slowly begins to see through his life. He is shocked to realize that he hardly knows his family at all; he has been absent so much. As his withdrawal from the drug of career becomes surer, he sees things differently. The failure could not actually have come at a better time. If this had not happened now, his grown-up children would have left home without his really knowing them. This experience of discovery often happens when people retire or are made redundant; they learn to reclaim and enjoy the life they never knew they had lost, until retirement. There is a beautiful verse from Antonio Machado:

> Last night I dreamed—blessed illusion—
> that I had a beehive here
> in my heart
> and that
> the golden bees were making
> white combs and sweet honey
> from my old failures.
>
> *Translated by Robert Bly*

Failure is the place where destiny swings against our intentions. What you wanted and worked for never came. Your energy and effort were not enough. Failure also happens in the inner world, the times when your own smallness and limitation ruined things; you reached deep into yourself for something kind or creative and caught only smallness. Failure often gnaws most deeply in the territory of relationships. Times when you have caused damage. Failure also includes personal weakness. This is often a subject that evokes great feeling in literature. This was a theme that haunted Joseph Conrad's characters in the novels *Heart of Darkness* and *Lord Jim*. Conrad explores failure in the challenging area of affinity. One character sees himself in an other and the other's failure gnaws at him and threatens to unravel a life built on standards and achievement. In *Heart of Darkness*, Marlow only catches glimpses of Kurtz, but he already has foreknowledge of his own failure. Failure is then often the place where you suffered unintentionally. Reflection on our failures brings home to us the hidden secrets of our nature. Failure is the place where longing is unexpectedly thwarted. This often brings interesting discovery and reintegration.

Unconscious Suffering

Below the surface in the night-side of your inner world, there is suffering happening. Given that suffering usually causes pain, it sounds strange to suggest that you might actually be suffering without knowing it. Yet there seems to be something in this idea the more one thinks about it. There is a vast area of the human soul that is totally unknown to us. Let us not equate it simply with the subconscious. This holds us too firmly within the idiom of psychoanalysis. In that unknown region, many things happen of which you are afforded no glimpse. It is probable that quite a lot of suffering happens there that never ascends to the surface of your mind. Quietly in the night of our souls, everyone suffers. This suffering can be quietly at work, refining, tempering, and balancing your presence here in the world. Patiently it turns the charred icon of your falsity into the luminous icon of real presence.

Perhaps this perspective can open a little window into the dark mystery of how children suffer. There is the awful reality of children who are suffering horribly in the world through abuse, poverty, and wars. Yet there is also the fact that in some way all children suffer. Behind the playful world of every child there is some unconscious darkness deciphering itself and working itself through. Every child carries even in its innocence some of the burden of the pain of the world. This is akin to the unknown suffering in which every adult also participates. Something in the very nature of suffering loves the darkness of the unknown and hurts us and lessens us even without our being fully conscious of it.

Suffering in the Animal Kingdom

There are different forms of suffering. There is also much suffering in the world that humans are too unrefined to carry. This is where our more ancient sisters and brothers, the animals, come in to carry part of the world's pain. This pain for which our minds are as yet too coarse. Sometimes when you look into an animal's face, you see great pain. This is not pain brought about by the consciousness negatively targeting itself. Animal consciousness is more lyrical and free. An animal does not burden itself in the way a human can.

Many of our burdens are false. Animals do not spend years inventing and constructing burdens for themselves. You do not walk into a field and encounter a cow who is seriously self-analysing and in deep turmoil, because she is failing to connect with her inner calf! It is highly improbable that you will ever meet a cow who is seriously swamped by the fact that her project of self-improvement has unleashed this huge ancestral cow thing in her life, and now she can hardly walk because she knows she is carrying all the cow karma of her ancestry! Neither will you find a cow who is fatally depressed because she has discovered that on the night she was born the astrological structure of her destiny was negatively set, and she is just reluctantly grazing in the sweet grass knowing that soon the very fields will rise up against her! As far as we know, cows are not burdened in this manner by ultimate questions. Nevertheless, you often encounter such loneliness in animal presence; animals seem to receive it from elsewhere. It belongs somehow to the intimate pain of the world. An animal's face can often be an icon of profound lonesomeness. It is said that Nietzsche, before one of his major breakdowns, was walking down a street in Turin. Coming up the street in the opposite direction was a horse and cart. He looked deeply into the horse's face and went up and put his arms around its neck and embraced it. The sadness in the old horse's face was a perfect mirror of his own torture. Every form of life participates in the light of soul and also in the darkness of suffering. A kind of voluntary kinship is made possible through suffering.

Suffering Brings Compassion

One of the great fruits of suffering is compassion. When you have felt and experienced pain, it refines the harshness that may be in you. Tolstoy said that our great duty as humans was to sow the seed of compassion in each other's hearts. This happens in friendship. If you are in pain and your friend knows pain, you feel the kinship and understanding that can really shelter you. Understanding is one of the few shelters that are capable of standing in the suffering place.

I was in China once, and I visited many Buddhist temples. My favourite Buddha was one I discovered at the back of the altar in one of the temples. He was a Buddha with hundreds of hands, and in each hand there was an eye. I asked a young Buddhist monk who this Buddha was. The monk explained that this was a Buddha who had lived a wonderful life. He had reached such a level of soul-refinement that he was about to go into Nirvana; before crossing this threshold he took one look back and saw that there was still one person suffering in the world. He was then given the choice, either to go into Nirvana or go back to help the suffering one. He chose to come back. The very moment he made that choice, he was raised immediately into Nirvana. He was given a hand to help everyone who was suffering. And he was given an eye in each hand to see where the help and shelter were needed. This Buddha is a beautiful image of enlightened compassion which has strength, wisdom, and enlightenment within it.

Illness: The Land of Desolation

When suffering comes, the darkness has arrived. The light is out. Even your faith falls away. When you are at the heart of great pain, you enter a land of sheer desolation. A strange and strong poem by the Conamara poet Caitlín Maude captures this desolation:

> Between the rosary
> And the thirty acres
> The pearl of your belief fell
> On a land without blessing.
>
> *Translated by the author*

The land of suffering feels like a land that blessing has never touched. Illness is a form of suffering that quickly takes us into the land without blessing. Illness is a terrible visitor. We never value or even see some things in our lives until we are just about to lose them. This is particularly true of health. When we are in good health, we are so busy in the world that we never even notice how well we are. Illness comes and challenges everything about us. It unmasks all pretension. When you are really ill, you cannot mask it. Illness also tests the inner fibre and luminosity of your soul.

It is very difficult to take illness well. Yet it seems that if we treat our illness as something external that has singled us out, and we battle and resist it, the illness will refuse to leave. On the other hand, we must not identify ourselves with our illness. A visit to a hospital often shows that very ill people are more alive to life's possibilities than the medical verdict would ever allow or imagine.

When we learn to see our illness as a companion or friend, it really does change the way the illness is present. The illness changes from a horrible intruder to a companion who has something to teach us. When we see what we have to learn from an illness, then often the illness can gather itself and begin to depart. A friend of mine has been through an awful illness in the past three years. It was a strange viral illness. He lost his walk and his sight for a period. I was overwhelmed by the gentleness with which he was able to meet this hostile destroyer. Of course, he focused his mind firmly on the horizon of healing and tried to shelter in the luminosity of his soul. He did not constantly quarrel with the illness or turn it into an unworthy enemy. Sometimes, when you see a thing as the enemy, you only reinforce its presence and power over you. He befriended his illness; he travelled with it, remaining very mindful and holding on as far as he could to the shelter of blessing. Well, the illness took him on an amazing journey over mountains that he could never have anticipated. He has returned now and has entered health again. But he is a changed person. He has learned so much. His soul now enjoys a quiet depth; his gentleness has grown. His presence enriches you when you meet him.

To Befriend the Places of Pain

When different places within us are in pain, we should extend the care of deep friendship towards them. We should not leave them isolated under siege in pain. A friend of mine went to the hospital to have a hysterectomy. A priest friend came to visit her on the evening before her operation. She was anxious and vulnerable. He sat down, and they began to talk. He suggested to her that she have a conversation with her womb. To talk to her womb as a friend. She could thank her womb for making her a mother. To thank it for all her different children who had begun there. The body, mind, and Spirit of each child had been tenderly formed in that kind darkness. She could remember the different times in her life when she was acutely aware of her own presence, power, and vulnerability as a mother. To thank her womb for the gifts and the difficulties. To explain to it how it had become ill and having it removed was necessary to her continuing life as a mother. She was to undertake this intimate ritual of leave-taking before the surgeons came in the morning to take her womb away. She did this ritual with tenderness and warmth. The operation was a great success. Her conversation with her womb changed the whole experience. The power was not with the doctors or the hospital. The experience did not have the clinical, short-circuit edge of so much mechanical and anonymous hospital efficiency. The experience became totally her own, the leave-taking of her own womb. When a part of your body is ill, it must be a lonely experience for it. If we integrate its experience and embrace it in the circle of recognition and care, it alters the presence of the illness and pain. Externally, we should endeavour to remain alert to others and their distress at our condition. How often do we see sick people comfort their comforters?

The dark visitation of illness needs to be carefully encountered, otherwise the illness can become a permanent tenant. A friend of mine was involved in a terrible car accident and was seriously injured. One of her legs was badly damaged. She told me of being in hospital and thinking how her body and her life were terminally damaged. The darkness of this realization gripped her totally. She spent days locked into the prospect of her bleak future. She became addicted to the wounding of her body. She felt that she would never again be able to shake herself free of this burden. Then one day, it hit her, almost like a ray of light through a dark sky, that this was the wound that would make her a life prisoner. When she began to see the power it was assuming, she realized with desperation that she could not permit it permanent tenancy. So she began to distance herself from the wound. Gradually, over a period, she regained her confidence and poise and came back to healing.

There is perhaps a moment in every life that something dark comes along. If we are not very careful to recognize its life-damaging potential before it grips us, it can hold us for the rest of our lives. We can become addicted to that wound and use it forever as an identity card. We can turn that wound into sorrow and forsakenness, a prison of crippled identity. It is difficult to be objective and gracious about your wounds, because they can hurt and weep for years. Yet wounds are not sent to make us small and frightened; they are sent to open us up and to help graciousness, compassion, and beauty root within us. Wounds offer us unique gifts, but they demand a severe apprenticeship before the door of blessing opens.

The Vulnerability and Mystery of the Body

All our knowing is tenuous and shadowed. Our bodies, too, are so fragile. An accident can suddenly visit a life and completely change one's world. In one split second in a car crash, your whole world could be taken from you. You then have to enter the world of illness and pain and begin to learn how to reside there. Your body is your only home in the universe.

When you become ill or injured, you have to become used to your body as a new dwelling. All of a sudden, it is strange, vulnerable, and injured. Up to now it worked with you and for you; now it hesitates, it must be encouraged, and often it just squats there unable to move or partake. There is a desperate poignancy in the presence of a sick body. A friend of mine who now has the companionship of illness and cannot be left alone says, "I have had to get used to living with this third thing that is always there now between me and everything."

The body is such an intricate and complex place. The more you become aware of what a nuanced inner network it is, the more you wonder how it actually continues to function in secrecy and silence. The heart is the great warm centre of your life. All emotion and feeling lives here. Think of the faithfulness of your heart that has never once stopped. In every moment of work, relaxation, thought, pain, and sleep, it continues to keep your life flowing. Your heart reflects the movement of your experience. The heart is the place of great departure in the body. From here, all your blood flows out to every inner territory. The heart is also the place of great return, the place to where all the tired blood returns to be reinvigorated.

Though the body is splendid and mysterious, it is fragile, too. Joy and blessings, trouble and turbulence can reach us, because we are in these visible tents of clay. We live on an unseen threshold. The name of that threshold is fragility. Our courage breaks here "like a tree in a black wind," as Yeats put it. Consequently, we need the shelter and blessing of prayer. Our language instinctively expresses this. The greeting "Hello" expresses surprise and delight that you have survived since the last meeting. "Good-bye" invokes a blessing around you until we meet again. These rituals of greeting and valediction are secretly meant to appease the deities and invoke blessing on us. Yeats adverts to this hidden seam of vulnerability when he says:

> Come away o human child
> To the waters and the wild
> With a fairy hand in hand
> For the world's more full of weeping
> Than you can understand.

No Wound Is Ever Silent

There is no one—regardless of how beautiful, sure, competent, or powerful—who is not damaged internally in some way. Each of us carries in our hearts the wound of mortality. We are particularly adept at covering our inner wounds, but no wound is ever silent. Behind the play of your image and the style you cut in the world, your wounds continue to call out for healing. These cuts at the core of your identity cannot be healed by the world or medicine, nor by the externals of religion or psychology. It is only by letting in the divine light to bathe these wounds that healing will come. The tender kindness of the Divine knows where the roots of our pain are concealed. The divine light knows how to heal their sore weeping. Every inner wound has its own particular voice. It calls from a time when we were wronged and damaged. It holds the memory of that breakage as pristine as its moment of occurrence. Deep inner wounds evade time. Their soreness is utterly pure. These wounds lose little of their acid with the natural transience of chronological time. If we dig into ourselves with the fragile instruments of analysis, we can destroy ourselves. Only the voice of deep prayer can carry the gentle poultice inwards to these severe crevices and draw out the toxins of hurt. To learn what went on at the time of such wounding can help us greatly; it will show us the causes, and the structure of the wound becomes clear. Real healing is, however, another matter. As with all great arrivals in the soul, it comes from a direction that we often could neither predict nor anticipate.

Celtic Recognition and Blessing of the Dark Side

The Celtic tradition recognizes that we need to invoke blessing on our suffering and pain. It is wrong to portray Celtic spirituality as a tradition of light, brightness, and goodness alone; this is soft spirituality. The Celtic tradition had a strong sense of the threat and terror of suffering. One of the lovely rituals was the visit to the Holy Well. These wells were openings in the earth-body of the Goddess. The land of Ireland was the body of the Goddess Ériú. Wisdom and cures were to be found in the Holy Wells. In our valley, there are three such wells. Two have cures for sore eyes. All kinds of personal things were left here as "thanks offerings" for the cure. Many of these wells are in the mountains. It is quite a poignant thing in a bleak, stolid landscape to find these little oases of tenderness bedecked with personal mementos, sacred places where people have come for centuries to the goddesses of the earth looking for healing. These wells were places where the water element was used to bless and heal. In the Irish tradition, there is a wonderful respect for holy water. People put little bottles of holy water in the walls of their farms to keep away evil and sickness. Some carry it in their cars to prevent accidents. Others sprinkle it at night for the holy souls and for absent friends and loved ones. There is a lovely sense of how the water element can bring protection. A huge percentage of the human body is water. Blessing with water is beautiful; it is as if the innocent water of the earth which has flown wild and free in rain and ocean comes to bless its embodied human sister.

The Celtic tradition had a great sense of how the powers of Nature could be stirred to bring pain and destruction. There are many such stories. For instance, a woman who had special powers could cause a storm at sea by stirring water violently in a vessel. Or a fisherman at sea could raise wind by whistling for it. There are also many stories of people who had charms to cure animals. They could diagnose intuitively what was wrong with the animal and then use the charm to bring the animal back to health. Certain people also had the charm to cure people. In the invisible network of suffering, it is amazing how some have the power to heal us, and others help us carry the burden.

To Help Carry the Suffering of an Other

The loneliness of suffering targets each person individually. When you suffer, no one can really experience what it is like for you. Beneath this isolation of the individual, is there some way in which suffering contributes to the light and creativity of creation? The poet and theologian Charles Williams had a theory of "co-inherence." He understood creation as a web of order and dependency between all of us and God: "the web of diagrammatised glory." Within this belonging a secret exchange of Spirit continually flows between us. A person has, then, the choice to take on the sufferings of another and carry them.

In modern times, this courageous kindness is exemplified in the action of Maximilian Kolbe, a Polish priest who was a prisoner in Auschwitz. A prisoner had escaped from Block 14. The *Lagerkommandant* said that ten would die for the one who had escaped. He chose ten men. One of them cried as he was chosen; he knew he would never see his wife and children again. Maximilian Kolbe stepped up and asked the commandant if he could take the man's place. He was allowed. They were thrown in a death cell where he was tortured and eventually starved to death. This is a powerful story of the courage and kindness of taking the cross from the shoulder of another.

The Celtic tradition had similar beliefs. For instance, when a woman was in the throes and torture of childbirth, she might offer a waistcoat or some other item of her clothing to her man in the belief that she could transfer her pains to him. Or alternatively, the man might go out onto the farm and do some excruciatingly hard work in order to take some of the pain from his woman. Creation seems to have a secret symmetry in which we all participate without being aware of it. Suffering seems to awaken this and break our belonging. Yet, perhaps ironically, we are nearest then to the heart of intimacy.

Out of the Winter a New Spring

Parenthood is an ever-changing mystery. One of its most neglected regions is the time when the parents are old. Perhaps, in the last years of their lives, parents do actually carry some of the pain their children are now enduring in their own lives. There is a tendency in us to underestimate parents when we have outgrown them; they are old now and do not understand us. We tend to lock them inside the images they present externally. They circle around the same old stories, habits, and complaints. Perhaps there is something deeper going on behind the façade of ageing and helplessness. They hold our images in their hearts, and maybe they carry us in a tender way through certain difficulties and pain without our ever suspecting it.

In the land of suffering there is no certainty. We cannot understand suffering, because its darkness makes the light of our minds so feeble and thin. Yet we trust that there is great tenderness at the root of pain, that our suffering refines us, that its fire cleanses the false accretions from the temple of the soul. Out of the winter ground a new springtime of fresh possibility slowly arises. In its real presence suffering transfigures and enlarges the human being. We must be careful to distinguish it from the fabricated, self-imposed burdens we create out of our own falsity. Such burdens bring us nothing. They keep us circling in the same empty rooms of dead fact. They never open us to the fecundity of possibility. Real suffering calls us home in the end to where our hearts will be happy, our energy clear, and our minds open and alive. Furthermore, the experience of suffering calls our hearts to prayer; it becomes the only shelter. In this sense, suffering can purify our longing and call us forward into a new rhythm of belonging which will be flexible and free enough to embrace our growth. Real suffering is where the contradictions within us harmonize, where they give way to new streams of life and beauty. As a Zen monk said, "When one flower blooms, it is spring everywhere."

A BLESSING

*May you be blessed in the Holy Names of those who carry
our pain up the mountain of transfiguration.*

*May you know tender shelter and healing blessing when
you are called to stand in the place of pain.*

*May the places of darkness within you be turned towards
the light.*

*May you be granted the wisdom to avoid false resistance
and when suffering knocks on the door of your life,
may you be able to glimpse its hidden gift.*

May you be able to see the fruits of suffering.

*May memory bless and shelter you with the hard-earned
light of past travail, may this give you confidence and
trust.*

May a window of light always surprise you.

May the grace of transfiguration heal your wounds.

*May you know that even though the storm might rage yet
not a hair of your head will be harmed.*

5

Prayer:

A Bridge Between Longing and Belonging

The Human Body Gathered in Prayer
Configures Our Need

One of the most tender images is the human person at prayer. When the body gathers itself before the Divine, a stillness deepens. The blaring din of distraction ceases, and the deeper tranquillity within the heart envelops the body. To see people at prayer is a touching sight. For a while, they have become unmoored from the grip of society, work, and role. It is as if they have chosen to enter into a secret belonging carried within the soul; they rest in that inner temple impervious to outer control or claiming. A person at prayer also evokes the sense of vulnerability and fragility. Their prayer reminds us that we are mere guests on the earth, pilgrims who always walk on unsteady ground, carrying in earthen vessels multitudes of longing.

We look up to what is above. We look up in wonder and praise at the sun. At night our eyes long to decipher the face of the moon. Cathedral spires reach to the heavens and call our eyes towards the silent immensity of the Divine. Mountains and horizons lure our longing. We seem to believe that true reality could not be here among us; it has to be either above us or beyond us. In human society, we adopt the same perspective. We place our heroes and heroines on pedestals. They have power, charisma, beauty, and status. They are the ones we "look up to." Yet pedestals are usually constructed with the most fragile psychological materials. Once we have elevated someone, we begin to chip away at the pedestal until we find the fissures that will eventually topple the hero. The popular press perfectly illustrates this point; it unmakes the idols it has made. Despite the desire to look up and to elevate people, one of the most touching and truthful configurations of human presence is the individual gathered in prayer.

To sit or kneel in prayer is visually our most appropriate physical presence. There is something right about this. It coheres with the secret structure of existence and reality, namely that we have a right to nothing. Everything that we are, think, feel, and have is a gift. We have received everything, even the opportunity to come to the earth and walk awake in this wondrous universe. There are many people who have worked harder than we, people who have done more kind and holy things than we, and yet they have been given such sorrow. The human body gathered in prayer mirrors our fragility and inner poverty, and it makes a statement of recognition of the divine generosity that is always blessing us. To be gathered in prayer is appropriate. It is a gracious, reverential, and receptive gesture. It states that at the threshold of each moment the gifts of breath and blessing come across to embrace us.

There is so such beauty and goodness in the world. In our times, it is fashionable to paint everything first in its darkest colours. The darkness becomes so absorbing that we never reach the colour and light. To concentrate exclusively on the negative makes us feel powerless and victimized. It is only fair to underline the joy that is in creation, too. Joy is a dignified presence; if we insist on being morose and depressed, joy will not interrupt us or intrude on us. There is a subtle rhythm to joy. Until you break forth to embrace it, you will never know its power and delight. Every day of your life joy is waiting for you, hidden at the heart of the significant things that happen to you or secretly around the corner of the quieter things. If your heart loves delight, you will always be able to discover the quiet joy that awaits to shine forth in many situations. Prayer should help us develop the habit of delight. We weight the notion of prayer with burdens of duty, holiness, and the struggle for perfection. Prayer should have the freedom of delight. It should arise from and bring us to humour, laughter, and joy. Religion often suffers from a great amnesia; it constantly insists on the seriousness of God and forgets the magic of the divine glory. Prayer should be the wild dance of the heart, too. In the silence of our prayer we should be able to sense the roguish smile of a joyful god who, despite all the chaos and imperfection, ultimately shelters everything.

Prayer Is Ancient Longing

Prayer is an ancient longing; it has a special light, hunger, and energy. Our earliest ancestors knew and felt how the invisible, eternal world enveloped every breath and gesture. They recognized that the visible world was merely a threshold. Their very first representations on the walls of caves expressed the desire to name, beseech, and praise. To the ancient eye, the world was a mystery independent in its own rhythm and poise. Nature was a primal mother with an unfathomable mind; she could be tender or cruel. The force and surface of Nature were merely the exterior visage that concealed a wild, yet subtle mind. For the ancients, prayer was an attempt to enter into harmony with the deeper rhythm of life. Prayer tempered human arrogance; it became the disclosure point of the deeper, eternal order. In post-modern society, the isolated individual has become the measure of all things. It is no surprise that in our loss of connection with Nature, we have forgotten how to pray. We even believe that we do not need to pray.

Prayer Is the Narrative of the Soul

Prayer issues from that threshold where soul and life interflow; it is the conversation between desire and reality. It is not to be reduced to the intermittent moments when we say prayers in words. Prayer is a deeper and more ancient conversation within us. In this sense, the inner life of each person is prayer that commences in the first stir in the womb and ends with the last breath before returning to the invisible world. In a similar sense one could consider prayer as the soul-narrative of a people issuing from that threshold where the desire of a people negotiates the constraints and sufferings of its history. This is echoed in the haunted prayer of Lear: "Poor naked wretches, wheresoe'er you are, / That bide the pelting of this pitiless storm, / How shall your houseless heads and unfed sides, / Your looped and windowed raggedness, defend you / From seasons such as these? O I have ta'en / Too little care of this."

Near us is the ruin of an old penal church. It is a two-room limestone ruin set in a hazel wood on the side of the valley. It is called "coilltín phobail," i.e., "the little wood of the people." This was the church where our people gathered to pray in Penal Times, when there was a war against the faith (Penal Laws were those passed from the sixteenth century onward, prohibiting the practice of the Catholic faith in Britain and Ireland). There was a price on the head of every priest. My father often told us that during the Mass, watchmen kept lookout at different points on the horizon. The priest celebrated the Mass in one of the rooms, but never showed his face to the congregation. Remaining unknown, he protected himself and his people. This little penal ruin stands as a poignant metaphor of resistance and desire for the Divine that an empire could not kill. Prayer is often the space from which the poor and the oppressed retrieve and express their nobility and graciousness. Prayer awakens the soul and opens doors of possibility. In bleak and brutal times, it keeps the dream and longing of the heart alive. It is the only refuge of belonging in extreme times.

One Sunday morning in Manhattan, a friend took me up to a gospel community in Harlem. As an outsider, I felt that we might be intruding on their sacred space. But there was a wonderful, warm welcome. Up front, on the altar, more than fifty people in vestments led the congregation in singing the liturgy. The gospel singing was magnificent. The ebb and flow of its easy rhythm brought us gently and gradually into deeper tranquillity of soul. Yet there was such poignancy to the singing, because one realized that these were some of the songs that had kept the soul of these people alive in the brutal times under the slave owner's whip. These deep-hearted, earth-resonant prayer songs kept meaning in the kingdom of the heart. Though their bodies were owned as objects, prayer kept their souls free and their minds dreaming of a time when the new day would break and the shadows flee.

Prayer and the Desire to Survive

It is often at the extremes that the eternal comes alive. When we are safely cushioned in our daily routine of duties and expectations, we forget who we are, and why it is that we are here. When suffering chooses you, the fabric of self-protection tears. The old familiarities and securities fall away as if they had never been there. The raft of desires that guided daily life become utterly insignificant. Suddenly they seem like fantasies from another era. Every ounce of energy gathers into one intention: the desire to survive. In some subtle, animal sense, we always secretly know how precarious and vulnerable our presence here is. Suffering absolutely unveils this fragility. E. M. Cioran writes, "Without God, all is night, with him light is useless."

Our desire to endure and survive is a powerful instinct and it shows how desperately we long to belong to life. It takes immense pain to dislodge that ancient desire to belong. When that desire is driven to the edge of its own endurance, it can often endure there, turning to its own depth and taking the form of prayer. The prayer that calls out of this wilderness is one of the deepest cries of the human heart. Often this prayer is answered excruciatingly slowly. At the first stage, just enough light is released to enable you to hold on at the edge of the cliff. Then over time a stronger light gathers to guide you back to shelter. Such suffering radically refines the way you belong in your life. The true essence of your life becomes present to you. Real prayer opens at the heart of desire, at a level below your image, words, and actions. Real prayer is the liberation of that inner voice of the eternal.

A Prayer Is Never Wasted

Prayer is never wasted. It always brings transformation. When you really want something and you do not receive it, you tend to believe that your prayer was not answered. Such prayer has a powerful intentionality; and it is true that at times your prayer is not answered in this direct way. You do not receive what you long for. Unknown to you, that prayer has secretly worked on another aspect of the situation and effected a transfiguration which may become visible only at a later stage. Unknown to you, prayer is always at the service of destiny. Your days and ways are never simply as they appear on the surface. Human vision is always limited and selective, and you never see the whole picture. The Providence that weaves your days sees the greater horizon and knows what your life needs in order for you to come fully to birth as the person you are called to be. Prayer refines you, so that you may become worthy of your possibility and destiny. The irony of being here is that sometimes it is precisely what you want to avoid that brings you further towards creativity and compassion. The intensity of rejection is the index of need.

In Prayer We Learn to See with the Eyes of the Soul

Through prayer, we learn to see with the eyes of the soul. Your normal vision is always conditioned by the needs of the ego. Prayer helps you to clearer vision. It opens you up to experiences you would never otherwise entertain. It refines your eyes for the unknown narrative that is quietly working itself through your words, actions, and thoughts. In this way, prayer issues from and increases humility. The normal understanding of humility involves a passive self-deprecation in which any sense of self-worth or value is diminished. Humility has a more profound meaning. "Humility" is a derivative of the Latin word "humus," meaning "of the earth." In this sense humility is the art of being open and receptive to the inner wisdom of your clay. This is the secret of all natural growth: "Unless the seed dies it remains but a single seed." Meister Eckhart in speaking of the original Creation says, "The earth fled to the lowest place." Clay is not interested in any form of hierarchy; it is immune to the temptation and competition of the vertical line. Under the convenient guise of not being noticed and being lowest ground, it operates a vast sacramentality of growth which nourishes and sustains all of life. In our misguided passion for hierarchy, we put first things first and other things nowhere.

The earth welcomes difficulty as invitation to novelty and freshness; the earth is full of all kinds of individualities. Yet no individuality ever becomes isolated. Each remains porous, somehow receiving and returning growth. The humility that prayer brings educates your spirit in the art of inner hospitality. You slowly learn to lose your defensiveness. You enter more deeply into the wisdom of your clay, your humus nature. You learn not to be uneasy or afraid. When your deeper nature awakens and is allowed to work, you discover a new flexibility. You do not need to define yourself negatively in terms of avoidance. Humility brings a new creativity. You begin to glimpse possibilities in situations and experiences which up to now you had considered closed.

Humility also brings you a new self-possession. You no longer feel the need to vocalize in the current jargon, at every moment, what is going on inside you. Language itself is wedded to silence. Now, like the silent earth, the cradle of all growth, you, too, can watch the stirrings of a new springtime in the clay of your heart. You gain more courage. You become surer about who you are, and you no longer need to force either image or identity. When you come into rhythm with your nature, things happen of themselves.

The Deepest Prayer Happens Silently in Our Nature

It is important to acknowledge that our deepest prayer happens in our nature. Prayer is not the monopoly of the pious; neither is it to be restricted to the province of those who are religious or spiritual. Conversely, neither can we say that those who have no religion or belief are not in prayer. Neither is prayer to be equated with prayers—the sequence of holy words with which we attempt to reach God. Were the spiritual life to be reduced to what we can see and the categories we put around people, no one could ever be deemed spiritual. Prayer is the activity of the soul. The nature of each soul is different. The eternal is related to each of us in a unique way. Frequently, our outer categories of holiness are mere descriptions of behaviour. They are not able to mirror or reflect the secret and subtle way in which the divine is working in the individual life. The words we use to describe the holy are usually too nice and sweet. Sometimes, the Divine is awkward and contrary. God might be most active in an individual who just at that time invites our disappointment, judgement, or hostility. The prayer of the soul voices itself in each life differently. One of the wonderfully consoling aspects of the world of spirit is the impossibility of ever making a judgement about "who" someone is in that world. You may know "who" a person is in the professional or social world, but you can never judge a person's soul or attempt to decipher what his destiny is or what it means. No one ever knows what divine narrative God may be writing with the crooked lines of someone's struggles, misdeeds, and omissions. We are all in the drama, but no one has seen the script.

Deep below the personality and outer image, the soul is continuously at prayer. We need to find new words to help name the unusual and unexpected forms of the Divine in our lives. When we divide life into regions, we lose sight of the most interesting places in which the Divine is alive in us. It is difficult to trust most spiritual or pious talk; it inevitably seems to have either a dead or a domesticated God as its reference. The divine presence slips through the crevices between our words and judgements. Wall-to-wall spiritual talk leaves no oxygen for a living God to breathe or for the danger of the soul to quicken. Words map the world. When we attempt to name the Divine, we need words that illuminate its seamless and hidden presence. The Divine has no frontiers. Our fear and limitation invent the barriers that keep us locked out from our divine inheritance. That kind of banishment makes you a victim of your own loss. To the divine eye, creation in its diversity is one living field. Often where we consider the Divine to be absent, it is in fact present under a different form and name. Spiritual discernment is the art of critical attention that is able to recognize the Divine presence in its expected and unexpected forms. The Divine prayer sustains all life; it never ceases, in every place and in every moment its embrace is there.

The Prayer of Being

In the Christian tradition, there have been many different theories of prayer. One predominant explanation tended to consider prayer as withdrawal from the world. Away from distraction and confusion, prayer is the stillness of pure attention to the Divine. In its extreme form, this tendency encourages passivity and quietism. The other main theory understands prayer as action and engaged presence: "laborare est orare"—to work is to pray. Perhaps we do not need to choose between them because they may be false alternatives. Everybody should attempt both these forms of prayer, particularly the form they find uncongenial. Exclude nothing. Maybe it would also be possible to bring them together if we speak of the prayer of being. At its deepest level, creation is continuously at prayer. The most vital and creative prayer is always happening within us, even though we never fully hear it. Now and again, we catch the echoes of the music of inner prayer.

What Is It That Prays in Us?

In every breath and in every moment of your life, the Divine is in conversation with itself. You carry a world in your mind, which you only catch glimpses of on occasions. Your own mystery is never fully present to you. This means that your prayers in wishes and words are always partial and often blind. Yet the deep prayer of the heart continues within you in a silence that is too deep for words even to reach.

One of the fascinating things to ask about prayer is, What do you pray with? Put more tenderly: What is it that prays within you? If prayer is but the voice of the superficial mind, the result is endless inner chatter. Prayer goes deeper. More precisely: prayer issues from an eternal well within you. The presence that prays within you is your soul. It is interesting to read in the New Testament that the soul is always seen as a continuation of the Holy Spirit. No place does it ever say that we should pray *to* the Holy Spirit. The Holy Spirit is not different from the activity of your prayer. You pray *in* the Holy Spirit. The little preposition suggests how you are suffused with the Holy Spirit. Your body is the temple of the Holy Spirit and the deepest level in you is spirit.

One of the deepest longings in the human heart is the longing for a foundation to things. Because we sense how fragile and uncertain life can be, we long for a foundation that nothing can shake. The first stage in building a house is to dig out the foundation. If the house were simply built on surface ground, the walls would crack and come away from each other. Yet the irony is that we never penetrate past the surface layer. Being on earth, we feel we are on solid ground. Yet at its deepest foundation, the earth rests again on the nothingness of the empty air—but it is held there by the invisible force fields of gravity. In the inner world, the deepest foundation of the mind and the heart also rests on the invisible nothingness of the soul. The roots of all intimacy and belonging are planted powerfully in the invisible spirit. You belong ultimately to a presence that you cannot see, touch, grasp, or measure.

When you forget or repress the truth and depth of your invisible belonging and decide to belong to some system, person, or project, you short-circuit your longing and squander your identity. To have true integrity, poise, and courage is to be attuned to the silent and invisible nature within you. Real maturity is the integrity of inhabiting that "immortal longing" that always calls you to new horizons. Your true longing is to belong to the eternal that echoes continually in everything that happens to you. Real power has nothing to do with force, control, status, or money. Real power is the persistent courage to be at ease with the unsolved and the unfinished. To be able to recognize, in the scattered graffiti of your desires, the signature of the eternal. True prayer in the Holy Spirit keeps the graciousness and splendour of that vulnerability open.

Prayer and Wonder: The Art of Real Presence

Prayer is the art of presence. Where there is no wonder there is little depth of presence. The sense of wonder is one of the key sources of prayer. Wonder at the adventure of being here is one of the special qualities of humans. Plato said, "All thought begins in wonder." Even our older sisters and brothers, the animals, often seem to be enthralled in silent wonder at creation. Sometimes in humans profound wonder can only be expressed in silence. Perhaps the huge silence of the animal world is their expression of wonder at creation. It certainly seems that the excitement of being here often over-comes them. Animals at play express pure joy. When you see young foxes tussle and tumble with each other, or a brace of lambs frisk and canter in the spring, you sense the innocent delight of the animal world. Animals often seem so contem-plative in their presence. Often, when one goes out to the mountains to herd cattle, one comes upon them grazing slowly on the tough mountain grass. They raise their heads and look lingeringly into the middle distance. That still gaze resembles the human gaze of wonder. At times, they look at us not just with wonder, but in amazement. How strange we must seem to them, so full of talk and trembling restlessness.

Wonder is a beautiful style of perception; when you won-der at something, your mind voyages deep into its possibility and nature. You linger among its presences. You do not take it for granted and are not deceived or blinded by its familiar-ity. The sense of wonder keeps experience fresh and original. It is lovely to see a relationship that even after years has still retained its wonder. When the person you love still causes you to feel wonder, you are still alive to his or her mystery. Wonder is the child of mystery. It calls your heart to thanks and praise.

Wonder Awakens Us to the Magic of the World

Wonder enlarges the heart. When you wonder, you are drawn out of yourself. The cage of the ego and the rail tracks of purpose no longer hold you prisoner. Wonder creates a lyrical space where thought and feeling take leave of their repetitive patterns, to regain their original impulse of rever-ence before the mystery of what is. Such a tiny word; yet *is* confers the highest dignity and mystery. Most other words have such personal colour and promise. *Is* looks so tight; it is a little splinter of language. Yet the word *is* holds all reality and is the dividing line between existence and non-existence, truth and falsity. To say something *is* means that it has real presence, it is not a fantasy nor a mere notion. The greatest distance in the world is the distance between *is* and *is not*.

You have often had the experience of driving somewhere, your mind absorbed. You come over a hill and suddenly the wild ocean is there. When you leave the house on a frosty winter's night, you find outside the dark heavens braided with starlight and the silent moon presiding over the sleeping fields and mountains. Sometimes we abruptly wake up to the magic of things!

The Shawshank Redemption is a film about friendship in a depressing prison setting. Every kind of brutality operates there. In that prison, the sounds are sinister and the silence is eerie. One day, a prisoner who is working in the library manages to get into the main office. He locks the door and puts on a piece of wonderful classical music, a duet from Mozart's *Marriage of Figaro*, and plays it over the loudspeaker into the prison yard. As if from the eternal spheres, like an invisible manna, this beautiful music falls onto all the haunted lives in this dreary place. All the prisoners stop, entranced, and listen. There is total silence and stillness to receive the full visitation of the music. This is a moment of startling epiphany. The visit of the music is such a surprise. In the lovely shock of its beauty, the lost grandeur of creation is suddenly present. This is a moment of pure wonder in a black world.

Wonder never rests on the surface of a fact or situation. It voyages inwards to discover why something is the way it is. In this sense, wonder kindles compassion and understanding. When you meet someone with a difficult or abrasive personality, you move away from him or her. If you begin to wonder what made a person become like that, you may be more open to the hidden story that has shaped this awkward presence. Wonder can often be the key to compassion.

Wonder Invites Mystery to Come Closer

The sense of wonder can also help you to recognize and appreciate the mystery of your own life. There is always a vitality and excitement about a person who has retained a sense of his or her own mystery. They have passion to explore and discover new aspects of themselves. Such a person is a living presence. It is deadening to be trapped in the company of someone who has a predictable and ready-made reaction to everything. Conversation is carefully framed and directed. Should you risk leading the conversation into uncharted areas, you draw a blank. It is as if a whole inner domain has been robbed of its natural resonance. One gets the same feeling from people who have explored their inner world and describe their identity in terms of whichever syndrome is in vogue at the moment. The words they use to describe their self-discoveries are all borrowed. This jargon has no colour and no resonance of any mystery, opaqueness, or possibility. Real wonder about your soul demands words which come from the more submerged inner thresholds where different forces meet. These words would be stamped with the unique signature of your presence. They would be imaginative and suggestive of the depths of the unknown within you. Unlike the fashionable graffiti of fast-food psychology, they hold the reverence to which mystery is entitled. Respect is a close companion of wonder.

Wonder, as the child of mystery, is a natural source of prayer. One of the most beautiful forms of prayer is the prayer of appreciation. This prayer arises out of the recognition of the gracious kindness of creation. We have been given so much. We could never have merited or earned it. When you appreciate all you are and all you have, you can celebrate and enjoy it. You realize how fortunate you are. Providence is blessing you and inviting you to be generous with your gifts. You are able to bless life and give thanks to God. The prayer of appreciation has no agenda but gracious thanks. Nothing is given to you for yourself alone. When you receive some blessing or gift, you do it in the name of others; through you, they, too, will come to share in the kindness of Providence.

You Cannot Step Outside Your Life

The unknown evokes wonder. If you lose your sense of wonder, you lose the sacramental majesty of the world. Nature is no longer a presence, it is a thing. Your life becomes a dead cage of fact. The sense of the eternal recedes, and time is reduced to routine. Yet the flow of our lives cannot be stopped. This is one of the amazing facts about being in the dance of life. There is no place to step outside. There is no neutral space in human life. There is no place to go to get out of it. There is no little cabin down at the bottom of the garden where the force and familiarity of life stop, and you can sit there in a space outside your life and yourself and look in on both. Once you are in life, it embraces you totally.

This is most evident in the mystery of thinking. You cannot step outside your own thought. As Merleau-Ponty says, "There is no thought to embrace all thought." Most of the time, we are not even aware of how our thinking encircles everything. When we wake up to how our thoughts create our world, we become conscious of the ways in which we can be blind and limited. Yet even when we decide to be critical and objective about our own thinking, thinking is still the instrument we use in the practice of this criticism. We live every moment of our lives within this relentless reflexivity. Even when we are tired and weary of the patterns of our own thinking, they still shape our vision and guide our actions.

Amidst the Unknown Prayer Builds an Inner Shelter

Wonder at the unknown also calls forth prayer. The unknown is our closest companion; it walks beside us every step of our journey. The unknown is also the place where each of us has come from. From ancient times, prayer is one of the ways that humans have attempted to befriend the unknown. Prayer helps us to build an inner shelter here. Nature is the kind surface, the intimate face of a great unknown. It is uncanny to behold how boldly we walk upon the earth as if we are its owners. We strut along, deaf to the silence in the vast night of the unknown that lives below the ground. Above the slim band of air which forms the sky around our planet is the other endless night. Wonder makes the unknown interesting, attractive, and miraculous. A sense of wonder helps awaken the hidden affinity and kinship which the unknown has with us. Ancient peoples were always conscious of the world underneath. Special sacred places could be doorways into that numinous region. Odysseus and Aenaeas, the two mystical voyagers of classical antiquity, knew where to go in order to enter the world underneath. In Celtic mythology, this is where the Tuatha de Dannan secretly lived. They were residents at the roots of the earth. They controlled all fertility and growth. Offerings and libations were regularly made to them. In ancient culture, nature always had an elemental divinity which demanded respect and reverence. While holding its reserve, the unknown revealed dimensions of its numinosity. Places can be numinous, but so can people.

The Celtic Art of Approaching
the Unknown and Nature

The Celtic tradition was powerfully aware of the numinous power of the unknown. It had refined rituals for approaching it. The Celts had no arrogance in relation to mystery. The people who mediated the unknown were called Druids. They helped the people to understand that the elemental divinities were not anonymous or impersonal. The earth was a Goddess and all the elemental forces took on personality. The Druids offered gifts to the Gods and the Goddesses. They interceded for the people and initiated them into the rhythm of belonging that the Celtic deities required. The Druids often worshipped in sacred groves. They are associated with sacred trees, especially the oak. They were also skilled in the art of interpreting the dreams of the people. They frequently undertook shamanic feats. They were able to change into different shapes, and they could enter smoothly into the air element and escape from all force of gravity. They lit the sacred fires and watched to see how the flames would turn. In this way, they were able to divine the future of the people. The Celtic world had a deep sense of the appropriateness of approach to the unknown. The lyricism and sacredness of the approach drew from the unknown the blessings that the people needed.

Nature Is Always Wrapped in Seamless Prayer

Celtic wisdom was deeply aware that Nature had a mind and spirit of its own. Mountains have great souls full of memory. A mountain watches over a landscape and lures its mind towards the horizon. Streams and rivers never rest; they are relentless nomads who claim neither shape nor place. Stones and fields inhabit a Zen-like stillness and seem immune to all desire. Nature is always wrapped in seamless prayer. Unlike us, Nature does not seem to suffer the separation or distance that thought brings. Nature never seems cut off from her own presence. She lives all the time in the embrace of her own unity. Perhaps, unknown to us, she sympathizes with our relentless dislocation and distraction. She certainly knows how to calm our turbulent minds when we trust ourselves into the silence and stillness of her embrace. Amongst Nature we come to remember the wisdom of our own inner nature. Nature has not pushed itself out into exile. She remains there, always home in the same place. Nature stays in the womb of the Divine, of one pulse-beat with the Divine Heart. This is why there is a great healing in the wild. When you go out into Nature, you bring your clay body back to its native realm. A day in the mountains or by the ocean helps your body unclench. You recover your deeper rhythm. The tight agendas, tasks, and worries fall away and you begin to realize the magnitude and magic of being here. In a wild place you are actually *in* the middle of the great prayer. In our distracted longing, we hunger to partake in the sublime Eucharist of Nature.

Prayer: A Clearance in the Thicket of Thought

In prayer, we come nearest to making a real clearance in the thicket of thought. Prayer takes thought to a place of stillness. Prayer slows the flow of the mind until we can begin to see with a new tranquillity. In this kind of thought, we become conscious of our divine belonging. We begin to sense the serenity of this clearing. We learn that regardless of the fragmentation and turbulence in so many regions of our lives, there is a place in the soul where the voices and prodding of the world never reach. It is almost like the image of the tree. The branches can sway and quiver in the wind, the bark can drum to the frenzy of rain, and yet all the while at the centre of the tree, there pertains the stillness of its anchorage. In prayer, thought returns to its origin in the infinite. Attuned to its origin, thought reaches below its own netting. In this way prayer liberates thought from the small rooms where fear and need confine it. Despite all the negative talk about God, the Divine still remains the one space where thought can become free. There we will be liberated from the repetitive echoes of our own smallness and blindness. Prayer sets our feet at large in the pastures of promise. When you pray, the submerged eternal melody in the clay of your heart rises from the silence to infuse with blessing your life and your friendships in the seen and in the unseen world. Blessed be God who made us limited and gave us such longing! This is where prayer can heal thought. Prayer can make us aware of the clusters of presence that make up our secret companionship. Prayer is the path to the secret belonging at the heart of our other lives.

Prayer and the Voices of Longing

Prayer is the voice of longing; it reaches outwards and inwards to unearth our ancient belonging. Prayer is the bridge between longing and belonging. Longing is always at its most intense in the experience of vulnerability. There is a frightening vulnerability in being a human. Culture and society are utterly adept at masking this. Humans behave generally as if the world belongs to them. They exercise their roles with such seriousness. Life is guided by rules of action and power. Some people gain a certain control over our lives. We are very conscious of them and careful that they receive the necessary attention and affirmation. Sometimes you would find yourself at civilized gatherings of those worthy ones; the conversation and behaviour observe such a careful pattern of mannered unreality that you have to work at stifling the surrealistic inner voice that wants to declare some wild absurdity to stop the games and offer some respect to the concealed vulnerability. When it is present in its raw form, in poverty or pain, we prefer to look the other way.

The sight of extreme and unsheltered vulnerability makes us afraid that our good fortune too could turn. It also makes us feel guilty; we do so little for the abandoned and forgotten. Underneath all our poise and attempted control of life, there is a gnawing sense of vulnerability.

Mystical Prayer as a Mosaic of Presence

Because we are so limited, it is difficult for us to understand who we are and what happens to us. No human can ever see anything fully. All we see are aspects of things. Being human is like being in a room of almost total darkness. The walls are deep and impenetrable, but there are crevices which let in the outside light. Each time you look out, all you see is a single angle or aspect of something. From within this continual dark, you are unable to control or direct the things outside this room. You are utterly dependent on them to offer you different views of themselves. All you ever see are dimensions. This is why it is so difficult to be certain of anything. As the New Testament says, "Now we see in a glass darkly, then we shall see face to face."

Most of the time we are so rushed in our daily routine that we are not even aware of how limited our seeing actually is. In this century, Cubist painters attempted to paint what an object might look like if it were seen simultaneously from all perspectives. Picasso and Kandinsky often take simple objects like guitars or animals and portray them in a fascinating multiplicity of different visions. If you could only step back from your life and view it from different angles, you would gain a whole different sense of yourself. Aspects of you that may disappoint and sadden you from one perspective may be perfectly integrated in the image of you as seen from another angle. Sometimes things that really belong in your life do not seem to fit because the way you view them is too narrow. We see a good illustration of this in friendship. You have different friends. No two of your friends see you in exactly the same way. Each one brings a different part of your soul alive. Even though your friends all like you, they may not like each other at all. This is one of the sad and joyful things about the wake when someone dies. Different friends have diverse stories of the departed. A funeral involves the creation in a stricken community of a narrative whose ending makes a beginning possible. All the stories are like different pieces that combine to build a mosaic of presence. All the stories go to make up the one story. This is like mystical prayer. This wholesome and inclusive seeing, in which all the differences can be seen to belong together, is what mystical prayer brings. Mystical prayer brings you into the deepest intimacy with the Divine. Your soul receives the kiss of God. Such closeness has great beauty and frightening tenderness. Embraced in this belonging, all talk and theory of the Divine seem so pale and sound so distant.

Mystical prayer is never trapped. Most of our viewpoints are trapped like magnets to the same point on the surface. Mystical prayer teaches us a rhythm of seeing that is dynamic and free and full of hospitality. Far below and beyond the fear and limitation of the ego, mystical prayer teaches us to see with the wild eye of the soul. It sees the secret multiplicity of presences that are active at the edge of our normal field of vision. In this kind of prayer you will find what Paul Murray describes as

> A ground within you
> no one has ever seen
> a world beyond the limits
> of your dream's horizon.

Prayer as the Door into Your Own Eternity

There are no words for the deepest things. Words become feeble when mystery visits and prayer moves into silence. In post-modern culture the ceaseless din of chatter has killed our acquaintance with silence. Consequently, we are stressed and anxious. Silence is a fascinating presence. Silence is shy; it is patient and never draws attention to itself. Without the presence of silence, no word could ever be said or heard. Our thoughts constantly call up new words. We become so taken with words that we barely notice the silence, but the silence is always there. The best words are born in the fecund silence that minds the mystery.

As Seamus Heaney writes in *Clearances*, "Beyond silence listened for . . ." When the raft of prayer leaves the noisy streams of words and thoughts, it enters the still lake of silence. At this point, you become aware of the tranquillity that lives within you. Beneath your actions, gestures, and thoughts, there is a silent tranquillity.

When you pray, you visit the kind innocence of your soul. This is a pure place of unity which the noise of life can never disturb. You enter the secret temple of your deepest belonging. Only in this temple can your hungriest longing find stillness and peace. This is summed up in that lovely line from the Bible: "Be still and know that I am God." In stillness, the silence of the Divine becomes intimate.

On That Day You Will Know as You Are Known

The shape of each soul is different. No one else can ever get inside your world and experience firsthand what it is like to be you. This is at once the mystery of individuality and its great loneliness. Those close to you can best sense and imagine what it is like to be you, but they can never feel, see, or

know your life from the inside. The deeper ground of indi-
viduality is to be sought in the originality of the Divine
Imagination manifest in the relish of beginnings. The Divine
Artist is utterly creative, makes each thing new and differ-
ent. Each individual expresses and incarnates a different
dimension of divinity. Each one of us comes from a different
place in the circle of the Divine. Consequently each one of us
prays out of a different inner world and each one of us prays
to a different place in the Divine Circle. This is the place we
left to come here. This is the empty nest in the Divine where
the secrets of our origin, experience, and destiny are stored.
When we pray, we pray to that space in the Divine Presence
which absolutely knows us. This could be what is suggested
by that lovely moment in the New Testament when it says
of our return to the invisible world: "On that day you will
know as you are known."

All our time here, we are on a constant threshold between
the Divine and the human. The Divine knows us totally. We
only know ourselves partially. When we return home this
disproportion and blindness will be healed. Then our know-
ing will be equal to the divine knowing of us. This recogni-
tion confers great permission on the individuality of prayer.
You can only pray through the unique lens of your individu-
ality. There is no need for you to be in any way guilty about
your reluctance or inability to mimic the formal prayers of
your religion or the pious prayer of others. If you listen to the
deep voice of your heart, that voice is at one with the unique
melody of your soul. Your deepest prayer is the prayer of
your essence. When you move deeper into the inner world
and enter the temple of your essence, your prayer will be of
one pulse beat with the Divine Heart.

The Soul Is the Home of Memory

Prayer helps us to belong more fully in our own lives. Ingeborg Bachmann said, "It takes so long to learn to take your place in your own life." The more we come to recognize the subtle adjacencies in our lives, the more easily they can enter our belonging. The more we recognize the neglected and unseen dimensions of our lives, the more enriched and balanced we become. It takes a lifetime's work to belong fully in your life. It is almost as if each event, encounter, and experience is a pathway to be explored and lived. Then the wisdom of the soul harvests it and brings its treasures back in along that pathway until they belong to the deepest circle of your self. Each day we voyage outwards, and at evening our souls bring home what we have suffered, learned, and created. The soul is more ancient than consciousness and mind. Each day your soul weaves your life together. It weaves the opaque and ancient depth of you with the actual freshness of your present experience. The soul is the home of memory. When you pray, you enter that sanctuary where the repository of unlived and lived things opens to embrace the mystery of what you now live. You cannot break into this place inside you. All attempts to force entry will be circumvented by your wily soul. However, when you pray into your own depths, they might open for a moment to offer you a glimpse of the eternal artistry that is at work in you. This eternal longing is put beautifully by Fernando Pessoa:

> So all recalls my home self and, because
> it recalls that, what I am aches in me.

Because prayer comes from such a deep space within you, it can afford you glimpses of yourself. Prayer satisfies the longing of the unknown to find you. It helps transfigure the barriers to your inner world. You come to discover that there is no distance between you and the deepest core of your being.

To Breathe in Your Soul Light

Even though the body may kneel, or words may be said or chanted, the heart of prayer activity is invisible. Prayer is an invisible world. Normally, when we look at something with our eyes, we see it empirically. We notice its shape, colour, and limits. In prayer, we see with the eye of the soul. We see in a creative and healing way. A lovely way to pray is to engage this light of the invisible world. Because the body is in the soul, all around your body there is an embrace of subtle soul-light. When you pray with your breath, you breathe this soul-light into the deepest recesses of your clay body. When you feel isolated or empty or lonesome, it is so nourishing to draw the eternal shelter of soul-light deep into you. This helps to heal you and returns you to inner tranquillity. When you come into a rhythm of breathing, you get deeper than the incisions of thought and feeling which separate you. This prayer restores your belonging at the hearth of divinity, a belonging from which no thought or act can ever finally exile you.

Praise Is Like Morning Sun on a Flower

The Bible respects and extols particularly the prayer of praise. It is interesting to ask why the prayer of praise is honoured. Perhaps the reason is to be discovered in a consideration of the nature of praise. There is a lovely saying in Irish: "Mol an óige agus tiocfaidh sí," i.e., Praise youth and it will blossom. Praise issues from recognition and generosity. It has nothing to do with the politics and manipulation of flattery. Praise is truthful affirmation. God has no need of your praise. Yet the act of praising draws you way outside the frontiers of your smallness. To praise awakens the more generous side of your heart. It draws out the nobility, the úaisleacht, in you. When the soul praises, the life enlarges. We know as individuals how encouraging praise can be. It is like watching Nature on a spring morning. At first, the flowers are all closed and withdrawn. Then, ever so gradually, as the rays of the sun coax them, they open out their hearts to praise the light. The diminishing of praise is an acute poverty in post-modern culture. With the swell of consumerism and technology and the demise of religion, we are losing our ability to praise. We replace praise with banal satisfaction. The absence of praise reduces culture to a flat monoscape; the magic of its creative and imaginative curvature gets lost. A culture that cannot praise the Divine becomes a bare, cold place. The demise of religious and spiritual practice has contributed hugely to this flattening.

One can understand how a culture that has come of age can find little shelter or resonance in the way many of the rituals of institutional religion are practised. Increasing numbers of people stay away. Others attempt to develop their own rituals. The difficulty here is that a deeply resonant ritual emerges over years out of the rhythms of longing and belonging in a community. Great ritual creates an imaginative and symbolic frame which can awaken the numinous otherness, the tenderness, and the danger of the Divine. It is a subtle and infinitely penetrating form. Scattered, isolated individuals cannot invent ritual. Consumerism has stolen the sacred ritual structures of religion and uses them incisively in its liturgies of advertising and marketing. Meanwhile the post-modern soul becomes poorer and falls even further from the embrace and practice of sacred belonging. The great thing about a community at prayer is that your prayer helps mine—as mine helps yours. This makes no consumerist sense, but it is one of the most vivid enhancements of Being available to us. Individualism of the raw competitive kind is ignorant of this dimension.

Prayer Changes Space

Another beautiful thing about prayer is the way it changes space. Physical space is full of distance. It is distance that separates people and things. Even between two people who love each other and live with each other, the short distance between their bodies is the colossal distance between two different worlds. The magical thing about prayer is that it creates spiritual space. This alters physical distance. In spiritual space there is no distance. A prayer offered for someone in New Zealand reaches her as swiftly as the prayer offered for someone right beside you. Prayer suffuses distance and changes it. Prayer carries the cry of the heart innocently and immediately over great and vast distances. William Stafford evokes this in his poem "An Afternoon in the Stacks." He describes the aftermath of reading a book. The act of reading becomes a wild symbiosis of the reader's longing and the wise configuration of words. Stafford knows that the reverberation of this intimacy will continue: ". . . the rumour of it will haunt all that follows in my life / A candle flame in Tibet leans when I move." In spiritual space, the trail of intimacy can traverse any distance and still retain the intensity and belonging.

Graced Vision Sees Between Things

Prayer reveals a hidden world. The way we see things is heavily conditioned. The eye always moves to the object. In a landscape, the eye is drawn at once to a stone, a tree, a field, a wave, or a face. The eye has great affection for things. Only infants or adults lost in thought gaze lingeringly into the middle distance. These are moments when we literally look at nothing. This perennially neglected nothing is precious space, because it provides the medium and the trail of connection between all the separate, different things and persons. The artist Anish Kapoor, reflecting on his fascinating exhibition at the Hayward Gallery, said, "The void is not silent. I have always thought of it more and more as a transitional space, an in-between space. It's very much to do with time. I have always been interested as an artist in how one can somehow *look* again for that *very first moment* of creativity where everything is possible and nothing has actually happened. It's a space of becoming." This middle distance is not empty; it is a vital but invisible bridge between things. Distance is necessary to sight: bring a thing too close and it blurs to invisibility. If our vision were graced and we could really see between things, we could be surprised at the secret veins of connection which join all that is separate in the one embrace. We are a family of the one presence. This is the concealed belonging which prayer helps to unveil.

It is so important that prayer happens in the world, every day and every night. It is consoling to remember that there are old and feeble nuns in forgotten convents who live out their days by creating little boats of prayer to ferry nourishment to a hungry world. There are also monks in monasteries in cities and in lonesome mountains whose wonderful chorus of prayer keeps life civilized and somehow still balanced. In our precarious and darkening world, we would have destroyed everything long ago were it not for the light and shelter of prayer. Prayer is the presence that holds harmony in the midst of chaos. Every time you pray, you add to the light and harmony of creation. If you do not pray, if you do not believe in prayer, then you are living off the prayers of other people. Each day, when we wake to move out into the world, and each night, when we gather ourselves in sleep, we should gently send the light of prayer from our hearts. It is important that some light of prayer emanate from each individual. Prayer is the most beautiful poem of longing. Martin Buber said, "Prayer is not in time but time is in prayer." Prayer is eternity and, therefore, time inhabits prayer.

"Behold, I Am the Ground of Thy Beseeching."

Prayer is a light that once lighted will never fail. All prayer opens the Divine Presence. When you sit in prayer, the purest force of your own longing comes alive. Julian of Norwich has a wonderful poetic insight into prayer as longing. The Lord whispers to her, "Behold, I am the Ground of thy Beseeching." In other words, your longing for God is not a thrust through empty distance towards a removed God. No. The actual longing for God is not a human invention; rather it is put there by God. The longing for God is already the very presence of God. Our longing for God brings the kiss of the Divine to the human soul. Prayer is the deepest and most tender intimacy. In prayer the forgiving tenderness of God gathers around our lives. God infects us with the desire for God.

You can pray anytime and anywhere. You do not have to travel to some renowned spiritual guide to learn how to pray. You do not need to embark on a fifty-five-step spiritual path until you learn how to say a proper, super prayer. You do not have to sort out your life so that you can be real with God. You do not have to become fundamentalist, and hammer away your most interesting contradictions and complexities before you can truly pray. You need no massive preamble before prayer. You can pray now, where you are and from whatever state of heart you are in. This is the most simple and honest prayer. Many of our prayer preparations only manage to distract and distance us from the Divine Presence. We always seem to be able to find the most worthy of reasons for not just being quite ready to pray yet; this means that we never get to prayer. Prayer is so vital and transforming that the crucial thing is to pray now. Regardless of what situation you are in, your heart is always ready to whisper a prayer.

We are always in the Divine Presence, every second, everywhere. In prayer the Divine Presence becomes an explicit companionship that warms, challenges, and shelters us. We do not have to skate over vast, frozen lakes of pious language to reach the shore of the Divine. God is not so deadeningly serious. We need to be gentle and smile, as Hopkins so beautifully writes: "My own heart let me more have pity on; let / Me live to my sad self hereafter kind." God is wild and must also have a subtle sense of irony. In the lyrical unfolding of our days, we remain in the Presence. The simplest whisper of the heart is already within the Divine Embrace.

The Celtic tradition always had a very refined sense of the protective closeness of God. Prayers like this: "No anxiety can be ours, the God of the Elements, the King of the Elements, the Spirit of the Elements closes over us eternally." There was no distance between the individual and God. There was no need to travel any further than the grace of your longing in order to come into the Divine Presence. The Celtic imagination enfolded the prayer of Nature into the heart of their conception of God. It is the God of sun, moon, stars, mountains, and rivers. God has a dwelling in the earth and the ocean. He inspires all things, he quickens all things, he supports all things, and creates all things. The earth is the ever-changing theatre of Divine Presence. Celtic spirituality is imbued with a powerful fluency of longing and a lovely flexibility of belonging. It is the exact opposite of fundamentalism.

Prayer Is Critical Vigilance

Prayer is the liberation of God from our images of God. It is the purest contact with the wildness of the Divine Imagination. Real prayer has a vigilance that is constantly watching and deconstructing the human tendency towards idolatry. Despite our best sincerity, we still long to control and domesticate the Divine. Meister Eckhart says that the closer we come to God, the more it ceases to be God. He says God "entwird," i.e., God un-becomes. In other words, God is only our name for it. Elsewhere he writes: "Therefore, I pray to God that he may make me free of 'God,' for my real being is above God if we take 'God' to be the beginning of created things." Idolatry is the worship of a dead God. It is ironic that every human needs some God on the inner altar of the heart. We cannot live without some deity, whether it is Jesus, the Trinity, Allah, Mohammed, or the Buddha. The deity could also be money, power, greed, addiction, or status. The critical vigilance of real prayer endeavours to ensure that it is the flame of the living God that burns on the altar of our hearts. Such prayer longs for the real warmth of divine belonging. Real prayer helps you to live in the beauty of truth. It is a visitation from outside the frontier of your own limitation. The great Irish poet Sean Ó Riordan says, "Níl aon bhlas ag duine ar a bhlas féin," i.e., No one can taste his own tasting. Though you are the closest and nearest person in the world to yourself, you cannot taste your own essence. When it comes to truly enfolding yourself, you remain a stranger. Only in the embrace of prayer are you able to unfold and enfold yourself in truth, affection, and tenderness.

A Generous Heart Is Never Lonesome

It is important to pray for those who are given in to our care in the world. Each person walks a unique pathway through the world. You have your own work, gifts, difficulties, and commitments. In order to take your place and contribute to the light of the world, you need to honour all these different dimensions of your life. Adjacent to all your activity in the world, there is also present in your life a small group of people who are directly in your care. They are usually family and some intimate friends who come to dwell at the centre of your life. These people are sent to you with gifts and challenges. In turn, you have a duty to look out for them. These people are in your soul-care. When someone is really close to you, you are in each other's soul-care. Because of the calling of your own life, you cannot be continually there. Yet in the affection of prayer, you can carry the icons of their presence on the altar of your heart. Often unknown to the world, you secretly carry these friends in your heart and from heart to heart you bless, mind, and care for each other. In the Celtic tradition, it was always recognized that if you sent blessings out from your heart, they multiplied and returned again to bless your own life. A generous heart is never lonesome. A generous heart has luck. The lonesomeness of contemporary life is partly due to the failure of generosity. Increasingly, we compete with each other for the goods, for image, and status. The one can only ascend if the other is put down; there is only so much room on the pedestal. The old class system may have largely vanished, but our new system has a more subtle but equally lethal need for hierarchy. We forget that competition is false. An old rule in thought is that you can only compare like with like. No two individuals in the world are alike. Consequently, it is false to compare people and continue to foster such a destructive ideology of competitiveness. We damage the sanctuary of each other's presence by building such false standards of comparison and competition. We have been seduced by competitiveness. And so easily. Because of the bogus certainties it supplies.

The Beauty of the Prayer-Gift

It is a lovely gift when a person prays for you. One of the greatest shelters in your life is the circle of invisible prayer that is gathered around you by your friends here and in the unseen world. It is a beautiful gift to draw someone into the shelter of your circle of prayer. When you are going through difficult times or marooned on some lonesome edge in your life, it is often the prayer of your friends that brings you through. When your soul turns into a wilderness, it is the prayer of others that brings you back to the hearth of warmth. I know people who have been very ill, forsaken, and damaged; the holy travellers that we call prayers have reached out to them and returned them to healing. The prayer of healing has wisdom, discernment, and power. It is unknown what prayer can actually achieve.

When you meet someone at the level of prayer, you meet them on the ground of eternity. This is the heart of all kinship and affinity. When you journey in there to meet someone, a great intimacy can awaken between you. I imagine that the dead who live in the unseen world never forget us; they are always praying for us. Perhaps this is one of the ways that they remain close to our hearts: they extend the light and warmth of prayer towards us. Prayer is the activity of the invisible world, yet its effect is actual and powerful. It is said that if you pray beside a flower it grows faster. When you bring the presence of prayer to the things you do, you do them more beautifully.

To Frame Each Frontier of
the Day with Prayer

After the absolution of night, the dawn is a new beginning. All the mystical traditions have recognized that the dawn is a special time. They all have had rituals of prayer for beginning the day. They do not greet the day with worry or the anxiousness of how many items are on the agenda before twelve. They literally take time to welcome the new day. Acknowledging the brevity of our time on earth, they recognize the huge, concealed potential of a day for soul-making. This space to recognize each unique day invests the day with a sense of the eternal. The monastic tradition blesses this beginning with prayer. As children, we were taught to say the "morning offering" prayer. Though quite traditional, this was a nice prayer of care for the new day. It would be lovely in the morning if you could give thanks for the gift of the new day and recognize its promise and possibility, and, at evening, it would be lovely to gather the difficulties and blessings of the lived day within a circle of prayer. It would intensify and refine your presence in the world if you came into a rhythm of framing your days with prayer.

A wonderful teacher and inspiration in the West of Ireland has as a motto for his school the axiom "The mind altering alters all." This is a powerful dictum to have as central to the vision of a school. The mind is the eye of the world. When the mind changes, the world is different. In a transferred sense, the prayerful presence transfigures everything. We will never understand the power of our prayer to effect change and to bring shelter to others.

We should pray also for those who suffer each day: those in prison, hospital, and mental institutions; for refugees, prostitutes, the powerful, the destroyers. There are so many broken places where our prayer is needed each day. We should be generous with our prayer. It is important to recognize the extent and intensity of spirit that prayer awakens and sends out. Prayer is not about the private project of making yourself holy and turning yourself into a shining temple that blinds everyone else. Prayer has a deeper priority, which is, in the old language, the sanctification of the world of which you are a privileged inhabitant. By being here, you are already a custodian of sacred places and spaces. If you could but see what your prayer could do, you would always want to be in the presence that it awakens. There is a poem by Fernando Pessoa which articulates this:

TO BE GREAT, BE ENTIRE

> To be great, be entire:
> Of what is yours nothing
> exaggerate or exclude
> Be whole in each thing. Put all that you are
> Into the least you do
> Like that on each place the whole moon
> Shines for she lives aloft.

This is a lovely prayer poem; to put all that you are into the least that you do. When you hold back, you avoid the truth of situations, you diminish what a friendship or an experience can become. There are many people who love each other, who belong with each other, but their disappointment with each other, or the wounds they have caused each other, hold them out of reach from each other. Wouldn't it be great if they could risk again coming in on a wave of new hope to the shore of each other's lives? The greatest gift you can give is the gift of your self; it is a huge gift. The sun is the mother of life. She gives her light so generously and evenly all over the earth. Like the sun, each one of us should share the light of our souls with generosity.

To Create Your Own Prayer
That Speaks Your Soul

To pray is to develop and refine the light of your life. It smooths the coarseness in your vision. It brings you closer to the homeland of your heart. There are many wonderful ancient and classical prayers from the tradition. Yet there is something irrevocably unique and intimate about your own individual prayer. It would be lovely to create your own prayer. Give yourself time to make a prayer that will become the prayer of your soul. Listen to the voices of longing in your soul. Listen to your hungers. Give attention to the unexpected that lives around the rim of your life. Listen to your memory and to the inrush of your future, to the voices of those near you and those you have lost. Out of all of that attention to your soul, make a prayer that is big enough for your wild soul, yet tender enough for your shy and awkward vulnerability; that has enough healing to gain the ointment of divine forgiveness for your wounds; enough truth and vigour to challenge your blindness and complacency; enough graciousness and vision to mirror your immortal beauty. Write a prayer that is worthy of the destiny to which you have been called. This is not about any kind of self-absorbed narcissism. It is about honouring the call of your soul and the call of eternity in you. Take as much time as you need to find the shape of the prayer that is appropriate to your essence. It might take a month or a year. When you have it shaped, memorize it. When you have it learned by heart, you will always carry this gracious prayer around the world with you. Gradually, it will grow into a mantra companion. It will be the call of your essence, opening you up to new areas of birth; it will bring the wild and tender light of your heart to every object, place, and person that you will meet.

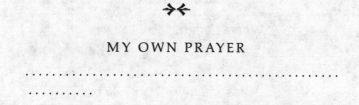

MY OWN PRAYER

. . . .
. . . .

6

Absence:

Where Longing Still Lingers

The Subtle Trail of Absence

Everyone who leaves your life opens a subtle trail of loss that still connects you with that person. When you think of these people, miss them, and want to be with them, your heart journeys out along that trail to where they now are. There are whole regions of absence in every life. Losing a friend is the most frequent experience of absence. When you open yourself to friendship, you create a unique and warm space between you. The tone and shape of this space is something you share with no one else. Your friend struck a note in the chamber of your heart that no one else could reach. The departure of the friend leaves this space sore with loss, some innocence within you is unwilling or unable to accept that one you gathered so close is now gone. It is the longing for the departed friend that makes the absence acute. Absence haunts you and makes your belonging sore.

Absence is never clear-cut; it reveals the pathos of human being. Physically each person is a singular, limited object. However, considered effectively, there are myriad pathways reaching outwards and inwards from your heart. The true nature of individuality is not that of an isolated identity; it is rather this active kinship with the earth and with other humans. When distance or separation opens, this connection is not voided—rather, the departed friend is now present in a different way. He is no longer near physically, in touch, voice, or presence. But the sore longing of his absence somehow still keeps him spiritually near. Longing holds pathways open to the departed; it does not erase people. Absence is one of the loneliest forms of longing, and when you feel the absence of someone, you still belong with the person in some secret way. There is a subtle psychic arithmetic in the world of belonging.

Absence and Presence Are Sisters

The ebb and flow of presence is a current that runs through the whole of life. It seems that absence is impossible without presence. Absence is a sister of presence. The opposite of presence is not absence but vacancy; where there is absence there is still energy, engagement, and longing. Vacancy is neutral and indifferent space. It is a space without energy. It remains blank and inane, untextured by any ripple of longing or desire.

By contrast, absence is vital and alert. The word "absence" has its roots in Latin "ab—esse," which means "to be elsewhere." To be away from a person or a place. Whatever or whoever is absent has departed from somewhere they belong. Yet their distance is not indifferent to the place or the person they have left. Though now elsewhere, they are still missed, desired, and longed for. Absence seems to hold the echo of some fractured intimacy.

And the Earth Knew Absence

The memory of the earth shrouds our thoughts with depth and mystery. In each individual, the earth breaks its silence. In human gesture, its primal stillness becomes fluent. Because we are so driven by thought we often forget our origin. We are seldom sensitive and patient enough to recognize in the mirror of thought the shadow of clay. The mind echoed back the earth's deepest dreams and longing, yet its original break from the earth must remain the earth's deepest experience of absence and loss.

In us, the earth experiences absence. Certain moments in nature seem to crystallize this loneliness. Often at night, when you hear the wind mourning around the house, it seems to be an elegy for us, its vanished children. Among animals the experience of loss often comes to poignant expression. When the calves were weaned from the cows on our farm, the mothers would cry all night the long wail of grief for their lost calves. Nature is elemental longing. The ancient stories of a culture frequently offer insights into absence and how it crosses all boundaries between the elements, the animal and the human.

The Legend of Midhir and Etain

One of the most beautiful stories in the Irish tradition on the theme of the ebb and flow of presence and absence is the story of Midhir and Etain. The fairy prince Midhir fell in love with Etain. His wife, Fuamnach, was furious, and with the help of a Druid changed Etain into a butterfly, and she raised a storm that buffeted the butterfly for seven years up and down the country. One day, a gust of wind blew her into the palace of Aengus the god of love. Even in butterfly form, he recognized her, but he was not able to remove the spell.

She did manage to change into a woman from dusk until dawn. He had a garden with the most beautiful flowers, and he put invisible walls around her so that she could enjoy the garden. But Fuamnach found out and sent a storm that buffeted Etain around the country again. Meanwhile, Midhir was not able to bear her absence. He searched every corner of the land for her. One day, she was blown in through the window of the king's palace. She fell into a goblet of wine that the queen was drinking. After nine months, she was born again as the king's daughter and again was named Etain. She grew up to be a very beautiful woman, and the High King took her for his wife. Midhir came to the great assembly at Tara and recognized her again, but she did not remember him. Beating the High King at a game of chess, all he asked was that he would receive one kiss from Etain. After meeting Midhir, Etain began to dream of her former life. Little by little, she began to recall all she had forgotten and she pined and fretted for Midhir. On the evening that he was to return for the kiss, Tara was armed against him like a forest of steel. Magically, he appeared in the midst of the banqueting hall and he embraced Etain. The alarm was raised. The king and his army rushed out after them but there was no sign of them in front of the castle. They all looked up to see two white swans encircling the starry sky over the palace.

The structure of this story is fascinating in what it reveals about the longing that lingers so potently at the heart of absence. When they fall in love, they create a unique space with each other, a special echo in each other's hearts. The intensity of this claim on each other sets the whole direction of the story from this point on. Once she is changed into a butterfly and driven away, Midhir is haunted by her absence. His life becomes one long search for her, who awakened his heart and then vanished. Her metamorphosis as a new child of the king erases her memory of him. But the longing at the heart of the absence he feels ensures that his power of recognition stays alert and patient. He finds her in a totally unexpected place and in the most extreme form of otherness, namely, in the form of a completely different person. Yet he still recognizes her. After the initial encounter, her absent former life begins to return in dream. This becomes an intense and exclusive longing. Transformed finally into swan shape, they are now united as graceful artists of the air; the sweet irony here is that this was precisely the element which had so tortured Etain and ensured her demented absence and separation from her lover. Now air is the element of their escape and unification.

The Longing for Real Presence

The deeper the intimacy and belonging, the more acute the sense of absence will be. It seems that real intimacy brings us in from the bleakness of exile. Intimacy is belonging. We come in from the distance and grow warm at the hearth of the friend's soul. Now there are places within us that are no longer simply our own. Rather they are inhabited with the taste and colour of the friend's presence. When the friend departs, the inner house of belonging falls to ruins; this is why absence holds such acute presence and poignancy. True belonging alters and re-creates your identity. When that belonging is fractured or lost, something of our deepest self departs. To open yourself is to risk losing yourself. Emily Dickinson says:

> Absence disembodies
> so does Death
> hiding individuals from the Earth.

Absence hides the one you love. You desire to be with the beloved, to see her, hear her, rest in her presence. But she is hidden from your eyes though not hidden from your heart. Letters and photographs are no longer objects of joy to raise your heart; now they are filled with pathos. You find yourself in places you were together, and your heart is seared with absence.

We are vulnerable to absence because we so deeply desire presence. Some writer, referring to another, said, "He has quite a delightful presence but a perfect absence." Obviously, happiness increased when the other was absent! The mind separates us, makes us absent from the earth. The privilege of the mind is its capacity for presence. There seems to be nothing else in Nature that can focus in such conscious presence. The deepest longing of the mind is for real presence. Real presence is the ideal of truth, love, and communication. Real presence is the ideal of prayer here and the beatific vision in the hereafter. Somewhere deep in the soul, our longing knows that we break through to the eternal when we are gathered in the shelter of presence. These are the moments of our deepest belonging. For a while, the restlessness and hunger within the heart grows still. The sense of being an outsider, a stranger here, ceases. For a while, we are home. This is such a satisfying and refreshing experience; it nourishes us to the roots.

Yet the experience of presence always remains fleeting and temporary. Not often do hunger, readiness, and grace conspire to bring our souls home; and when they do, the visit is inevitably short. The mind and time are doomed to move relentlessly onwards. All we achieve is the glimpse, the taste; we are not allowed to linger. We plunge forth again into the ever-diverse fields of new experience. Presence becomes broken, scattered, and fragmentary. We endeavour to be real. Yet so much of our presence is diminished by our role and its functions. Behind our many intricate and necessary social masks, we often secretly wonder who we are and daydream of letting everything derivative and secondhand fall away and living the life we love. We dream of leaving the daily round in which absence, rather than presence, seems to control and determine things. Most of our social world is governed by a sophisticated and subtle grammar of absence. In post-modern culture, we tend more and more to inhabit virtual reality rather than actual reality. More and more time is spent in the shadowlands of the computer world; this is a world which is all foreground but has no background. Many people have to earn their living in the world of function. Imagine someone in a factory assembly line who has to hit the same bolt every twenty seconds for the rest of his working life. You could not stay present in that kind of work unless you were a saint or a Zen mystic. In your heart you would have to be elsewhere. This work makes you absent. This is the absence that Karl Marx referred to as alienation. Much of modern life is lived in the territory of externality; if we succumb completely to the external, we will lose all sense of inner and personal presence. We will become the ultimate harvesters of absence, namely, ghosts in our own lives.

The Homeless Mind

In post-modern culture, the human mind seems particularly homeless. The traditional shelters no longer offer any shelter. Religion often seems discredited. Its language and authority structures seem to speak in the idiom of the distant past and seem powerless to converse with our modern hunger. Politics seems devoid of vision and is becoming ever more synonymous with economics. Consumerist culture worships accumulation and power; it establishes its own gaudy hierarchies. In admiring the achievement and velocity of these tiger economies, we refuse to notice the paw marks of its ravages and the unglamorous remains of its prey. All these factors contribute to the dissolution of real presence. The homeless mind is haunted by a sense of absence that it can neither understand nor transfigure. Indeed, in its desperation, it endeavours to fill every moment with some kind of forced presence. Our poor times suffer from unprecedented visual aggression and cacophony.

There is a great story about the loss of belonging in Gershom Scholem's book *Major Trends in Jewish Mysticism*. In the eighteenth century, there arose in Eastern Europe a remarkable mystical movement called Hassidism. Its founder was known as the Baal Shem Tov, and he was a religious genius and pioneer. One day, a calamity threatened the community in which he lived, and so he called his chief disciple and said, "Come, let us go out into the woods."

And they went to a certain very special spot that the master seemed to know about, and he built a very special kind of fire, and then he offered a special prayer. He said, "Oh, God, Thy people are in dire need. Please help us in this moment of distress, etc." Then to his disciple, he said, "It is all right now. Everything will be all right."

They went back and found that, indeed, the calamity that had been impending somehow had been averted. The master died, and in the next generation, this disciple became the leader of the same group. And in his day, likewise, another major disaster threatened to wipe out the community.

Now, he took his chief disciple and they set out for the woods, but he had forgotten just where the exact place was, though he did remember how to light the fire. So he said, "Oh, God, I don't know where the place is, but you are everywhere, so let me light the fire here. Your people need you, calamity threatens. Please, help." And then after the prayer he turned to his disciple and said, "It is all right now."

And when they returned to the town, they were greeted with the joyful news that the threat had been removed. Well, then, that disciple became the master in the next generation, and once again, a catastrophe was imminent.

This time he went out with his disciple. He no longer knew the place, and he had forgotten how to make the fire, but he still knew the prayer and he said, "God, I don't know this place very well, but you are everywhere. I don't know how to make the fire, but all the elements are in your hands. Your people need you. We ask your help." Then he turned to his disciple and said, "Now it is all right. We may go back."

They went back and everything indeed was all right. The story concludes by stating that today, we don't know the place; we no longer know how to make the fire; we don't even know how to pray. So all we can do is to tell the story, and to hope that somehow, the telling of the story itself will help us in this hour of need.

Psychology and Self-Absence: Talking Ourselves Out

Our culture is fragmented; the old shelters are gone and the sever of the cold breeze of isolation is everywhere. This has made our desire for belonging all the more intense. We search continually for connection. Today many people find this in therapy and psychology. If you find a wise guide to lead you on the inner quest, you are a fortunate person. It is dangerous to open your self to another in such a total way. Opening your soul to an unworthy guide can have negative consequences. When you really tell how and who you are, you offer your listener a key to the temple of your life. You allow that person a huge voice in your conversation with yourself. Listening is such an underrated activity. In fact it is hugely subversive. Because when we listen deeply, we take in the voice of the other. The inner world is so tender and personal, and the voices that really enter assume great power.

I like to think of psychology as soul-searching: you search your soul and you also search for your soul; and, of course, on the quest your soul is searching with you. The journey has diverse paths, and different voices surface suggesting a real adventure and the possibility of awakening and healing. Good soul-searching refines and heals your presence. It helps you to belong more honestly to yourself. If you are driven by needs and inner forces of which you are unaware, then your behaviour and actions are not free; you only partly belong to yourself. To bring these subtle forces into the light helps change their negative control over you.

The magic of psychology is how powerfully it underlines the effect that awareness can have. When you come to know yourself, you come home to yourself and your life flows more naturally. As you become more integrated, your integrity deepens. You inhabit the heart of your life; you become the real subject of your life rather than its target or victim.

When the wall came down in Germany I remember meeting a friend who had been in Berlin that week. She said, "Man erlebt sich als reines Subjekt," i.e., in Berlin in those days "You experience yourself as pure subject." This was a lovely statement of the immense personal power of feeling, thinking, and seeing that is in each of us. When the run of life and possibility is with you, you feel as if you are riding a wave of energy. Unfortunately, much of the time we are not gathered in the grace of such inner fluency. More often than not we are split asunder within, one part fighting against the other. To learn the art of being the subject of your own life and experience enlarges your spirit.

It would be great as we grow older to become more free and fluent. You often see old people who have grown into this grace. Though their bodies are old, their presence is as majestic and swift as a ballet dancer. They have somehow entered the mystery of true unity. They are at one with themselves. It is interesting to hyphenate the word "atonement," the religious ideal, as at-one-ment. This unity is the heart of all belonging; without this hidden unity of everything, no belonging would be possible. The unity is also the secret. Elsewhere that now holds the presence of those who have vanished from our lives; it ensures that absence is not vacancy.

Good soul-searching helps you to sift the past. Often you only begin when you find yourself in crisis. The word "crisis" comes from the Greek word "krinein," meaning "to decide" or "to sift." When you take time to search your soul and its past you will know more clearly what belongs to you and what does not. When you sift your soul, you are better able to identify the host of various longings you carry. When you listen to your longings coming to voice, you can discern which horizons they have in mind. You understand that to pursue certain longings would probably destroy you. Certain voices would love to seduce you.

It is interesting that at the source of the Christian tradition, in the Genesis story, the future of creation is determined by longing. The desire to eat of the fruit of the tree of good and evil caused the rupture in creation. When Adam followed his longing, its immediate effect was the loss of the ideal belonging of Paradise. In Christian mythic terms, the perennial tension between longing and belonging is to be traced back to this fracture. Expelled as we were from the harmony of Paradise, our belonging will always be fractured and temporary. Our longing will be permanent and full. Towering over the Greek tradition is the longing of the wanderer to return home. The huge longing of Odysseus is going in the other direction. He is already an exile, he wants to return to the belonging of his home and homeland. The true search for soul brings longing and belonging into a creative tension of harmony. Mediocre therapy could haunt your soul with absence by reducing each inner presence to a function.

Brittle Language Numbs Longing

It is a testimony to the relevance of a science when it finds its way into the heart of a culture. In this crossing, the science is often vulgarized. Contemporary culture is riddled with psychologese. So many people speak of themselves now in the brittle clarity of disembodied psychological terms. One such powerful term is "process": "I am looking at my own process," or "Let us try and process that for a while," or "You can trust the process." In many cases "processing" has become a disease; it is now the way in which many people behave towards themselves. This term has no depth or sacredness. "Processing" is a mechanical term: there are processed peas and beans. The tyranny of processing reveals a gaping absence of soul.

The only wisdom required nowadays consists of managing to get the right emotional components and complexes onto the appropriate assembly line so that they can go through the correct solidifiers and emerge in the correct packaging so that they can be "dealt with." A "deal" is a business or contractual arrangement; it also happens to cards, especially in casinos. When you hear someone say "I am having to deal with this feeling right now," you may wonder whether the emotion has been secretly absent for a while doing a crash course in Wall Street and is now forcing its "owner" into an unexpected corner. Such terminology is blasphemous; it belongs to the mechanical world. When you use it on your inner life, it "formats" your holy wildness. You become an inner developer, turning the penumbral meadows of the heart into a concrete grid. No wonder the tone of the modern soul sounds like the prison language of a ghetto. Such brittle cold language numbs your longing and unravels the nuance and texture of your presence; it can turn you into a ghost in your own life, a custodian of absence, a grey visitor of vacancy.

The obsession with such turgid analysis betrays how suspicious we have become of our own experience. We treat our experience, not as the sacramental theatre of our numinous lives, but rather as if it did not belong to us at all or as if it were merely public property. Unless you trust your experience and let it happen, you cannot be present for yourself or anything else in a natural way. When you lose this hospitality to yourself, there is no longer any welcome for the surprise and wonder of new things. Your experience becomes poor, and, ironically, the poorer it gets, the more obsessive is the desire to analyse it to bits. When your experience is rich and diverse, it has a beautifully intricate inner weaving. You know that no analysis can hold a candle to the natural majesty and depth of even the most ordinary moment in the universe. Every moment holds a gallery of sacred forms. Soul-searching is the activity of respectful and critical wonder at the drama of your biography. As with any worthy story, it has its own inner destiny and form independent of its author. When you keep scraping at your soul, you damage your very ability to experience anything. If you lose your sensibility, you have nothing to open the door to welcome the world.

Beyond Being an Observer— Becoming a Participant

When you become an interfering observer in your own life, you cease to be a living participant. Much modern therapy trains people to be rigid observers of themselves. They never sleep on the job. Like heroic cowboys, they manage to sleep with one eye open. It is, then, extremely difficult to let yourself become a whole-hearted participant in your one beautiful, unrepeatable life. You are taught to police yourself. When you watch a policeman walk down a street, he does it differently. He is alert, his eyes are combing everything. He does not miss a thing. When you police yourself, you are on the beat alone, you are in such alert that the usual inner suspects inevitably surface and suddenly you are in your element, you can exercise your full authority. You will put them through the full process: identification, arrest, and conviction. You know how to "deal" with them. Such an approach to the self highlights the modern reduction of the "who" question to the functionalism of the "how." We need a new psychology to encourage us and liberate us to become full participants in our lives; one that will replace self-watch with self-awakening. We need a rebirth of the self as the sacred temple of mystery and possibility; this demands a new language which is poetic, mystical, and impervious to the radiation of psychologese. We need to rediscover the wise graciousness of spontaneity. The absence of spontaneity unleashes us negatively on ourselves.

Certain cultures practise wholesome spontaneity; others are somewhat more rigid and considered in their behaviour. An Irish friend lived in Berlin for a while in the eighties; at this time punk culture was still strong. One day, he was walking down a street and there were two disciples of punk ahead of him. Each had an architecture of hair that must have taken months to perfect, a series of unbelievable shapes and colours. He walked faster and reached the pedestrian light first. It was still on red; he looked up and down the street, there was no traffic coming. Having a functional rather than sacred attitude to such objects, he crossed the forbidden street on red and continued along the other side.

He looked over his shoulder to see how far behind him the punks were now. But he could not see them. When he looked farther back, he saw that they were still waiting on the other side for the green light. It struck him that the programming had penetrated far below the hairline. And these were the anarchists! When spontaneity is absent, longing and belonging rigidify. Yet who we are and what happens to us in the world occur spontaneously. Meister Eckhart says, "Deus non habet quare," i.e., God does not have a why. There is huge spontaneity in the Divine which graces life. God is no functionalist Driven by the mechanics of agenda or programme. As our lives flow into the absence of the past, it is the spontaneity of memory we can neither control nor force which gathers and keeps that absence for us.

Memory Is Full of the Ruins of Presence

As we journey onwards in life, more and more spaces within us fill with absence. We begin to have more and more friends among the dead. Every person suffers the absence of their past. It is utterly astonishing how the force and fibre of each day unravel into the vacant air of yesterday. You look behind you and you see nothing of your days here. Our vanished days increase our experience of absence. Yet our past does not deconstruct as if it never was. Memory is the place where our vanished days secretly gather. Memory rescues experience from total disappearance. The kingdom of memory is full of the ruins of presence. It is astonishing how faithful experience actually is; how it never vanishes completely. Experience leaves deep traces in us. It is surprising that years after something has happened to you the needle of thought can hit some groove in the mind and the music of a long vanished event can rise in your soul as fresh and vital as the evening it happened. Memory provides such shelter and continuity of identity. Memory is also fascinating because it is an indirect and latent presence in one's mind. The past seems to be gone and absent. Yet the grooves in the mind hold the traces and vestigia of everything that has ever happened to us. Nothing is ever lost or forgotten. In a culture addicted to the instant, there is a great amnesia. Yet it is only through the act of remembrance, literally re-membering, that we can come to poise, integrity, and courage. Amnesia clogs the inner compass and makes the mind homeless. Amnesia makes the sense of absence intense and haunted. We need to retrieve the activity of remembering, for it is here that we are rooted and gathered. Tradition is to the community what memory is to the individual. The absence of the past remains subtle yet near.

Ruins: Temples of Absence

The human heart longs to dwell. The root of the word "dwelling" includes the notion of lingering or delaying. It holds the recognition of our pilgrim nature, namely, the suggestion that it will only be possible to linger for a while. From ancient times, we have carved out dwelling places on the earth. Against the raw spread of Nature, the dwelling always takes on a particular intensity. It is a nest of warmth and intimacy. Over years and generations, a large aura of soul seeps into a dwelling and converts it in some way into a temple of presence. We leave our presence on whatever we touch and wherever we dwell. This presence can never be subsequently revoked or wiped away; the aura endures. Presence leaves an imprint on the ether of a place. I imagine that the death of every animal and person creates an invisible ruin in the world. As the world gets older, it becomes ever more full with the ruins of vanished presence. This can be sensed years and years later even more tangibly in the ruins of a place. The ruin still holds the memory of the people who once inhabited it. When the ruin is on a street, its silence is serrated because it endures the import of surrounding echoes. But when a ruin is an isolated presence in a field, it can insist on its personal signature of presence in contrast to the surrounding nature. A ruin is never simply empty. It remains a vivid temple of absence. All other inhabited dwellings hold their memory and their presence is continually added to and deepened by the succeeding generations. It is, consequently, quite poignant that a long since vacated ruin still retains echoes of the presence of the vanished ones. The German poet Friedrich Hölderlin captures this unstated yet perennial presence of the echo of touch in abandoned places:

> When night is like day
> And over slow footpaths,
> Dense with golden dreams,
> Lulling breezes drift.

The abandoned place is dense with the presence of the absent ones who have walked there. Another region of absence is the absence of what is yet to come.

The Absence of the Future

There is also a whole region of the absent which embraces not the vanished, but that which has not yet arrived. On the pathway of time, the individual is always somehow in the middle. There are events, persons, thoughts, and novelties ahead that have not yet arrived. This is the territory of the unknown. We are always reaching forward with open gestures into the future. Much of our thinking endeavours to invite the unknown to disclose itself. This is especially true of questions. The question is the place where the unknown becomes articulate and active in us. The question is impatient with the unrevealed. It reaches forward to open doors in the unknown. The question attempts to persuade absence to yield its concealed presences. All perception works at this threshold. Unknown to ourselves we are always unveiling new worlds that lie barely out of reach. This is where the imagination is fully creative. All language, thought, creativity, prayer, and action live out of that fissure between word and thing, longing and fulfilment, subject and object.

There are invisible furrows of absence everywhere.

Towards a Philosophy of Loss

Life is rich and generous in her gifts to us. We receive much more than we know. Frequently life also takes from us. Loss is always affecting us.

A current of loss flows through your life like the tide that returns eternally to rinse away another wafer of stone from the shoreline.

You know the sore edges in your heart where loss has taken from you. You stand now on the stepping stone of the present moment. In a minute it will be gone, never to return. With each breath you are losing time. Absence is the longing for something that is gone. Loss is the hole that it leaves. The sense of loss confers a great poignancy on your longing. Each life has its own different catalogue. Some people are called to endure wounds of loss that are devastating. How they survive is difficult to understand. Each of us in our own way will be called at different times to make its sore acquaintance. From this angle, life is a growth in the art of loss. Eventually, we learn to enter absolute loss at death. In Conamara, when someone is dying, they often say "Tá sí ar a cailleadh," i.e., She is dying—literally, "She is in her losing."

In a certain sense, there can be no true belonging without

the embrace of loss. Belonging can never be a fixed thing. It is always quietly changing. At its core, belonging is growth. When belonging is alive, it always brings new transitions. The old shelter collapses; we lose what it held; now we have to cross over into the beginnings of a new shelter of belonging that only gathers itself slowly around us. To be honest and generous in belonging to the awkward and unpredictable transition is very difficult. This happens often in friendship and love. Your relationship may be changing or ending. Often the temptation is to suppress this, or avoid it or cut it off in one brutal, undiscussed stroke. If you do this, you will not belong to the changing, and you will find yourself an intruder on the emerging new ground. You will not be honourably able to rest in the new belonging because you did not observe the dignity of painfully earning your passage. Loss always has much to teach us; its voice whispers that the shelter just lost was too small for our new souls. But it remains hard to belong generously to the rhythm of loss.

The beauty of loss is the room it makes for something new. If everything that came to us were to stay, we would be dead in a day from mental obesity. The constant flow of loss allows us to experience and enjoy new things. It makes vital clearance in the soul. Loss is the sister of discovery; it is vital to openness; though it certainly brings pain. There are some areas of loss in your life which you may never get over. There are some things you lose and, after the pain settles, you begin to see that they were never yours in the first place. As the proverb says: What you never had you never lost.

Loss qualifies our whole desire to have and to possess. It is startling that you cannot really hold on to anything. Despite its intensity, the word "mine" can only have a temporary and partial reference. Ironically, sometimes when we desperately hold on to something or someone, it is almost as if we secretly believe that we are going to lose them. Holding on desperately cannot in any way guarantee belonging. The probability is that it will in some strange way only hasten loss. True belonging has a trust and ease; it is not driven by desperation to lose yourself in it or the fear that you will lose it.

The loneliest wave of loss is the one that carries a loved one away towards death.

Grief: Longing for the Lost One

As a child you think death is so strange. You anticipate that when it comes, it will be accompanied by major drama. Yet so often death arrives with uncanny quiet. It steals into a room and leaves an awful silence. A loved one is gone. The first time that death takes someone close to you, it breaks your innocence and your natural trust in life. It is strange to lose someone to death. The shock should paralyse you, but the disturbing quiet somehow makes everything sufficiently unreal, and the force of the loss is dissipated. Unlikely as it may sound, though death has indeed occurred and you were there, you do not truly know yet that your friend has died. You go through the funeral days, their drama and sympathy buoyed up by the certainty and shelter of rhythm which this whole ritual provides. It is only later, when the new silence gathers around your life, that you realize your awful loss. You have been thrown out of the shelter of a belonging where your heart was at home.

The time of grief is awkward, edgy, and lonesome. At first, you feel that it is totally unreal. With the belonging severed, you feel numbed. When you love someone, you are no longer single. You are more than yourself. It is as if many of your nerve lines now extend outside your body towards the beloved, and theirs reach towards you. You have made living bridges to each other and changed the normal distance that usually separates us. When you lose someone, you lose a part of yourself that you loved, because when you love, it is the part of you that you love most that always loves the other.

Grief is at its most acute at death. There is also a whole unacknowledged grief that accompanies the breakup of a relationship. This indeed can often be worse than death, at least initially, because the person is still around and possibly with someone else. The other is cut off from you.

Grief is the experience of finding yourself standing alone in the vacant space with all this torn emotional tissue protruding. In the rhythm of grieving, you learn to gather your given heart back to yourself again. This sore gathering takes time. You need great patience with your slow heart. It takes the heart a long time to unlearn and transfer its old affections. This is a time when you have to swim against the tide of your life. It seems for a while that you are advancing, then the desolation and confusion pull you down, and when you surface again, you seem to be even further from the shore. It is slow making your way back on your own. You feel so many conflicting things. You are angry one minute; the next moment you are just so sad. After a death there are people around you, yet you feel utterly isolated: no one else has the foggiest notion of your loss. No one had what you had, therefore, no one else had lost it. Yet when friends try gently to accompany you, you find yourself pulling back from them, too. In a remarkable collection of modern elegies to mourn the loss of his wife, the Scottish poet Douglas Dunn ends his poem "The Clear Day" with this verse:

> I shall sieve through our twenty years, until
> I almost reach the sob in the intellect,
> The truth that waits for me with its loud grief,
> Sensible, commonplace, beyond understanding.

Because your loss is so sore, something within you expects the world to understand. You were singled out. Now you are on your own. Yet life goes on. That makes you angry: sometimes, you look around at your family or the others who have been hit by this loss; it does not seem to have hurt them as much. But you remember that behind the façade they are heartbroken too. You have never experienced anything like this. During grief, the outer landscape of your life is in the grip of a grey weather; every presence feels ghostly. You are out of reach. You have gone way into yourself. Your soul lingers around that inner temple which is empty now save for the sad echo of loss.

Grief Is a Journey That Knows Its Way

Despite its severity, the consolation at a time of grief is that it is a journey. Grief has a structure; it knows the direction and it will take you through. It is amazing how time and again, one of the most consoling factors in experience is that each experience has a sure structure; this is never obvious to us while we are going through something. But when we look back, we will be able to pick out the path that offered itself. Experience always knows its way. And we can afford to trust our souls much more than we realize. The soul is always wiser than the mind, even though we are dependent on the mind to read the soul for us. Though travel is slow on the grief journey, you will move through its grey valley and come out again onto the meadow where light, colour, and promise await to embrace you. The loneliest moment in grief is when you suddenly realize you will never see that person again. This is an awful shock. It is as if all the weeks of sorrow suddenly crystallize in one black bolt of recognition. You really know how total your loss is when you understand that it is permanent. In this life there is no place that you will ever be able to go to meet again the one who has gone. On the journey of grief, this is a milestone. You begin thereafter to make your peace with the shock.

We Grieve for Ourselves

Gradually, you begin to understand more deeply that you are grieving primarily over your own loss. The departed one is gone home and is gathered now in the tranquillity of Divine Belonging. When you realize that it is for yourself that you are grieving, you begin to loosen your sorrowful hold on the departed one.

Part of what has had you holding on so desperately is the fear that if you let go, you would lose that person forever. Now you begin to glimpse the possibilities of being with him or her in a new way. If you loosen the sad grip of grief, a new belonging becomes possible between you. This is one of the most touching forms of belonging in the world: the belonging between us and our loved ones in the unseen world. It is a subtle and invisible belonging for which the crass obviousness of modern culture has no eye. Yet this invisible belonging is one in which so many people participate.

Though the silent weeping of your heart lessens, you get on, more or less, with your life, yet a place is kept within you for the one who is gone. No other will ever be given the key to that door. As years go on, you may not remember the departed every day with your conscious mind. Yet below your surface mind, some part of you is always in the person's presence. From their side, our friends in the unseen world are always secretly embracing us in their new and bright belonging. Though we may forget them, they can never forget us. Their secret embrace unknowingly shelters and minds us.

The bright moment in grief is when the sore of absence

gradually changes into a well of presence. You become aware of the subtle companionship of the departed one. You know that when you are in trouble, you can turn to this presence beside you and draw on it for encouragement and blessing. The departed one is now no longer restricted to any one place and can be with you anyplace you are. It is good to know the blessings of this presence. An old woman whose husband had died thirty years earlier told me once that the last thing she did each night before sleep was to remember him. In her memory, she went over his face detail by detail until she could gather his countenance clearly in her mind's eye. She had always done this since he died, because she never wanted him to fade into the forgetfulness of loss.

While it is heartbreaking to watch someone in the throes of grief, there is still a beauty in grief. Your grief shows that you have risked opening up your life and giving your heart to someone. Your heart is broken with grief, because you have loved. When you love, you always risk pain. The more deeply you love, the greater the risk that you will be hurt. Yet to live your life without loving is not to have lived at all. As deeply as you open to life, so deeply will life open up to you. So there is a lovely symmetry and proportion between grief and love. Conamara is a dark landscape full of lakes and framed with majestic mountains. If you ask any person here how deep a lake is, they say that they often heard the ancestors say that the lake is always as deep as the mountain near it is high. The invisible breakage of grief has the same symmetry. Meister Eckhart said, "Depth is height." There is a haunting poem from the third century B.C. by Callimachus which imaginatively captures grief and the richness of absence as memory:

They told me, Heraclitus,
They told me you were dead.
They brought me bitter news to hear
And bitter tears to shed.
I wept as I remembered,
How often you and I
Had tired the sun with talking
And sent him down the sky.
But now that you are lying,
My dear old Carian guest,
A handful of grey ashes,
Long, long ago at rest.
Still are your gentle voices,
Your nightingales, awake—
For death he taketh all away
But these he cannot take.

Translated by William Cory

The Imagination and the Altars of Absence

In contrast to the discursive mind, the imagination seems more at home in its portraiture of absence and loss. This should not surprise, since the hallmark of the imagination is suggestion rather than description. The imagination offers you only the most minimal line in order to permit and encourage you to complete the picture for yourself. Consequently, the most enthralling part of a poem or a story is actually that which is omitted or absent. It is often at the very end of a short story that the threshold that would lead into the real story is reached. The writer has not cheated you but rather brought you to a door that you must open yourself. You are invited to people this absence with your own imagined presence. Your imagination begins to take you into a shape of experience that calls you beyond the familiar, the factual, and the predictable. By imaginatively acquainting you with places from which you have been absent, it enlarges and intensifies your presence. This often happens magically when you visit an art gallery. Art galleries are temples to colour. Art reminds one of what Keats said so memorably: "I am sure of nothing but the holiness of the heart's affections and the truth of the imagination."

The imagination teaches us that absence is anything but empty. It also tries to mirror the complexity of the soul. In order to function, society always tries to reduce things to a common denominator or code. Politics, religion, and convention are usually committed to looking away from the raging complexity that dwells under the surface in every human heart.

The penumbral and paradoxical world of the soul is taken for all practical purposes as absent. The external world deals with the individual by first engaging in this act of subtraction. Consequently, we depend desperately on the imagination to trawl and retrieve our poignant and wounded complexity, which is forced to remain absent from the social surface. The imagination is the inspired and incautious priestess who against all the wishes of all systems and structures insists on celebrating the liturgy of presence at the banished altars of absence.

In this sense, the imagination is faithful and hospitable to everything that lives in the house of the heart. It is willing to explore every room. Here the imagination shows courage and grace. Literature's most fascinating and memorable characters are not saints or cautious figures who never risked anything. They are characters who embody great passion and dangerous paradoxical energy. In this way, the imagination mirrors and articulates that constant companion dimension of the heart that by definition and design remains perenially absent, namely, the subconscious.

Absence is such a powerful theme and presence precisely because such a vast quantity of our identity lies out of reach in this unknown and largely unknowable region. Though predominantly absent from our awareness, the rootage of the subconscious accounts for so much of what happens above in the days of our lives. Because the imagination is the priestess of the threshold, she brings the two inner territories together. The imagination unifies the inner presence and the inner absence of our lives—the daylight outside self by which we are known and the inner night-time self whose dimensions remain unknown even to ourselves. The artist is the one who is committed to the life of the imagination.

The Artist as Permanent Pilgrim

For most roles in life, there are structures of study and apprenticeship to acquire the skill to function, be it as teacher, mechanic, or surgeon. Though certain structures exist for training in the arts, the artist is different. The artist trains himself; it can be no other way. Each artist is animated by a unique longing. There are no outer ready-made maps for what the artist wants to create. Each is haunted by some inner voice that will not permit any contentment until what is demanded is created. The artist cannot settle into the consensus of normal belonging. His heart pushes him out to the edge where other imperatives hold sway. There is great lonesomeness in becoming implicated in the creation of something original. The French poet Arthur Rimbaud said, "I have no ancestors." In a sense, the artist is called not so much from outside as from the unknown depths within.

The invitation to create comes from elsewhere. Artists are the priestesses and priests of culture. They coax the invisible towards a form where it becomes faintly visible, silence towards voice, and the unknown towards intimacy. Artists help us to see what is secretly there. No artist stands alone in a clear space. Every artist works from the huge belonging to the tradition, but yet does not repeat anything. The artist belongs in a strange way. He inhabits the tradition to such depth that he can feel it beat in his heart, but his tradition also makes him feel like a total stranger who can find for his longing no echo there. Out of the flow of this intimate foreignness something new begins to emerge.

The artist is fiercely called to truth. Despite all the personal limitation and uncertainty, he has to express what he finds. Sometimes the findings are glorious. Rilke's poetry gladdens the heart and makes you aware of the secret eternity of everything around you. The music of Beethoven gives huge voice to the dense cadences of creation. At other times, the artist has to name and portray the crippling and poisonous forms of belonging for which we settle: Kafka's meticulous articulation of the surrealism of bureaucracy; Beckett's portrayal of the famine of absence that can never be warmed or filled. In this way the artist calls us to freedom and promise. In art, we see where the lines of our belonging have become tight and toxic.

The artist is always faithful to longing, first. This willingness to follow the longing "wherever it leads" demands and enables all kinds of new possibilities of belonging. Hölderlin says: "Was bleibt aber stiften die Dichter," i.e., What endures, / the poets create.

The creation of such permanence is the result of following longing to the outposts, beyond every cosy or settled shelter, until some echo of the eternal belonging is sounded.

A large number of our brothers and sisters are also at the outposts we never visit.

The Ones We Never Hear From

This absence also works at the social level. Society is coming more and more to mirror the media, yet the media are no innocent surface or screen on which anything and every-thing is welcome to appear. No. The media work with a pow-erful selectivity. They construct their world around carefully chosen, repetitive, and loud chronicles. Yet there are so many people we never hear from. We never read of them in the papers. We never hear of them in the news. A whole range of people are absent. They are usually the poor, the vulnerable, the ill, and prisoners. Their voices would be slow and direct and would gnaw at our comfort and endanger our compla-cency. Most of us who are privileged live quite protected lives and are distant from and blind to what the poor endure. Out of sight, out of mind. What is absent from our view does not concern us.

Addiction: Obsessed Longing

One of the terrible metaphors of post-modern society is the drug. The addiction to drugs is arguably one of the greatest problems facing Western society. When drugs hook you, they make your longing captive. The depth and complexity of your life telescopes into one absolute need. Regardless of the presence of others who love you, the gifts that you have, the life that you could have, your life now has only one need, the drug. The longing of the addict is a craving for which he will sacrifice all other belonging. It is astounding how the inner world of the human heart has a capacity for such absolute single-mindedness. Addiction is longing that is utterly obsessed. There is no distance anymore between the longing and the drug. The longing determines the life. The drug has the power of a sinister God; it awakens absolute passion and demands absolute obedience.

A drug is an anonymous and unattractive piece of matter. For the addict, however, this banal stuff shines like the most glorious diamond imaginable. When the eye sees it, the longing is already travelling in the direction of pure joy; no wonder they choose names for drugs like "Ecstasy." The addict has no memory. All time is now; either the now of joy or the tortured now of longing for the fix. Far away from the dingy streets where the addict moves, probably out in the most scenic and beautiful area of the city, live the suppliers. They make their wealth from the misery of those poor demented ones for whom the city streets are an underworld. The suppliers work international routes which are the same as the international routes for arms. At a broader cultural level, drug addiction is a profound metaphor for contemporary society. The marginalized addicts are the scapegoats for the collective addiction in contemporary society. The obsessive nature of our culture comes to expression in the addict. The addict is visible, tangible, and vulnerable. The addict is always on the margins of belonging.

Another group who have to endure absence through losing or giving up belonging are those who are emigrants.

The Emigrants

Contemporary society is deeply unsettled. Everywhere a new diaspora is emerging because of hunger and poverty. The subjects of this diaspora are the emigrants. Exile is difficult and disconcerting. You are uprooted. Something within us loves the continuity, shelter, and familiarity of our home place. Among your own people, you can trust the instinctive compass of your words and actions. You move in a natural rhythm that you never notice until you are away. Exile is difficult because you find yourself among strangers. And it is slow work to find a door into the house of their memory.

While at university, I worked a summer on the buildings in America. I met an old man from our village in the West of Ireland. He was over eighty and had left home at eighteen and never returned. He talked so wistfully of home. He could remember the name of every field and well. As he intoned the litany of Gaelic place-names, his eyes kindled in the warmth of belonging. Even though he had lived in exile all his adult life, there was a part of his heart which never left home. I imagine that he withdrew into this private sanctuary of memory when times were raw and lonely. Those in exile understand each other. You'd see it in the way they meet and talk. What they can presume about each other. How easily they slip into the rhythm of companionship. You'd see it in the Irish in a Kilburn pub, a group of Turkish people sitting by a river at the weekend in a German town, or the Filipina girls who gather near a bridge in Hong Kong every Sunday to talk of home. When you emigrate, you fracture your belonging to the language of your homeland.

Language and Belonging

Each language has a unique memory. The thoughts, whispers, and voices of a people live in their language. Gradually, over time, all the words grow together to build a language. The sound of the wind, the chorus of the tides, the silence of stone, love whispers in the night, the swell of delight and the sorrow of the darkness, all came to find their echoes in the language. As it fills out, the language becomes the echo-mirror of the people and their landscape. No one knows the secret colour and the unique sound of the soul of a people as their language does. A language is a magical presence. It is utterly alive. Because we use it every minute to feel and think and talk, we rarely stop to notice how strange and exciting words are. It is like the air: we cannot live one moment without it, yet we rarely think of it. The most vital centre of your life is your mind. Your world is moored to your mind. Now there is no power that awakens and opens the mind as language does. Words form our minds, and we can only see ourselves and the world through the lenses of words. As they age over centuries, words ripen with nuance and deeper levels of meaning. The memory of a people lives in the rich landscape of its language. The destructive things done by them and to them live there too.

When strangers intrude and take over what is not their own, everything in the place reminds them that they do not belong there. Their guilt and unease can be assuaged by making the take-over as clean and thorough as possible. They must control everything. This is what a colonizer does. Our Irish language was targeted in this way. The flow between the feeling and the language was broken. Your own language fits your mind. Ancestral memory and nuance break on the shores of thought.

A Philosophy of Dúċas

The longing of a people is caught in the web of their language. Dreams and memories are stored there. A language is the inner landscape in which a people can belong. When you destroy a people's language through colonization or through the more subtle, toxic colonization of consumerism, you fracture their belonging and leave them in limbo. It is fascinating how a language fashions so naturally the experience of a people into a philosophy of life. Sometimes one word holds centuries of experience; like a prism, you can turn it at different angles and it breaks and gathers the light of longing in different ways.

In the Irish language, there are no specific substantive nouns of longing and belonging. This must mean that the Irish mind never saw them as fixed, closed realities, nor as separate things; or perhaps it means that the experience of them was constantly in the consciousness. Both belonging and longing come together in a wider, implicit sense of life and living. The word "dúcas" is the larger embrace. Dúcas captures the inner sense and content of belonging in that it means one's birthright and heritage. This brings to expression the particular lineage of belonging to which one became heir on entering the world. The act of birth brings possibility and limitation, but it also confers rights. Dúcas also means one's native place. This is where you were born and the networks of subtle belonging that will always somehow anchor you there. There are many deep and penumbral layers to the way we belong in the world. There is none more dense and difficult to penetrate than the time and place of our first awakening as children. In the Irish tradition, there would be a deep sense of the way a place and its soul-atmosphere seep into you during that time.

The phrase "ag fillead ar do dúcas" means returning to your native place and also the rediscovery of who you are. The return home is also the retrieval and reawakening of a hidden and forgotten treasury of identity and soul. To come home to where you belong is to come into your own, to become what you are, to awaken and develop your latent spiritual heritage. Dúcas also means the nature of the relationship you have with someone when there is a real affinity of soul between you both. When you have dúcas with someone, there is a flow of spirit and vitality between you. The echo of each other's longing brings and holds you both within the one circle of belonging. In this sense, dúcas is what enables and sustains the anam-ċara affinity.

Dúcas also refers to a person's deepest nature. It probes beneath the surface images and impressions of a life and reaches into that which flows naturally from the deepest well in the clay of the soul. It refers in this sense to that whole intuitive and quickness of longing in us that tells us immediately how to think and act; we call this instinct. An old Irish proverb believes that instinct is a powerful force within us. It may remain latent for ages but it can always break out: "Briseann an dúcas amac trí súile an cait," i.e., Dúcas will break forth even through the eyes of the cat. Dúcas is often used to interpret, explain, or excuse something in a person. "He cannot help it—he has the dúcas for that. In some sense, dúcas seems to be a deeper force than history. You belong to your dúcas; your dúcas is your belonging. In each individual there is a roster of longing that nothing can suppress.

Dúcas suggests the natural wildness of uninhibited Nature. There is also the proverb which says dúcas is impervious to outside training: "Is treise an dúcas na an oilúint," i.e., Dúcas is stronger than education or upbringing. Dúcas shows the faithfulness of memory but accents the inevitable results of instinct. Without an awareness of dúcas, we are blind to what we do. Soul-searching is the excavation of the dúcas in and around us in order to belong more fully to ourselves and to participate in our inner heritage in a critical and creative way. Given the sense of homelessness in modern life, there is anxiety and fear and a tendency to prescribe a style of belonging that has no self-criticism and wants to corral longing in fixed, empirical frames. This is fundamentalism.

Fundamentalism: False Longing and Forced Belonging

Unable to read or decipher the labyrinth of absence, the homeless mind often reverts to nostalgia. It begins to imagine that our present dilemma, rather than being a new threshold of possibility, is in fact a disastrous fall from an ideal past. Fundamentalism laments the absence of the time when everything was as it should be. Family values, perfect morality, and pure faith existed without the chagrin of question, critique, or the horror of such notorious practices as alternative lifestyles or morality. Such perfection of course never existed. Neither experience nor culture has ever been monolithic. Fundamentalism is based on faulty and fear-filled perception. It constructs a fake absence, the absence of something that never in fact existed in the first place. It then uses this fake absence to demand a future constructed on a false ideal. Fundamentalism pretends to have found an absolute access point to the inner mind of the mystery. Such certainty cannot sustain itself in real conversation that is critical or questioning.

Fundamentalism does not converse or explore. It presents truth. It is essentially noncognitive. This false certainty can only endure through the belief that everyone else is wrong. It is not surprising that such fundamentalism desires power in order to implement its vision and force the others to do as prescribed. Fundamentalism is dangerous and destructive. There is neither acceptance nor generosity in its differences with the world. It presumes it knows the truth that everyone should follow. There is often an over-cosy alliance between fundamentalism and official religion. Disillusioned functionaries sometimes see fundamentalism as the true remnant which has succeeded in remaining impervious to the virus of pluralism. When people on the higher rungs of hierarchy believe this, the results are catastrophic. Blind loyalty replaces critical belonging. The creative and mystical individuals within an institution become caricatured as the enemy; they become marginalised or driven out. Some of the most sinister forms of fundamentalism are practised in cults.

Cults and Sects

Spirituality that cuts itself off from religion can go totally astray and become entangled in the worst networks of deception, illusion, and power. We are all aware of the horror stories of individuals whose minds have been taken over by cults and sects. These individuals are offered emotional warmth and belonging. The price is the handing over of the individual mind. Cults are instinctively adept at mind altering. They seduce and exploit the natural longing for the spiritual. Unlike a great religious tradition which demands and requires the critical loyalty and inner opposition of its theologians, a cult has no theology. The counter-questions are neither invited nor allowed. The cult manages to hold you prisoner while making you feel and believe you are liberated and free. You could even feel pity and worry for those outside the cult, the lost ones who have not yet seen your light. The cult operates an efficient dualism, which separates mind and heart and splits self and society. It snares your longing in a sinister trap. The rise of cults testifies to the awful loneliness of post-modern culture. They are attractive because they seem to present a way of belonging that offers consolation, certainty, and purpose. Even though they do not actually deliver any of these possibilities in any real or truthful sense, their followers certainly invite us to look at the crisis of belonging in our society and religions.

Our Longing for Community

Each one of us wants to belong. No one wants to live a life that is cut off or isolated. The absence of contact with others hurts us. When we belong, we feel part of things. We have a huge need to participate. When this is denied us, it makes us insecure. Our confidence is shaken, and we turn in on ourselves and against ourselves. It is poignant that we actually are so fragile inside. When you feel rejected, it cuts deep into you, especially if you are rejected by those whose acceptance means a lot to you. The pain of rejection only confirms the intensity of our longing to belong. It seems that in a soul-sense we cannot be fully ourselves without others. In order to *be*, we need to *be with*. There is something incomplete in purely individual presence. Belonging together with others completes something in us. It also suggests that behind all our differences and distances from each other, we are all participating in a larger drama of spirit. The "life and death of each of us" does indeed affect the rest of us. Not alone do we long for the community, but at a deeper level we are already a community of spirit.

There is a Providence that brought us here and gave us to each other at this time. In and through us, a greater tapestry of creativity is being woven. It is difficult for us to envisage this. We live such separate and often quite removed lives. Yet behind all the seeming separation a deeper unity anchors everything. This is one of the powerful intimations of the great religious traditions. The ideal of community is not the forcing together of separate individuals into the spurious unity of community. The great traditions tell us that community somehow already exists. When we come together in compassion and generosity, this hidden belonging begins to come alive between us. Consequently, a community which is driven by power or too great a flurry of activity and talk will never achieve much more than superficial belonging. The attempt to force community usually drives the more creative and independent people away. We do not so much build community as if it were some external and objective structure as we allow community to emerge. In order for community to emerge, we need time, vision, and a certain rhythm of silence with each other. It is impossible to grasp what makes community at its heart. We often hear the phrase "community spirit," which recognizes that community is not so much an invention or construction of its members, but a gift that emerges between them and embraces them. We do not make community. We are born into community. We enter as new participants into a drama that is already on. We are required to maintain and, often, reawaken community.

Perhaps community is a constellation. Each one of us is a different light in the emerging collective brightness. A constellation of light has greater power of illumination than any single light would have on its own. Together we increase brightness. Yet no star can move away outside the constellation in order to view the overall brightness. It is interesting how perspective is such a powerful force in determining what we see and what we miss.

Many of the astronauts who have voyaged into space have had amazing experiences. As they moved further and further away from the earth, many of them were overcome with emotion and affection for that diminishing little blue planet called earth. Raised infinitely out of their individual communities, they gradually had a total view of the earth. Looking through the accelerating infinity of space, their hearts were touched with tenderness for home. Similarly with us, within the solitude of our own individual light we can never glimpse our collective brightness. All we see are frail candles, stuttering in the wind and the dark. Yet this should not make us insensitive to the embrace and the potential of our greater light. What kind of luminous view the dying must have as they slowly ascend to leave here?

The Shelter of Community

One of the great dreams of humanity is the founding of a perfect community where longing and belonging would come into sublime balance. From Plato's *Republic* to the Basic Community in Latin America of contemporary times, the realization of the ideal has continually called the human heart. In the Christian story, it is the dream of the realization of the Kingdom of God. The perfect community would be a place of justice, equality, care, and creativity. Humans have wonderful abilities and gifts. Yet our ability to live together in an ideal way remains undeveloped. All community life seems to have its shadows and darkness. In contrast to many communities in Nature, human intensity in its brightness and darkness makes it difficult to envisage or inhabit ideal community.

The ideal of creation is community, a whole diversity of presences which belong together in some minimal harmony. It is fascinating to lift a stone in a field and find a whole community of ants in such active rhythm. Though we would not suspect it, ants also have their shadowed order whereby some colonies actually have their own slave-ants to work for them. Who would ever suspect that such negative hierarchy can be found in miniature under a stone? Nature is a wonderful community that manages to balance light and dark, destructiveness and creativity, with incredible poise. Think of the sequence of the seasons and the waves and the force-fields that hold planets in rhythm. When you examine closely any piece of a field or bog, your eyes slowly begin to discern the various communities of insect, bird, animal and plant life that coexist. What to the glance seemed to be just another bit of a field reveals itself as a finely tuned, minia-ture community. Each little self has its own space and shelter. It is an organic and diverse community. If humankind could only let its fear and prejudice go, it would gradually learn the inestimable riches and nourishment that diversity brings. Community can never be the answer to all our questions or all our longings, but it can encourage us, and provoke us to raise questions and voice our desires. It cares for us, whether we know it or not.

Rural communities have a special, distinctive essence. In bygone days here in Conamara, when a person got married, the whole village would gather and build a simple but sufficient house for the couple in one day. In our village, neighbours would work in groups to get the harvest in. One day, everyone would gather at our farm to bring home the hay or turf, or to cut the corn; the next day we would go to your farm. This is the old Irish notion of the "Meitheal": the community gathered as an effective group to do the work for each other that an individual working alone would not have done in ages.

Each one of us is a member of several communities simultaneously: the community of colleagues at work, neighbours, family and relations, and friends. Such communities develop naturally around us. No individual can develop or grow in an isolated life. We need community desperately. Community offers us a creative tension which awakens us and challenges us to grow. No community we belong to fits our longing exactly. Community refines our presence. In a community no one person can have his own way. There are others to be considered and accommodated, too. In this way, we are taught compassion and care. We learn so much from community without ever realizing how totally we absorb its atmosphere.

The community also challenges us to inhabit to the full our own individuality. No community can ever be a total unity that embraces and fulfils all the longing of its individuals. A community can only serve as a limited and minimal unity. Community becomes toxic if it pretends to cover all the territories of human longing. There are destinations of longing for each individual that can only be reached via the path of solitude.

The most intimate community is the community of understanding. Where you are understood, you are at home. There is nothing that unites or separates us like the style and species of our perception. Often in a close friendship, the different ways of seeing are what bring most hurt, not the things that each does. When the perceptions find a balance in their own difference, then the togetherness and challenge can be wonderfully invigorating. When there is an affinity of thought between people and an openness to exploration, a real community of understanding and spirit can begin to grow. Where equality is grounded in difference, closeness is difficult but patience with it brings great fruits. Such community is truthful and real. There is a deep need in each of us to belong to some cluster of friendship and affinity in which the games of impression and power are at a minimum, and we can allow ourselves to be seen as we really are, we can express what we really believe and can be challenged thoroughly. This is how we grow; it is where we learn to see who we are, what our needs are, and the unsuspecting effect our thinking and presence have on other lives. The true realization of individuality requires the shelter of acceptance and the clear pruning blade of criticism. Our post-modern culture has enshrined the cult of individualism as authenticity. The irony here is that the pursuit of individualism is abstract and empty. Real individuality in all its bright ambivalence is forgotten. Individualism is the enemy of real individuality. The true path of individual longing always avoids the fast highway and travels the solitary boreens which traverse the true landscapes of creativity, difficulty, and integration.

Our world desperately needs to come in from the lost islands of desiccated individualism and learn to stand again on the fecund earth where vibrant and vital interaction can happen between people. Matthew Arnold speaks of islands separated by the "unplumbed, salt, estranging sea." Our world is facing so many crises ecologically, economically, and spiritually. These cannot be overcome by isolated individuals. We need to come together. There is incredible power in a community of people who are together because they care, and who are motivated by the ideals of compassion and creativity. When such a community develops and maintains its own vision, it will not fall into the trap of being the prisoners of reaction and beginning to resemble more and more the opposition. It will not deconstruct in the introverted power games, but maintain its care and critical focus. When such a prophetic community is nourished by prayer and animated by Divine Longing, the harvest of creativity and belonging which it can bring is unlimited. True community transfigures absence.

Towards a New Community

Our culture is complex and fast moving. We have a sharp eye for authoritarianism and control in their direct and obvious forms. We are, in ironic contrast, almost completely blind to the huge control and subtle authoritarianism of consumerist image culture. On the one hand, we are warriors for the freedom view and on the other, simultaneously, are absolute disciples of the God of Quantity. Our crisp cynicism and compliant greed have meant that we have unwittingly severed huge regions of the invisible tissue which holds community and civility together. Our society is addicted to and incessantly nourishes and inflates the spectacular. The invisible tissue which sustains real belonging is never spectacular; it is quiet and unostentatious. In order to survive as a planet and as a society, we need to reawaken and retrieve these lost and forgotten capacities of ours. Such virtues may heal our absence from our true nature.

One of these quiet virtues is honour. Contemporary psychology and spirituality speak of "honouring your gifts," etc.; the focus is inevitably subjective and sometimes narcissistic. Honour is a broader and deeper presence. The Irish word "úaisleacht" is lovely. Úaisleacht means "nobility"; it also carries echoes of honour, dignity, and poise. A person can be wild, creative, and completely passionate, and yet maintain úaisleacht. This is in no way an argument for some kind of code of honour; such codes inevitably become external and arrogant. It is more a plea for the retrieval of a sense of honour. This reawakening would gradually ensure the lessening of our tabloid convention and obsession. The sense of honour would also begin to reveal the vast fissures in and the hollowness of the huge kingdom of image and PR. Television might cease to be a soap kingdom. At evening, the empty screen might indeed become some kind of genuine mirror for our real concerns. Some of the huge questions which now confront us might actually begin to come alive in our homes, to replace the pursuit of fake questions which further nothing but gossip and passivity. Imagine a programme called "The Awkward Question," which would genuinely pursue many of the fundamental questions that the media avoid. A sense of honour in the way we relate to each other would invite the return of respect; the recognition that every person is worthy of respect. No one should have to earn respect. It could also mean a reawakening of our sense of courtesy. There is something very fine about a courteous person. Our times are often vulgar.

Compassion is another such quiet virtue. There is a huge crisis of compassion in contemporary society. This crisis has nothing to do with our inability to feel sympathy for others. It has more to do with the numbing of our compassion because of our image exposure to so many of the horrors that are happening around the world. We feel overwhelmed and then hopeless. It is important to remember that a proportion of our numbness is convenient. We avoid the harrowing images or allow ourselves to be immediately overwhelmed. Most of us continue our privileged lives within our complacent cocoons. Outside of the normal pain and difficulties of our lives and those of our friends, we rarely come into contact with the hungry, the destitute, and the oppressed. Their convenient absence from our lives means that we can never follow through and make the connection between the way we live and the awful lives to which our more helpless and vulnerable sisters and brothers are condemned. Not far from any of us are the poor, the homeless, the prisoners, the old people's homes, and the addicts. Because we are privileged, we have great power. We have a duty to speak out for those who have no voice or are not being listened to. The practice of compassion would show us that no sister or brother deserves to be excluded and pushed onto the bleak margins where life is sheer pain and endurance. We should at least begin to have some conversations with these members of our human family. It would open our eyes. When our compassion awakens, our responsibility becomes active and creative. When we succumb to indifference, we blaspheme against the gifts that we could never earn, that have been so generously given to us. The duty of privilege is absolute integrity.

Hope is another quiet virtue. We live in a culture where information is relentlessly meted out to us in abstract particles. So much of our information is a series of facts about how disastrous everything is. When we listen to the voices of doom, we become helpless and complicit in bringing the doom nearer. It is always astounding to see how willing humans are to give away their power and become disciples of helplessness. This accounts for the chromatic cynicism which reigns in our times. Cynicism is very interesting. Behind the searing certainty of the cynic, there is always, hidden somewhere, disappointed longing. It takes quite a good deal of energy to be a committed cynic. Time and again, life offers opportunities and possibilities. Time cannot help being a door into eternity. Within even the most cynical heart, eternity is a light sleeper. It takes considerable energy continually to quell the awakening invitation. Argument with a cynic merely serves this sliced certainty. A more subtle approach that addresses, not the argument, but the residue of disappointed longing can bring change. Our world is too beautiful and our human eternity too magnificent that we should succumb to hopelessness and cynicism. The human heart is a theatre of longings. Under every hardened and chromatic surface, be it system, syndrome, or corporation, there is a region of longing that dreams as surely of awakening to a new life of freedom and love as winter does of the springtime.

There are many other quiet virtues like care, sympathy, patience, confidence, loyalty. A new sense of community could gradually surface if we called upon some of these virtues to awaken. The great religious traditions advocate these as ideals. Increasingly, the custodianship and representation of these traditions have fallen into the hands of frightened functionaries who can only operate through edict and prescription. Few of them have the sensibility and imagination to address our longings in a way that respects our complexity and wildness of soul. They are unable to invite our sense of freedom and creativity to awaken and begin the new journey towards belonging. We need to take back our own power and exercise our right to inhabit in a creative and critical way the traditions to which we belong. We have allowed the functionaries to persuade us that they have the truth and that they own our traditions. A great tradition is a spacious and wonderful home for our nobility of soul and desperation of longing. We need to exercise our belonging in a new and critical way.

Divine Longing Transfigures Absence

One of the lovely things about longing is that it is not merely an abstract concept. Every heart has longing. This means that longing is always full of feeling. There is great concentration now on "getting in touch with your feelings" and "expressing your feelings." There is often more than a whiff of narcissism about these projects. In this practice we have increasingly lost sight of the beauty and wholesomeness of feeling itself. Feeling is a powerful disclosure of our humanity. A person who can really feel things is fully in touch with his or her own nature. Such nature is difficult to grasp and define, but we do know that we can trust someone who has nature. When we say "There is great nature" in a person, we mean that there is a presence of feeling in them that is passionate, deep, and caring. We can trust that even in awkward times of confusion and conflict the pendulum of nature will eventually come to rest in truth and compassion. It also suggests a deeper substrate of presence than personality, role, or image. When we lose touch with our Nature, we become less human. When we discover our own nature, we find new belonging.

The feeling of longing in your heart was not put there by yourself. We have seen how each of us was conceived in longing, and every moment here has been a pilgrimage of longing. Your life is a path of longing through ever-changing circles of belonging. Your longing echoes the Divine Longing. The heart of transcendence is longing. God is not abstract or aloof. We have done terrible damage to the image of God. We have caricatured God as an ungracious moral accountant and done what we should never have done: We have frozen the feeling of God and drawn the separated mind of God into war with our own nature. God has not done that; our thinking has. The results have been terrible. We have been abandoned in an empty universe with our poor hearts restless in a haunted longing; furthermore, this has closed the door on any possibility of entering into our true belonging. We are victims of longing, and we cannot come home. The thinking that has invented and institutionalized this way of life has damaged us; we are at once guilty and afraid. Of such a God E. M. Cioran writes: "All that is Life in me urges me to give up God." Our vision is our home. We need to think God anew as the most passionate presence in the universe—the primal well of presence from which all longing flows, and the home where we all belong and to which all belonging returns. God is present to us in a form that endlessly invites our longing, namely, in the form of absence. Simone Weil said, "The apparent absence of God in this world is the actual reality of God."

God has a great heart. Only a divine artist with such huge longing would have the beauty and tenderness of imagination to dream and create such a wonderful universe. God is full of longing: every stone, tree, wave, and human countenance testifies to the eternal and creative ripple of Divine Longing. This is the tender immensity of Jesus. He is the intimate linkage of everything. William Blake used the phrase "Christ the Imagination." The deepest nature of everything is longing. This is why there is always such hope of change and transfiguration. Beneath even the most hardened surfaces longing waits. Great music or poetry will always reach us because our longing loves to be echoed. Neither can we ever immunize ourselves against love; it knows in spite of us exactly how to whisper our longing awake. It is as if, under the clay of your presence, streams of living water flow. Great moments always surprise you. The routine is broken, and unexpected crevices appear on the safe surface of your life. Such moments dowse you—they make you recognize that within you there is eternity.

You should never allow any person or institution to own or control your longing. No one has a right to deny you the beautiful adventure of God by turning you into a serf of a cold and sinister deity. When you let that happen, it makes you homeless. You are a child of Divine Longing. In your deepest nature you are one with your God. As Meister Eckhart says so beautifully, "The eye with which I see God is God's eye seeing me."

That circle of seeing and presence is ultimate belonging. It is fascinating that Jesus did not stay on the earth. He made himself absent in order that the Holy Spirit could come. The ebb and flow of presence and absence is the current of our lives; each of them configures our time and space in the world. Yet there is a force that pervades both presence and absence: this is spirit. There is nowhere to locate spirit and neither can it be subtracted from anything. Spirit is everywhere. Spirit is in everything. By nature and definition, spirit can never be absent. Consequently, all space is spiritual space, and all time is secret eternity. All absence is full of hidden presence.

In the pulse-beat is the life and the longing, all embraced in the great circle of belonging, reaching everywhere, leaving nothing and no one out. This embrace is mostly concealed from us who climb the relentless and vanishing escalator of time and journey outside where space is lonesome with distance. All we hear are whispers, all we see are glimpses; but each of us has the divinity of imagination which warms our hearts with the beauty and depth of a world woven from glimpses and whispers, an eternal world that meets the gaze of our eyes and the echo of our voices to assure us that from all eternity we have belonged, and to answer the question that echoes at the heart of all longing: While we are here, where is it that we are absent from?

A BLESSING

May you know that absence is full of tender presence and
  that nothing is ever lost or forgotten.

May the absences in your life be full of eternal echo.

May you sense around you the secret Elsewhere which
  holds the presences that have left your life.

May you be generous in your embrace of loss.

May the sore well of grief turn into a well of seamless
  presence.

May your compassion reach out to the ones we never hear
  from and may you have the courage to speak out for
  the excluded ones.

May you become the gracious and passionate subject of
  your own life.

May you not disrespect your mystery through brittle
  words or false belonging.

May you be embraced by God in whom dawn and twilight
  are one, and may your belonging inhabit its deepest
  dreams within the shelter of the Great Belonging.

VESPERS

As light departs to let the earth be one with night
Silence deepens in the mind and thoughts grow slow;
The basket of twilight brims over with colours
Gathered from within the secret meadows of the day
And offered like blessings to the gathering Tenebrae.

After the day's frenzy may the heart grow still,
Gracious in thought for all the day brought,
Surprises that dawn could never have dreamed,
The blue silence that came to still the mind,
The quiver of mystery at the edge of a glimpse,
The golden echoes of worlds behind voices.

Tense faces unable to hide what gripped the heart,
The abrupt cut of a glance or a phrase that hurt,
The flame of longing that distance darkened,
Bouquets of memory that gathered on the heart's altar,
The thorns of absence in the rose of dream.

And the whole while the unknown underworld
Of the mind turning slowly in its secret orbit.

May the blessing of sleep bring refreshment and release
And the Angel of the moon call the rivers of dream
To soften the hardened earth of the outside life,
Disentangle from the trapped nets the hurt and sorrow
And awaken the young soul for the new tomorrow.

Suggested Further Reading

Gaston Bachelard. *The Poetics of Space*. Boston, 1969.

Jean Baudrillard. *Fatal Strategies*. New York, 1990.

Wendell Berry. *Collected Poems*. North Point Press, 1984.

Saint Bonaventure. *The Journey of the Mind to God*. Translated by
P. Boehner, O.F.M. Hackett, 1993.

Jorge Luis Borges. *The Book of Sand*. London, 1980.

Ian Bradley. *The Celtic Way*. London, 1993.

Albert Camus. *Exile and the Kingdom*. New York: Vintage, 1991.

Alexander Carmichael. *Carmina Gadelica*. Edinburgh, 1994.

William Desmond. *Being and the Between*. New York, 1995.

Myles Dillon. *Early Irish Literature*. Dublin, 1994.

Robert Graves. *Greek Myths*. BCA, 1993.

Seamus Heaney. *The Haw Lantern*. London, 1987.

Philippe Jaccottet. *Selected Poems*. Translated by Derek Mahon.
London, 1988.

John of the Cross. *The Collected Works*. Translated by K.
Kavanagh, O.C.D., and O. Rodriguez, O.C.D. ICS, 1979.

Thomas Kinsella, trans. *The Tain*. Oxford, 1986.

Ivan V. Lalić. *The Passionate Measure*. Tranlsated by Francis R.
Jones. Daedalus, 1989.

Mary Low. *Celtic Christianity and Nature*. Edinburgh, 1996.

Iris Murdoch. *Metaphysics as a Guide to Morals*. London, 1992.

Gerard Murphy. *Early Irish Lyrics*. Oxford, 1996.

P. Murray, ed. *The Deer's Cry: A Treasury of Irish Religious Verse*.
Dublin, 1986.

Pablo Neruda. *Selected Poems*. Translated by N. Tarn. London,
1977.

Noel Dermot O'Donoghue. *The Mountain Behind the Mountain: Aspects of the Celtic Tradition.* Edinburgh, 1993.

John O'Donohue. *Person als Vermittlung: Die Dialektik von Individualität und Allgemeinheit in Hegel's 'Phänomenologie des Geistes.' Eine philosophisch-theologische Interpretation.* Mainz, 1993.

____. *Anam Cara: A Book of Celtic Wisdom.* New York: HarperCollins, 1997.

____. *Echoes of Memory.* Dublin, 1994/1997.

Daithi O hógain. *Myth, Legend and Romance: An Encyclopaedia of the Irish Folk Tradition.* New York, 1991.

Liam de Paor. *Saint Patrick's World.* Four Court's Press, 1996.

Fernando Pessoa. *Selected Poems.* Translated by J. Griffin. Harmondsworth: Penguin, 1982.

M. Merleau-Ponty *Phenomenology of Perception.* London, 1981.

Kathleen Raine. *The Lost Country.* Dolmen Press, 1971.

____. *On a Deserted Shore.* Dolmen Press, 1990.

Rupert Sheldrake. *The Rebirth of Nature.* London, 1990.

Cyprian Smith. *The Way of Paradox: Spiritual Life as Taught by Meister Eckhart.* London, 1987.

George Steiner. *Real Presence.* London, 1989.

Esther de Waal. *The Celtic Way of Prayer.* London, 1996.

David Whyte. *The Heart Aroused.* New York, 1995.

© 1999 by Gerry O'Gorman

JOHN O'DONOHUE lives in Ireland. He is a Catholic scholar who lectures and conducts workshops in the United States and Europe. He was awarded a Ph.D. in philosophical theology from the University of Tübingen in 1990, and his book on the philosophy of Hegel, *Person als Vermittlung*, was published in Germany in 1993. His collection of poetry *Echoes of Memory* was published in 1994. John O'Donohue is the author of the award winning *Anam Ćara*, which has been a number one bestseller in Ireland for more than a year.